A. D. Cousins

SHAKESPEARE'S SONNETS AND NARRATIVE POEMS

week

 LONGMAN

An imprint of **PEARSON EDUCATION**

Harlow, England · London · New York · Reading, Massachusetts · San Francisco · Toronto · Don Mills, Ontario · Sydney
Tokyo · Singapore · Hong Kong · Seoul · Taipei · Cape Town · Madrid · Mexico City · Amsterdam · Munich · Paris · Milan

Pearson Education Limited
Edinburgh Gate
Harlow
Essex CM20 2JE
United Kingdom
and Associated Companies throughout the world.

Visit us on the World Wide Web at:
http://www.pearsoneduc.com

First published 2000

ISBN 0-582-21513-7 [CASED]
ISBN 0-582-21512-9 [LIMP]

British Library Cataloguing-in-Publication Data

A catalogue record for this book is available from the British Library

Library of Congress Cataloging-in-Publication Data

Cousins, A. D., 1950–
    Shakespeare's sonnets and narrative poems / A. D. Cousins.
        p.   cm. — (Longman medieval and Renaissance library)
    Includes bibliographical references and index.
    ISBN 0–582–21512–9. — ISBN 0–582–21513–7 (cased : alk. paper)
        1. Shakespeare, William, 1564–1616—Poetic works.   2 Shakespeare,
    William, 1564–1616. Venus and Adonis.   3. Shakespeare, William,
    1564–1616. Rape of Lucrece.   4. Narrative poetry, English—History
    and criticism.   5. Shakespeare, William, 1564–1616. Sonnets.
    6. Sonnets, English—History and criticism.   I. Title.   II. Series.
    PR2984.C68   1999
    821'.3—dc21   99–16779
                                                                        CIP

Set by 35 in 10.5/12pt Bembo
Printed and bound by CPI Antony Rowe, Eastbourne

Transferred to digital print on demand, 2006

Contents

To my Family

Acknowledgements

In writing a book one incurs many debts and I am glad to have the opportunity here to thank friends and colleagues for their generosity. With the aid of research grants from Macquarie University and from the Ian Potter Foundation, I was able to work at the Massachusetts Center for Renaissance Studies in 1995 as an Adjunct Professor and at the English Department of Pennsylvania State University as a Visiting Scholar in 1997. Doing so gave me the chance to consult respectively with Arthur F. Kinney and with Linda Woodbridge, Shakespeare scholars whose learning and good counsel have helped me considerably. Heather Dubrow kindly made time to read the initial versions of chapters 1 and 2; I am grateful to her for her many suggestions which have made those chapters better than they would otherwise have been. Neil Keeble, the general editor responsible for Renaissance titles in the series in which this book appears, has been a constant source of encouragement and helpful comment. I should like also to thank Michael Ackland, Normand Berlin, Jim and Maureen Cahillane, Patrick Cheney, Conal Condren, Jim Dutcher, Tony Gibbs, Damian Grace, Bob Hoopes, Manfred Mackenzie, Earl Miner, Mauro Di Nicola, Liam Semler, Malcolm Smuts and Boyd Vickery.

Parts of Chapter 1 have appeared, in earlier versions, in *Studia Neophilologica*. Part of Chapter 2, also in an earlier version, has appeared in *Studies in English Literature*. Part of Chapter 3, likewise, has appeared in *Imperfect Apprehensions: Essays in English Literature in Honour of G. A. Wilkes*.

Introduction

In studying Shakespeare's Sonnets and narrative poems, this book focuses in particular on their variously manifested scepticism, their concern both with what wisdom might be in human conduct and with the extent to which human conduct might be directed by wisdom, their preoccupation with knowing, inventing, or reinventing the past, their exploration of the relations among self-knowledge, sexuality and death, and their ambiguous figuring of gender.[1] As it does so the book considers how Shakespeare's poems compete with, rewrite, contradict or harmonize with those by some other writers, especially by English writers of the sixteenth and seventeenth centuries. And of course at different points the book considers similarities or differences between Shakespeare's non-dramatic verse and his plays.

What the book has to say about those things can be broadly described as follows. It suggests that in the Sonnets and narrative poems can be seen a scepticism which cannot be neatly or simply classified but which for the most part seems closer to Pyrrhonism than to scepticisms of other kinds.[2] It suggests as well that scepticism – of whatever kind – is not consistently exercised in the non-dramatic verse, for by no means all aspects of experience portrayed in the poems are subjected to a sceptical perspective; moreover, those aspects of experience which are sceptically examined do not receive scrutiny to the same degree. As regards the matter of wisdom, the book suggests that in his poems Shakespeare seems to examine prudence (*prudentia* rather than *sapientia*) as an ideal of wisdom for the conduct of life.[3] It proposes that he represents prudence as a problematic ideal and as notably absent from human conduct when most needed. Further, it also proposes that he does not merely attribute imprudence to personal failure. No less problematic, the book argues, is the preoccupation in the non-dramatic verse with knowing and evoking the past.[4] Different ways of viewing the past coexist in the poems. Sometimes the past appears to be regarded as if a pellucid, securely authorized narrative, at others not; and sometimes knowledge of the past is suppressed.

Sometimes the past is invented or reinvented – for purposes of play, or otherwise, but always so that control can be asserted over it, since it is not a neutral territory.

As one would expect, the non-dramatic verse indicates that neutrality does not feature in the relations among self-knowledge, sexuality and death. The book argues that, exploring the relations among them, the poems associate death with sexuality and self-knowledge denied but, in addition, death with sexuality unable to be denied and self-knowledge dubiously expressed. Consciousness of mortality (rather than death itself), sexuality and self-knowledge are also linked and explored, from startlingly unlike but not wholly dissimilar angles of vision. Their being thus explored, as the book suggests, is associated with the poems' recurrently ambiguous figuring of gender.[5] Shakespeare chiefly represents gender in the poems through classical myth and through the conventions of Petrarchan discourse. Given the pervasive allusions in the *Rime* to the *Metamorphoses*, the union of myth and of Petrarchism in Shakespeare's non-dramatic verse is unsurprising. It is even less surprising given the indebtednesses of *Venus and Adonis*, but also the Sonnets, to the *Metamorphoses* and of *Lucrece* to the *Fasti*. However, the main point here is that Venus, Adonis, Narcissus and Laura feature prominently in the figuring of gender, the androgyny of Adonis and of Narcissus enabling their implicit elision with Laura whereas Venus tends to be set in opposition to Laura, is at times masculinized, and is at times even distantly analogous to the speaker of the Sonnets.

Shakespeare's using the *Metamorphoses* and the *Rime* of course offered him the opportunity not merely to imitate Ovid and Petrarch but partly to rewrite them in attempts to renew, appropriate and overgo aspects of their achievements.[6] Studying the major non-dramatic verse in more or less chronological order, the book suggests that, taking the opportunity, he refashioned the minor epic in *Venus and Adonis*, the complaint in *Lucrece*, and the amatory sonnet sequence in his Sonnets.[7] Thereby, as the book argues, he engaged in rivalry neither with Ovid and Petrarch alone nor solely across the remove of centuries. In *Venus and Adonis* he went beyond Lodge and, perhaps, competed with Marlowe; in *Lucrece* he not so much rewrote as wrote over Daniel; in the Sonnets he gestured toward Sidney but used those allusions as elements of verse distinctly and transgressively his own. Some of the concerns and preoccupations marking that verse as his, and likewise the rest of the non-dramatic verse, also feature strongly in his plays – as is discussed in the subsequent chapters.

How the book's five chapters pursue the notions proposed above can be outlined briefly in this way. Beginning with consideration of *Venus and Adonis* as a poem through which Shakespeare sought the patronage of the Earl of Southampton, the first chapter proceeds to consider his choice of genre: that of the minor epic. *Scillaes Metamorphosis* (1589), by Thomas Lodge, seems to have initiated the genre in England and the chapter examines how Lodge recreated Ovidian narrative in generating that new kind of writing. Also considered are the primary audience for *Scillaes Metamorphosis* and the narrator, modelled on the narrator of the *Metamorphoses*, who figures so obtrusively in the poem. It is suggested that Lodge's minor epic offered Shakespeare an opportunity: a way of writing for a more specific audience – including and especially Southampton – than that for which he usually wrote. Shakespeare can be seen, then, as having appropriated a new genre aimed at a sophisticated readership – including, of course, his potential patron – and as having sought to make it his own. In part, the chapter argues, he sought to do that by fashioning the poem's narrator so as to imply his insight into and ability to recreate the teller of the *Metamorphoses*. However, as is then discussed more closely, he sought chiefly to make the minor epic his own by ingenious and elaborate play with myth.

Shakespeare does not have his narrator merely play with the plot of the Venus and Adonis fable as recounted by Ovid. In effect he has his narrator play with the mythography of Venus and of Adonis themselves. Two things are suggested in connection with that. First, the characterization of Venus has more diversity than has been recognized, most of her manifold aspects according with (perhaps deriving from) ancient representations of her that were still known and studied in Shakespeare's time. It is argued that the conventional elements in Venus' characterization are subverted and that, in presenting the goddess of love as having a great variety of aspects, Shakespeare's narrator indicates love's incongruous multiplicity. Amid consideration of her all but infinite variety, emphasis is given to the humanizing of Venus and its implications. Particularly emphasized is this: herself transformed, to a degree, by discovering the familiar, human experience of loving another in vain, the goddess offers Adonis her love as a means for his achieving self-transformation, a redefined subjectivity. Second, it is suggested that the characterization of Adonis forms a curious counterpart to that of Venus. Adonis appears to be given a female rhetoric for rejecting love and a Platonic, male rhetoric for evaluating it – in addition to an adolescent rhetoric of indignation and impatience at harassment. Moreover, rejecting the goddess's offer of metamorphosis, he becomes an antithesis to Narcissus.

In the context of those characterizations are discussed the poem's ambiguous figuring of gender, its exploring the relations among death, sexuality and self-knowledge, and its scepticism. Venus seems from the start of the poem to be masculinized in terms of Petrarchan and libertine discourses; the former is used likewise to feminize Adonis. Furthermore, Shakespeare's narrator devalues the sexual attractiveness of Venus but, himself seemingly appreciative of Adonis as an object of desire, sets up the feminized Adonis for the gaze of the implied male reader. Rejecting the offer of metamorphosis through introduction to heterosexual erotic experience, Adonis is shown by the narrator to repudiate as well the gaining of self-knowledge; in fact, the reader sees Adonis trying to keep the acquisition of self-knowledge altogether separate from initiation into sexual experience. His denial of sexuality and thus of self-knowledge leads, it is argued, to his becoming an antithesis to Narcissus but, ultimately, to his parodic sexual encounter with the boar. In rejecting sexual initiation Adonis may evade the insistence and egocentrism of sexual desire, and loss of his present, incomplete subjectivity for the gaining of a diminished, eroticized one, but he likewise evades self-knowledge: if sexual desire is problematic, so too can chastity be. The poem sceptically balances opposites such as those in its Ovidian play with myth. However one finds a deeper, more Pyrrhonian scepticism, and inquiry into what wisdom might be in human conduct, in Shakespeare's second narrative poem.

When trying to persuade Adonis to make love to her, Venus relates an important episode from her past but suppresses a crucial detail; that significant suppression aside, the mythic past is freely invented or reinvented in Shakespeare's first narrative poem. But control of the past is not so lightly treated in *Lucrece*. The poem's scepticism, its inquiry into wisdom, its figuring of gender, its exploring the interactions of death, sexuality and self-knowledge, are all part of a more serious focus on controlling the past: an examination of how people seek to control it in order to shape the future. The second chapter, like its predecessor, begins with consideration of Shakespeare's quest for patronage from Southampton and in doing so considers ways in which *Lucrece* is an opposite to *Venus and Adonis*. Then studying how, in his second narrative poem, Shakespeare rewrote one of the oldest stories in western culture, Chapter 2 discusses likenesses and differences between Shakespeare's version of the Lucretia story and some earlier, influential versions of it.

As regards the genre of *Lucrece*, the chapter argues that the poem is a minor epic but one that emphasizes the epic no less than the erotic, juxtaposing two mythologized, supposedly foundational moments in Roman history: the rape of Lucrece and the fall of Troy; the notional moment of the republic's beginning and likewise that of Rome's origin. It suggests, too, that the poem has affinities with *de casibus* tragedies, with the complaint, and with the tyrant play. Insofar as *Lucrece* has affinities with the complaint it has connections especially with Daniel's *Rosamond* (1592), which revived the complaint form. The chapter examines how *Lucrece* seems calculatedly to rework its predecessor, as if Shakespeare's poem were designed both to acknowledge and to transcend Daniel's, to acknowledge the renewal of the complaint genre but to transcend the genre itself.

Proceeding to study the characterizations of Tarquin, Collatine and Lucrece, the chapter proposes that to recognize the mutually defining nature of those characterizations is to see that they are more complex in their discursive relations than has been so far acknowledged. It is argued in particular that Tarquin is distinctly a Platonic type of the tyrant and, as well, a demonic parody of the Petrarchan lover, being the latter insofar as he pursues a lady, Lucrece, who is portrayed as an exemplar of the chaste Roman matron and an incarnation of the Petrarchan mistress. Collatine, redirecting Tarquin's violence from the siege of Ardea onto Lucrece, seems to figure as a self-betraying Adam who brings the serpent – Tarquin – to his domestic Eden and tempts the serpent into violating his unwilling Eve, his wife who is like an innocent from the Golden Age and an earthly paradise. Collatine is thus at once a type of hubris and of imprudence.

The chapter suggests that one of the most important elements of Lucrece's characterization is her externalized sense of her ultimate self: her existence as chaste Roman matron. That sense of who she is clarifies her profound consciousness of herself as an exemplar of chastity and her profound fear of becoming an exemplar of unchastity. She knows that others have established her as the first and can turn her into the second. Her consciousness of herself as exemplar seems in turn to clarify her sense of being immersed in historical process. Rape impels Lucrece to look anxiously to the future and likewise to the past, as well it might. But for her there is a special reason for its doing so. Anticipating misrepresentation of her role as exemplar, its unjustly parodic inversion, Lucrece simultaneously anticipates the falsification of history. To preserve her existence as an exemplar of chastity is at once, for her, significantly if partly to save the present from future misinterpretation, to protect history from false tradition. The chapter explores what the poem indicates as the problematics of exemplarity. Thus the chapter considers chiefly these questions: how reliable can exemplarity be as a means of defining subjectivity? Can exemplarity be regarded as a reliable means of interpreting history, of clarifying and stabilizing it? What does it indicate about exemplarity if Lucrece has to kill herself in order to preserve its (her) integrity and hence the integrity of historical tradition? In response to those questions the chapter suggests that exemplarity appears not merely to be subverted in the poem, though aspects of it certainly are; rather, it is subjected to close and sceptical examination which implies both that it works and that it does not.

Whether or not the Sonnets overlap chronologically with *Venus and Adonis* and with *Lucrece*, though it seems likely that they do, they certainly share many of the narrative poems' concerns and preoccupations. Prudence is, for example, a concern revealed early in the Sonnets and one that is given various emphases throughout the Sonnets as a whole. In considering continuities and discontinuities between the Sonnets and the narrative poems, the third chapter begins with discussion of the discourse that dominated the writing of secular sonnet sequences in Shakespeare's time: the Petrarchan discourse of love, though not merely of love, manifested in the *Rime*. The Petrarchan language and rhetoric of love are discussed, particular attention being given to the desire-riven persona fashioned by Petrarch in his poems. Then the chapter examines the entry of that Petrarchan discourse into English verse. It focuses on Sidney's *Astrophil and Stella*, which created the fashion for secular sonnet sequences in the 1590s, examining how Petrarchan motifs are used by Sidney as elements of a meta-Petrarchan text. The characterization of Astrophil is studied in relation to that of Petrarch's persona in the *Rime*. It is suggested that self-division links them but that courtiership and unrepudiated desire, along with other things, distinguish Astrophil from his Petrarchan antecedent. It is also suggested that, in the love-engendered conflict which largely characterizes Astrophil, one witnesses conflict among authorities and discourses important to, if not only to, the Elizabethan courtly world.

As the chapter subsequently argues, the relations between Shakespeare's Sonnets and the Petrarchan discourse of love are intricately initiated in the early poems, the Petrarchan elements of which mingle sometimes harmoniously, at others not, with the non-Petrarchan. Attempting to clarify those relations, the chapter considers the use of the Narcissus myth in the initial four sonnets, a myth used by Petrarch and his successors including Sidney. Shakespeare uses it to have his speaker suggest the androgyny as well as the self-love of the young man to or about whom Sonnets 1–19 are written, the first seventeen

of which counsel marriage and procreation. That counsel, its recipi-
ent and the representation of his gender are identified as immediately
differentiating the use of the Narcissus myth in the early sonnets
from its uses in the *Rime* and in *Astrophil and Stella*. Of course they
immediately and generally differentiate the Sonnets from the *Rime*
and from *Astrophil and Stella*. It is suggested that, although the young
man figures primarily as Narcissus, he appears as well to be another
Adonis and a counterpart to the ideal lady of Petrarchan tradition.

This Narcissus, the chapter argues, is called to account: in his role
as Narcissus the young man is told to what and to whom he must
answer for his narcissism. Shakespeare's speaker urges him to learn
prudence and to fulfil his part in the economy of nature; before the
young man are set imperatives natural and social rather than divine.
Narcissus is, then, to gain wisdom. He must gain it, the speaker
insists, because to be human means to be subject to the tyranny of
Father Time. The speaker implies that, having been confronted with
self-knowledge, the young man must overcome death through the
power of his sexuality. But the rest of the early sonnets indicate
clearly enough that the speaker's elegant attempts at persuasion are in
vain. As the chapter proceeds to show, the speaker then challenges
Father Time on the young man's behalf, doing so carefully since he
does not wish his role as hero – as giver of immortality – to obscure
the aristocratic youth to whose service he proffers himself. His chief
strategies of mediation are praise and professions of devotion.

Those strategies pervade the sonnets subsequently written to or
about the young man (20–126), yet they do not simply recur. From
the start, for example, the youth is celebrated for his perfect, an-
drogynous beauty, and celebrated for it at the expense of women; he
is indicated to be like, but to transcend, Laura. However, Shakespeare's
speaker also implies from the start that the young man shares with
women the very instability which supposedly makes them inferior
to men in general and to the young man in particular. The fourth
chapter argues that there is throughout Sonnets 20–126 a continuous
and radical equivocation in the speaker's celebration of the youth.
Praise of the young man in some poems is marred or undermined, at
times by allegations of ostentatiously imprudent behaviour; alternatively,
praise of him in one poem is countered by depreciation of him in
another. Wavering and oscillation characterize the speaker's celebra-
tion of the young man. As the chapter suggests, to a lesser degree
they mark as well the speaker's professions of devotion. Consequently,
it is proposed, there can be seen a scepticism in the speaker's por-
trayal of the youth – something like a Pyrrhonian scepticism without

the comfort of suspended judgement – that coexists with idealization of him. And idealization can be seen likewise in the speaker's self-portrayal. He often represents himself as the totally devoted friend of the young man, empowered by love for him, or as the young man's totally devoted but powerless and unworthy friend: two versions of self-idealization. He offers two versions of farewell to friendship with the young man. Thus in portraying himself the speaker invites, deliberately or otherwise, wary if not sceptical examination. He reveals the precariousness of the fictions that he imposes on himself as well as the precariousness of those that he imposes on the youth.

One of those fictions is that of friendship and, as the chapter suggests, the representation of the friendship asserted to exist between the speaker and the young man is ambiguous both because of the androgyny attributed to the young man and because of the homoerotic as well as misogynic elements within the discourse of male friendship as it had been inherited from ancient times. Furthermore, relations between the discourses of friendship and of patronage are certainly not clear in Sonnets 20–126; neither are the relations between asserted friendship and acknowledged differences of class or of age. Shakespeare's speaker seems to imitate the Petrarchan motif of the ageing, obsessed lover. He seems to suggest that his awareness of mortality sharpens his devotion to the youth – and brings him a mostly powerless, various insight into the nature of his devotion and its imprudences, an often hapless wisdom. His much proclaimed sense of social, but not only social, inferiority to the youth seems to be identified, too, as heightening his devotion and his insight into it. On the other hand, he seems at least once to suggest that the imprudent, aristocratic young man is in fact capable of exercising a certain cold prudence born of his aristocratic narcissism.

By that point in the Sonnets the speaker has indicated his own narcissism. He has also anxiously and not infrequently reconstructed the past in order to justify his frequently wilful understanding of the present. The last of the Sonnets, 127–154, begin with precisely that: a reconstruction of the past in order to justify a wilful view of the present. The fifth chapter of the book explores how the final sonnets, opening with a duplicitous mock-history of 'black' as opposed to 'fair' beauty, then rewrite Petrarch's drama of the divided self. That drama, performed so cunningly by Sidney's Astrophil, is played out by Shakespeare's speaker in relation to two objects of desire. It seems that the fair-haired youth remains a focus of his attachment; the so-called Dark Lady likewise enthrals him. The chapter suggests that, although there are clear and important differences between the

earlier sonnets and the later, there are nevertheless important sim-
ilarities. For example, before depicting the Dark Lady as a truly 'ugly
beauty', as profoundly antithetic both to Laura and to the young
man, Shakespeare's speaker portrays her through a process of waver-
ing and of oscillation, imposing fictions precariously upon her much
as he did upon the youth. Thus the chapter proposes that if the
speaker's perspective on the Dark Lady is initially ambiguous it is not
sceptical. Another similarity between the earlier and later sonnets is
that the speaker continues his unstable portrayal of the youth, evoking
the contraries that pervade his earlier representations of the 'master
mistress'.

The speaker's divided desire, the chapter argues, brings powerfully
and duplicitously together the discourses of misogyny and of friendship,
already often linked in male writings about the nature of friendship.
The chapter studies the doubleness of the speaker in attributing
doubleness to the Dark Lady, his assertions that she can arouse and
experience only concupiscence, his disgust with his own concupiscence
and impotent wisdom, his exaltation of the evidently flawed male
friend: the process by which he caricatures her and, at the same time,
all but caricatures himself. In the last sonnets, both the speaker and
the Dark Lady seem to resemble the Venus of *Venus and Adonis*;
although flawed, the youth seems nevertheless to resemble Laura,
while the Dark Lady appears to be Laura's antithesis. That having
been said, Cupid is perhaps more important than either Venus or
Laura in Sonnets 127–154. The speaker recurrently alludes to Cupid,
implies that he has become a counterpart to Blind Cupid, and plays
with the lore of Cupid in Sonnets 153–154. Cupid symbolizes de-
sire, after all, and desire is the speaker's chief preoccupation. Bitterly
playful acknowledgement of desire's power ends the Sonnets. It may
be that there the speaker indicates resignation to his being dominated
by desire; whatever the case, his final words concede his desire to be
without end and his predicament to be without resolution.

NOTES

1. This study does not take a biographical approach to the non-dramatic
   verse, as is iterated at relevant points in the following chapters. As is also
   iterated in the following chapters, the editions used are: S. Booth,
   Shakespeare's Sonnets (New Haven and London: Yale University Press,
   1977); F. T. Prince, *William Shakespeare: The Poems* (1969; rpt. London:
   Methuen, 1976). I have also consulted other editions of the non-
   dramatic verse, chiefly these: W. G. Ingram and T. Redpath, *Shakespeare's
   Sonnets* (1964; rpt. London: Hodder & Stoughton, 1978); J. Kerrigan,

The Sonnets and A Lover's Complaint (Harmondsworth: Penguin, 1986);
G. Blakemore Evans, *The Sonnets* (Cambridge: Cambridge University
Press, 1996); H. Vendler, *The Art of Shakespeare's Sonnets* (Cambridge,
Mass. and London: Harvard University Press, 1997) – which was not
available to me when I was writing on the Sonnets but which I have
since consulted; J. Roe, *The Poems* (Cambridge: Cambridge University
Press, 1992).

2.   And therefore closer at times to the scepticism in some of Montaigne's
Essays. My research into scepticism and Shakespeare's non-dramatic
verse has grown out of work I began many years ago in connection
with scepticism, mannerism and the writings of Ralegh and of the early
Donne. That work first took the form of two articles: 'The Coming of
Mannerism: the Later Ralegh and the Early Donne', *English Literary
Renaissance*, 9 (1979), 86–107; 'The Cavalier World and John Cleve-
land', *Studies in Philology*, 78 (1981), 61–86. Since that time there has of
course been much research into varieties of philosophical scepticism in
the Renaissance and into philosophical scepticism in relation to Shake-
speare. As regards the former, see especially: M. Burnyeat (ed.), *The
Skeptical Tradition* (Berkeley: University of California Press, 1983);
R. H. Popkin, 'Theories of Knowledge', in *The Cambridge History of
Renaissance Philosophy*, eds C. B. Schmitt and Q. Skinner (Cambridge:
Cambridge University Press, 1988), pp. 668–84 (building in part on his
monograph of 1979); B. P. Copenhaver and C. B. Schmitt, *Renaissance
Philosophy* (Oxford: Oxford University Press, 1992), pp. 196–284; S.
Gaukroger, *Descartes: An Intellectual Biography* (Oxford: Clarendon Press,
1995), pp. 184–6, 309–21. As regards the latter, relevant work is cited
in the notes to the following chapters. However, for widely ranging
and quite different introductions to the topic see G. Bradshaw, *Shake-
speare's Scepticism* (Brighton: Harvester, 1987) and S. Cavell, '*Coriolanus*
and Interpretations of Politics', in *Themes Out of School: Effects and
Causes* (San Francisco: North Point, 1984), pp. 60–96, also S. Cavell,
'Macbeth Appalled', in *The Cavell Reader*, ed. S. Mulhall (Oxford:
Blackwell, 1996), pp. 198–220. In relation to Cavell see S. Mulhall,
Stanley Cavell: Philosophy's Recounting of the Ordinary (Oxford: Clarendon
Press, 1994), pp. 185–206, and Gaukroger, cited above.

3.   Introductions to debates about the notion of wisdom in the Renaissance
can be found in E. F. Rice, *The Renaissance Idea of Wisdom* (Cambridge,
Mass.: Harvard University Press, 1958); R. Hoopes, *Right Reason in the
English Renaissance* (Cambridge, Mass.: Harvard University Press, 1962);
V. Kahn, *Rhetoric, Prudence, and Skepticism in the Renaissance* (Ithaca and
London: Cornell University Press, 1985).

4.   Introductions to Renaissance historiography, to its 'sense of the past',
can be found in: P. Burke, *The Renaissance Sense of the Past* (London:
Arnold, 1969); D. Hay, *Annalists and Historians: Western Historiography
from the Eighth to the Eighteenth Centuries* (London: Methuen, 1977),
pp. 87–168; E. Breisach, *Historiography Ancient, Medieval, and Modern*

(Chicago and London: University of Chicago Press, 1983), pp. 153–95; J. M. Levine, *Humanism and History: Origins of Modern English Historiography* (Ithaca and London: Cornell University Press, 1987), pp. 19–154; D. R. Woolf, *The Idea of History in Early Stuart England* (Toronto: Toronto University Press, 1990), pp. 3–104. See also: R. L. Smallwood, 'Shakespeare's Use of History', in *The Cambridge Companion to Shakespeare Studies*, ed. S. Wells (Cambridge: Cambridge University Press, 1986), pp. 143–62; P. Rackin, *Stages of History: Shakespeare's English Chronicles* (Ithaca and London: Cornell University Press, 1990); J. Bate, *The Genius of Shakespeare* (London: Picador, 1997), pp. 200–30.

5. For introductions to the current debate about male homosociality and homosexuality in Renaissance Europe, and especially in Shakespeare's England, see: A. Bray, *Homosexuality in Renaissance England* (London: Gay Men's Press, 1982); E. K. Sedgwick, *Between Men: English Literature and Male Homosocial Desire* (New York: Columbia University Press, 1985); J. M. Saslow, *Ganymede in the Renaissance: Homosexuality in Art and Society* (New Haven and London: Yale University Press, 1986); B. R. Smith, *Homosexual Desire in Shakespeare's England: A Cultural Poetics* (Chicago and London: Chicago University Press, 1991); J. Goldberg, *Sodometries* (Stanford: Stanford University Press, 1992); C. J. Summers (ed.), *Homosexuality in Renaissance and Enlightenment England: Literary Representations in Historical Context* (New York: Haworth Press, 1992); S. Orgel, *Impersonations: The Performance of Gender in Shakespeare's England* (Cambridge: Cambridge University Press, 1996). For introductions to the current debate, likewise, about femaleness: R. Kelso, *Doctrine for the Lady of the Renaissance* (Urbana: University of Illinois Press, 1956); I. Maclean, *The Renaissance Notion of Woman: A Study in the Fortunes of Scholasticism and Medical Science in European Intellectual Life* (Cambridge: Cambridge University Press, 1980); L. Woodbridge, *Women and the English Renaissance: Literature and the Nature of Womankind, 1540–1620* (Urbana: University of Illinois Press, 1984); P. J. Benson, *The Invention of the Renaissance Woman: The Challenge of Female Independence in the Literature and Thought of Italy and England* (University Park: Pennsylvania State University Press, 1992); G. Duby and M. Perrot (gen. eds), *A History of Women: Renaissance and Enlightenment Paradoxes* (Cambridge, Mass. and London: Harvard University Press, 1993); O. Hufton, *The Prospect Before Her: A History of Women in Western Europe*, vol. 1 (London: HarperCollins, 1995); A. Laurence, *Women in England 1500–1760: A Social History* (1994; rpt. London: Phoenix, 1996). Many of the books listed above refer to or discuss Shakespearean texts.

6. That is to say, using the *Metamorphoses* and the *Fasti* as narrative sources offered him that opportunity in general; using the former and the *Rime* in order to represent gender offered it to him in specific ways.

7. The chronology of the poems is not absolutely clear, it should be added. Their chronology is discussed at the beginnings of Chapters 1–3.

Chapter 1

Venus and Adonis

(I) THE MINOR EPIC. LODGE'S *SCILLAES METAMORPHOSIS*

Venus and Adonis was the first of Shakespeare's poems to be published. It was registered at Stationers' Hall on 18 April 1593 and may have been begun in the summer of the previous year.[1] For much of the time, approximately between that summer and May 1594, the London theatres were closed because of the plague.[2] His career as a playwright interrupted, Shakespeare took the opportunity to present himself publicly as someone who could write not only plays.[3] He dedicated his poem to Henry Wriothesley, Earl of Southampton, who was then nineteen years old, prominent at court and a sought-after patron.[4] As has often been pointed out, the wording of the dedication gives one no reason to believe that Shakespeare knew the Earl well, or even at all.[5] Moreover, what he hoped to gain from dedicating the poem to Southampton is not clear. Shakespeare no doubt desired the prestige of patronage by the Earl; he also probably wanted more than prestige. It may be that he wanted hospitality in a comfortable residence outside London and hence away from the plague. Perhaps he wanted, indirectly or directly, financial support now that his livelihood as a dramatist was under threat.[6] Whatever his likely hopes, his gains – if any – are unknown.

The poem through which Shakespeare courted the Earl's attention is in kind a minor epic, or epyllion.[7] Some reasons for poems such as Shakespeare's *Venus and Adonis*, Marlowe's *Hero and Leander*, and others by their contemporaries or successors being called 'minor epics' have been usefully suggested by Clark Hulse:

> Minor epic is linked most closely to epic in its materials; its characteristic diction, verse forms, and mythological imagery all seek out the marvelous and often the extravagant. Its amorous action is quite literally the minor action of epic, set in counterpoint to the major themes of public and military virtue. . . . And, like so many epics, it is a mixed genre, presenting its objects with motifs from drama and lyric, especially the sonnet and pastoral.[8]

Thomas Lodge's *Scillaes Metamorphosis* (1589) appears to have been the first of the English minor epics. Like most of the minor epics subsequent to it, the poem is partly an imitation of and partly an elaboration on a story as re-told by Ovid. Not solely the *Metamorphoses* was used, of course, in Lodge's making of his poem – something that also links it to others of its kind. Furthermore Lodge does not merely re-tell Ovid's version of the Glaucus and Scilla myth; nor does he suggest that it has a moral content, as English verse translations or imitations of Ovidian narratives, prior to his poem, tended to do.[9] He playfully revises the Ovidian narrative on which he draws – just as Ovid, in his epic, playfully revised the familiar form of the myth.[10] Glaucus, for instance, becomes in Lodge's poem a deft, amusing parody of the unhappy male lover to be seen in so much other Elizabethan verse: the sea-god ponderously complains, at comically tedious length, of his unrequited love (as in stanzas 18–32); he is comic, too, in his long-winded self-pity (as in stanzas 43–69). Then, too, in the *Metamorphoses* Scilla is transformed by a jealous rival, a witch, who poisons her, whereas in Lodge's poem Cupid punishes her for disdaining Glaucus, her loyal suitor, but her consequent transformation results from her mental sufferings (see stanzas 115–24). Lodge's revision of Ovidian fable is wittily parodic. Creating a (mostly) comic Glaucus, he parodies Ovidian narrative in order to parody an aspect of current literary fashion. And instead of tacking on or inserting a moral to legitimize his doubly parodic fiction, for the quite different benefit of an apparently young, male audience he offers male wish-fulfilment (a disdainful object of desire is punished) and male sexual fantasy (a bevy of attractive, sympathetic, sexually aware females surrrounds Glaucus, and he is freed from unrequited love).[11] The poem ends with the narrator's repetition, notionally to the female reader but, more likely, for the male reader's delectation, of a message from Glaucus: '*Nymphs must yield, when faithful lovers stray not*' (L'ENVOY, l.3).

The narrator, who in repeating that message confirms the poem's abandonment of the convention that the *Metamorphoses* should be read as moral allegory, is himself one of the poem's significantly new elements. He is the frame to the poem's action; he is also closely involved in its action; in fact, he is a main figure in the poem from its beginning. Represented as mingling ironic ingenuousness with a more overt sophistication, a sensitivity to pathos with a sense of the ludic and the ludicrous, he is as well a quite distinctly characterized figure: like others in the tale in as much as he is a disappointed lover and (or) preoccupied with the psychology of sexual experience, but unlike those others in having the traits of ironic ingenuousness and so on.[12] Because he is indeed a main figure in the poem and quite distinctly individualized, Lodge's narrator would seem to be new to Tudor verse narrative derived, by imitation or by translation, from the *Metamorphoses* – new, that is to say, with the appearance of the minor epic itself.[13] Moreover, those features that seem to make him novel – and one would want to emphasize here his obtrusiveness in conjunction with the specific traits that distinguish him from the other figures in the poem – seem at the same time to make him resemble the narrator fashioned by Ovid in his epic.[14] Lodge appropriately gave a poem close in spirit to the *Metamorphoses* a narrator recalling the ironic, sophisticated, game-playing narrator who guides the reader through Ovid's tales of transformation.[15]

No one, I think, would want to argue that *Venus and Adonis* is both directly and heavily indebted to *Scillaes Metamorphosis*, although there have been suggestions that at some moments Shakespeare's poem clearly echoes Lodge's.[16] Yet it would seem reasonable to argue that Lodge's poem provided Shakespeare with an opportunity. *Scillaes Metamorphosis* was written primarily for a specific, sophisticated audience, the young men at the Inns of Court. When Shakespeare wrote *Venus and Adonis* he was, apparently, no longer writing for the very diverse audience of the playhouse but for an audience similar to that of Lodge's poem; for a similar audience he wrote a poem of the same kind as Lodge's.[17] Of course one member of that new audience was hopefully identified by his poem's being dedicated to the Earl of Southampton. Shakespeare, then, in his new role as non-dramatic poet, wrote for a new audience – particularly including the Earl as (possibly) also a patron – a new poem of a new kind.[18] It now seems appropriate to look at the concerns and strategies of Shakespeare's poem, and at how his poem relates not only to *Scillaes Metamorphosis* but, as well, to other poems by his contemporaries or successors.

(II) THE POEM'S NARRATOR. VENUS AND THE
MULTIPLICITY, THE OTHERNESS OF LOVE

Before discussion of Venus and Adonis as they are fashioned in Shakespeare's poem, something must be said of the poem's narrator, for in presenting Venus and Adonis to the reader he himself is carefully presented. Unlike Lodge's narrator he is not a character in the story he relates, yet like Lodge's narrator he is distinctly individuated as a storyteller. He has some characteristics in common with the narrator of *Scillaes Metamorphosis* but those seem to derive from the characterization of Ovid's narrator in the *Metamorphoses*. It may be that Shakespeare modelled his narrator on Lodge's, elaborating on Lodge's achievement; it is also possible, and I think more probable, that Lodge's poem suggested to Shakespeare how effectively Ovid's narrator could be recreated in English verse.[19] Like the speaker of Ovid's epic, Shakespeare's urbanely plays with myth, implicitly being far too sophisticated to accept it merely at face value. He brings out its comic incongruities (like Ovid's speaker, however, he does not always bring out merely the comic aspects or possibilities of ancient myth); he brings out its paradoxes (enlarging on or inventing them). He seems at a distance from what he describes (though, like Ovid's speaker, he can also at times seem very responsive to scenes of pathos or of suffering); he confronts the reader with the unexpected; he favours epigrams and the epigrammatic – and also luxuriant description. One result of the many specific similarities between Shakespeare's narrator and Ovid's is a further and more comprehensive similarity: the former, like the latter, appears to be in almost total control of the mythic world that he pictures.[20] Thus Shakespeare's narrator indicates his creator's insight into and ability to recreate the narrator of Ovid's *Metamorphoses*; nonetheless, when one sees the narrator presenting and, hence, represented with Venus and Adonis, one sees that Shakespeare's poem as a whole signals its maker's mastery of the genre that Lodge had recently introduced into Tudor literature.

The Venus presented by Shakespeare's narrator has been studied in recent times from mainly two angles. Sometimes she has been looked at as if a character in a play, which seems appropriate enough given that her creator was a playwright and that he gave her speech after speech. As a result, the consistencies, fluctuations and contradictions in her characterization have been often discussed, with a good deal of agreement but by no means with unanimity.[21] Sometimes she has been studied in connection with particular aspects of Renaissance symbolism or thinking about ancient myths. Critical commentary adopting that angle of approach has occasionally interpreted Venus as a simple, symbolic figure but, more usually, as an evocatively allegorical one – especially, of course, in the context of some Renaissance interpretations of the Venus and Adonis story.[22] Here, employing both well-established ways of approach, I want to offer a new account of Venus' presentation in the poem. First it will be argued that the characterization of Venus, although often acknowledged to be various, is in fact far more diverse than has been recognized. Most of the manifold aspects of her, it will be suggested at the same time, accord with (maybe derive from, partly or wholly) ancient representations of her that were still known and studied in Shakespeare's time, as can be seen from a range of contemporary books about the meanings of ancient myths.[23] The main points of that first argument will be: that even if most of the different aspects of Venus' characterization seem conventional, frequently their conventionality is subverted; that, in presenting the goddess of love as having a great variety of aspects, Shakespeare's narrator implies not merely love's many-sidedness but its often incongruous multiplicity. The second argument put forward will be that one of the more important aspects of Venus' characterization is her discovering the familiar, human experience of loving another in vain.[24] It will be suggested that her experiencing the misery of unrequited human love has significance for a couple of reasons. She comes to know something of not only the unhappiness to be found in human love but, as well, of how love can usurp control over a human consciousness.[25] Therefore the goddess of love comes experientially to know – to a degree – a phenomenon that she has necessarily seen yet never felt. For her, the experience of loving Adonis both in vain and obsessively is a new, alien experience: ultimately, the experience of love as otherness. The third and last major argument proposed in what follows will be that Venus, herself partly transformed by her unrequited love for Adonis, offers him her love as a means for his achieving self-transformation. To be more specific, it will be argued that, in offering Adonis her love, Venus simultaneously offers him metamorphosis, a redefined subjectivity, in which self-perfection and safety will be supposedly gained but a loss of self will be inevitable.

Venus had been seen since ancient times as having a wide range of aspects; there were, as various writers had demonstrated, many Venuses. Early in her initial wooing of Adonis, Venus uses a tactically considered, schematic language of sexual seduction, and it characterizes her as a goddess of physical desire, wise in the techniques of enticement. That characterization is developed when she goes on to say:

'Vouchsafe, thou wonder, to alight thy steed,
And rein his proud head to the saddle-bow;
If thou wilt deign this favour, for thy meed
A thousand honey secrets shalt thou know.
        Here come and sit, where never serpent hisses,
        And being set, I'll smother thee with kisses.

'And yet not cloy thy lips with loath'd satiety,
But rather famish them amid their plenty,
Making them red, and pale, with fresh variety:
Ten kisses short as one, one long as twenty.
    A summer's day will seem an hour but short,
    Being wasted in such time-beguiling sport.'

                                                                    (ll. 13–24)

The rest of Venus' opening speech suggests both the mingling of
imagination with sensuality in her attempt to seduce Adonis and
how intensely, almost boundlessly physical her desire for him is. The
speech as a whole, then, shows the goddess of love to be skilled in
the deceptive language and rhetoric of seduction; it shows, too, that
she is obsessive in her desire, in effect seeking infinite physical enjoy-
ment of Adonis who, in his physicality, is finite. Yet while Venus'
opening speech vigorously characterizes her, it does so in accord
with two ancient versions of the goddess which were still current in
the sixteenth century. Insofar as she is the calculating rhetorician of
love, Shakespeare's Venus recalls the *Venus Mechanitis* of the ancient
world, the Venus practised in love's verbal and other artifices.[26] Insofar
as she is the goddess of virtually limitless physical desire, she recalls
Venus Vulgaris, an ancient representation of Venus as the goddess of
wholly sensual love.[27] Venus' opening speech at once forcefully pre-
sents her and offers what can be seen as a conventional representation
of her. It seems clear, however, that whether Shakespeare's Venus
merely harmonizes with or actually derives from convention, the
conventional elements in her characterization are treated ironically.
For a start, Venus fails as a rhetorician of love. Her language and tactics
of seduction are problematic because some of their main images for
praising Adonis' exceptional beauty also highlight its transience and
(or) vulnerability ('flower', 'doves', 'roses'). But a far more important
problem is that in trying to seduce Adonis she uses the wrong language
– the wrong language and rhetoric for her particular audience.[28]
Maybe Venus does not fully recognize that Adonis is not only very
young and inexperienced but very reluctant as well; it seems likelier,
though, that in her urgency she just pays too little attention to those
things. Whatever the case, her speech implies that she is both a
connoisseur of the erotic ('A thousand honey secrets shalt thou know')
and smothering ('I'll smother thee with kisses'), greedy in her passion
(see ll. 19–24, *passim*). Adonis has, clearly enough, no wish to be
smothered by Venus' greedy passion, something the introductory
stanza of the poem has indicated and that the rest of it makes explicit.
Therefore her words of love repel him; and, failing to express her

desire persuasively in words, she gets no chance to express it physic-
ally to her satisfaction. In effect, she fails as *Venus Mechanitis* and so is
frustrated as *Venus Vulgaris*. It could be suggested that her opening
speech even has the result of turning her into a parodic *Venus
Verticordia*, the Venus who promotes chastity in women – given that
Adonis is described as having some female attributes.

Perhaps two other features of Venus' presentation here might be
briefly considered before further aspects of her in the poem are dis-
cussed. When Venus tries to seduce Adonis she acts, according to the
poem's initial stanza, like an assertive, male lover. Some of the words
she chooses and her tactics of persuasion distinctly suggest that. For
example, her insistence that the beauty of her beloved is unique,
although justified by its actually being so, is of course conventional
in sixteenth- and seventeenth-century English love verse written in
imitation of Petrarch's, and by men to or about women. No less con-
ventional in that love verse are celebrations of female beauty in terms
of emphatic images of whiteness and redness, such as appear in
Venus' praise of Adonis' beauty.[29] Likewise, the male speakers in that
love verse sometimes offer their ladies gifts in order to win their affec-
tions. To cite a pair of obvious instances, Marlowe's speaker in 'Come
live with me and be my love' offers gifts to his beloved; Damon, in
Marvell's 'Damon the Mower', tells of the gifts with which he has
wooed his beloved Juliana.[30] Venus, too, offers Adonis a gift, an
elaborate enticement in order to bring him physically close to her
('A thousand honey secrets . . .'). As those examples reveal, Venus uses
a predominantly male, assertive (Petrarchan) language and rhetoric of
love. The outcome is, though, that when Venus acts 'like a bold-fac'd
suitor' in using such a language/rhetoric she uses it inappropriately,
after the fashion described above, and appears comic. Shakespeare's
Venus seems, as it were, to be a *Venus Mechanitis* who simultaneously
fails and acts out a comedy of gender-reversal. And that doubly ironic
presentation of her is immediately developed. Having misemployed
language in her initial attempt to make Adonis love her, she then
successfully persuades herself of his sexual inclinations by misreading
the body language of his 'sweating palm' (l. 25). She cannot or will
not read his 'sweating palm' as signifying physical discomfort and (or)
emotional distress. Moreover the comedy of gender-reversal becomes
almost grotesque when Venus subsequently 'pluck[s]' Adonis from his
horse (l. 30), tucks him under her arm (l. 32) and finally 'thrust[s]' him
to the ground (l. 41). The comedy of gender-reversal is, nonetheless,
more shrewd than such an instance of it might indicate, and that more
interesting dimension to it will be considered later in this discussion.

(III) VENUS AND METAMORPHOSIS

The final feature of Venus' presentation here that I wish to glance at is this: in her attempt to seduce Adonis she offers him a heightening of his beauty to be achieved through transformation. Playfully assuring Adonis that when 'smother[ing him] with kisses' (l. 18) she will 'not cloy [his] lips with loath'd satiety' (l. 19), Venus goes on to assert that in fact she will enhance their beauty, '[m]aking them red, and pale, with fresh variety' (l. 21). She will add, that is, to the 'white and red' of Adonis' natural beauty (l. 10) – and specifically to the natural beauty of his (red) lips – through her art of sexuality, making his lips startlingly change in colour and thus into instances of the Renaissance aesthetic principle of *varietà* (variety: connected with the principle, or ideal, of *grazia* – that is, an elegance delightful to the observer/ reader).[31] To receive that heightening of his beauty, Adonis must allow himself to be transformed from an asexual to a sexual being. For his beauty to be transformed, in other words, he must allow himself to be metamorphosed. The 'time-beguiling sport' (l. 24) of sexual play will involve at once his superficial aesthetic transformation and a metamorphosis of his subjectivity. Venus' offer of metamorphosis will be repeatedly made to Adonis throughout the poem. One of those offers, in particular, is both challenging and complex. The motif's introduction occurs, however, in her first speech; its initial, ludic appearance suggests the aesthetic element in Venus' connoisseurship of the erotic and Adonis' presentation in the rest of the poem as an aesthetic/sexual object.

It seems reasonable to argue that the aspects of Venus so far discussed (*Venus Mechanitis* and *Venus Vulgaris*, to put it briefly) recur more often throughout Shakespeare's poem than do virtually any of the others contributing to her many-sided characterization, and hence their elaborate, initial encoding has been examined in some detail. There is no need, I think, for the subsequent treatment of those aspects to be completely traced since in that initial encoding their defining features are indicated. Some of the modifications to them, nonetheless, do have to be looked at and now will be, in the context of an account of Venus' other guises in the poem. One of those, another major aspect of the goddess in the poem, is that of *Venus Genetrix*: the Venus, from ancient times to those of Shakespeare, associated with the generative power in nature, fertility and the desire to reproduce beauty through offspring (to take the most obvious illustration, the beauty of one's beloved). There has often been mention of Shakespeare's Venus in that role but the question remains as to how the role functions.[32] Insofar as Shakespeare's Venus resembles *Venus Genetrix*, she does so problematically. When Adonis' stallion breaks away from where it has been tied and runs after '[a] breeding jennet' (l. 260), it forcefully displays the generative impulse. Venus, turning the horse into an example for its master, suggests that he too should do, with her, what comes naturally:

'Let me excuse thy courser, gentle boy,
And learn of him, I heartily beseech thee,
To take advantage on presented joy;
Though I were dumb, yet his proceedings teach thee.
    O learn to love. . . .

                                                                (ll. 403–7)

But in fact Venus argues there that Adonis, in acting 'naturally', should imitate solely animal desire: that his natural love for her should be only of and for the body. Her love for him is certainly of that kind, what Pico called 'Bestial . . . Love' as distinct from human or divine love.[33] It is natural and obsessively physical, as the image of the 'glutton eye' in her immediately preceding words makes startlingly clear:

'Who see his true-love in her naked bed,
Teaching the sheets a whiter hue than white,
But when his glutton eye so full hath fed,
His other agents aim at like delight?

                                                                (ll. 397–400)

That 'glutton eye' image, furthermore, connects with other images in the poem that insistently imply Venus' devouring sexuality.[34] And all those link with the images suggesting that her desire is predatory as well as natural, the best known of which are probably the simile of the 'empty eagle . . . devouring all in haste, /Till either gorge be stuff'd or prey be gone' (ll. 55–8, a comparison made by the narrator), and the metaphor likening her to the boar (ll. 1117–18, a comparison made by Venus herself). If she resembles *Venus Genetrix* she is a parodic, a narrowly and brutally 'natural' version of that divinity: in effect, another manifestation of *Venus Vulgaris*. That being granted, the problematics of Venus as *Venus Genetrix* do not, even so, end there.

The similarity between Shakespeare's Venus and *Venus Genetrix* also seems ironic in at least a couple of other ways. First, when Venus speaks in effect as *Venus Genetrix* – celebrating the generative impulse in nature, urging Adonis to reproduce his unique beauty through offspring – she speaks primarily, at the very least, to seduce

him.[35] What could be called the *Venus Genetrix* aspect of her character-
ization is therefore subordinate to the (*de facto*) *Venus Mechanitis* and
Venus Vulgaris aspects.[36] Second, when Venus searches desperately for
Adonis after he has gone to hunt the boar, there occurs this description
of nature impeding the preoccupied goddess:

> And as she runs, the bushes in the way
> Some catch her by the neck, some kiss her face,
> Some twine about her thigh to make her stay:
> She wildly breaketh from their strict embrace,
> > Like a milch doe, whose swelling dugs do ache,
> > Hasting to feed her fawn hid in some brake.

(ll. 871–6)

The elision of the sexual and the maternal in that description of Venus
incongruously mingles her *Vulgaris* and *Genetrix* aspects.[37] However
it is ironic, too, that the goddess whose love almost smothered Adonis
now finds herself almost imprisoned by a sexually assertive natural
world with which, as *Venus Genetrix*, she is associated. She comes to
experience something of what Adonis appears to have been undergoing
throughout much of the poem, and 'wildly breaketh' indicates her
response. The final function of Venus as *Venus Genetrix* may, then, be
twofold. In that particular role she seems to imply the natural brutality
and reductiveness, rather than the natural, creative beneficence, of
sexual desire. Perhaps more important, in that role she seems also to
help make problematic the nature of 'nature' in Shakespeare's poem.
When trying to seduce Adonis she appeals recurrently to 'nature';
Adonis appeals to 'nature' in rejecting her. But if she is, at least in
part, a nature/fertility divinity who is incomplete as well as self-
divided in being so – while, moreover, Adonis' perception of 'nature'
differs in important respects from hers – her role as *Venus Genetrix*
seems to emphasize the ambiguity of 'nature' in her fictional world
and also in ours, its openness to appropriation for the justifying of
quite opposite ends.

There are a great many further aspects to Shakespeare's Venus.
For a start, she is also a deceiver. Just after telling Adonis that even
Mars the god of war has wooed her (ll. 97–102), she reassures him
that, if he makes love to her, no one will find out and therefore
secrecy will preserve his honour (ll. 121–6). She omits to tell Adonis
that Vulcan, her husband, not only caught Mars and her in bed but
added to their embarrassment by calling in the other gods to share
his discovery, an omission all too obvious to the reader. In trying to
trick Adonis – and she tries more than once in the course of the tale

– she bears a clear likeness to the conventional *Venus Apaturia* (Venus the Deceiver).[38] The poem reveals, though, that Venus has most success in unwittingly deceiving herself (as when, for example, she persuades herself that Adonis' 'sweating palm' indicates his amorous disposition). Venus the deceived Deceiver is, additionally, a prophet. She uncertainly foresees Adonis' death at the hunt (ll. 661–6). Soon after his death she deliberately and formally foretells what the experience of love will thenceforward be, always and everywhere (ll. 1135–64). Again, an old convention seems to underlie this aspect of her characterization: that of Venus as *Magistra Divinandi* (Mistress of/Instructor in Prophesying).[39] However, Shakespeare's Venus again parodically refigures convention. Jealousy prompts her first, accurate, hesitant foretelling (l. 657). Her second is anachronistic, for, as the myths show, love had already and widely been what she announces it will become. Her wholly negative vision of love's future seems, moreover, open to query since the reader could object that its truth is incomplete. The mock-explanatory prophecy, that is to say, actually tells more about Venus' bitterness, and selfishness, than it does about the nature of love supposedly since Adonis' death.

Although other aspects of Shakespeare's Venus in relation to conventional representations of the goddess still remain to be examined, for example, the link between her and *Venus Meretrix* (Venus the Prostitute; see ll. 511–22), there is space for study of only one more of her guises: her pervasive guise as *Venus Victrix* (Venus the Conqueror). The ancient title Venus the Conqueror referred, as is fairly well known, to Venus' overcoming Mars, the god of war, through the power of her beauty and of his desire for her. In the sixteenth century that title was often interpreted as signifying Love's capacity to overcome Strife, or even Love's capacity to bind the conflicting elements of the universe into an harmonious discord.[40] The connection between Shakespeare's Venus and *Venus Victrix* is made explicit in the poem. Venus boasts to Adonis:

'I have been woo'd as I entreat thee now,
Even by the stern and direful god of war,
Whose sinewy neck in battle ne'er did bow,
Who conquers where he comes in every jar;
     Yet hath he been my captive and my slave,
     And begg'd for that which thou unask'd shalt have.

'Over my altars hath he hung his lance,
His batter'd shield, his uncontrolled crest;
And for my sake hath learn'd to sport and dance,

To toy, to wanton, dally, smile and jest,
  Scorning his churlish drum and ensign red,
  Making my arms his field, his tent my bed.

'Thus he that overrul'd I oversway'd,
Leading him prisoner in a red rose chain:
Strong-temper'd steel his stronger strength obey'd,
Yet was he servile to my coy disdain.

(ll. 97–112)

But of what kind is that connection? Shakespeare's Venus seems to be a failed *Venus Victrix*; more important, the *Venus Victrix* motif itself – as an emblem of Love's salutary power – seems to be dismantled throughout the poem.

When Venus has finished recounting her victory over Mars, she immediately says to Adonis: ' "O! be not proud, nor brag not of thy might, /For mastering her that foil'd the god of fight" ' (ll. 113–14). Her point is, of course, that Adonis has made her love him (simply by being irresistible) and in doing so has conquered Venus the Conqueror, who overcame even the god of war. She consciously inverts the *Venus Victrix* motif and identifies herself as a now-failed, now-parodic Venus the Conqueror. As is obvious enough, her admission is partly true because she has indeed been overcome by Adonis' beauty. Yet it is also disingenuous, mere flattery to seduce Adonis: she reveals herself as a failed/parodic *Venus Victrix* so that she can subsequently conquer him and re-enact her role as victor. At this moment of the poem, that is to say, she puts her role as *Venus Victrix* in the service of her roles as *Venus Mechanitis* and *Venus Vulgaris* so that, ultimately, the first and third of those roles can be fused. Her failure to seduce Adonis means, however, that she remains just the failed and parodic *Venus Victrix* she disingenuously claims to be.

Nonetheless Venus does have her moments of victory. She 'pluck[s]' (l. 30) Adonis from his horse, for example, walks off with him under her arm and then pushes him to the ground (ll. 32–42). To take another example, she forces her kisses on him with the greed and dominance of an 'empty eagle' devouring its prey (l. 55; cf. ll. 57–8 and 61). Again, Adonis when imprisoned 'in her arms' (l. 68) is as helpless as a 'bird . . . tangled in a net' (l. 67). Likewise, her hand imprisons his as 'a gaol of snow' might 'a lily' or as 'an alabaster band' might a piece of 'ivory' (ll. 362–3). Her lips 'conquer' (l. 549) his and she preys on him like a 'vulture' (l. 551) or a plunderer (ll. 553–8). Those are indeed moments of victory but they are all flawed.[41] The reader sees Venus as a ludicrous, bestial, predatory or, at the least, visually perfect yet wholly undesired Conqueror. The narrator's ironic imaging of her as a Victor seems relentless: as the examples above indicate, he subverts the *Venus Victrix* motif not only once in the poem but throughout it. The implication would appear to be that, in the world of the poem, the *Venus Victrix* motif cannot function as an emblem of Love's overcoming Strife, or of Love's making the universe into an harmonious discord. The motif, as a signifier of love's benignly invincible power, is pervasively, comically, vehemently dismantled.

Those aspects of Venus' characterization which seem to accord with, and often to refigure, conventional representations of her suggest love to be not one thing, nor merely a number of things, but a great range of things. They emphasize love's multiplicity – both within and outside the fictive world of *Venus and Adonis* – and imply how unstable and protean, how incongruous and dangerous love can be in its manifold variety. In doing so they seem as well to imply that no single definition can encompass love. Notably absent among them, and therefore foregrounded by its absence, is a connection between Shakespeare's Venus and the conventional *Venus Urania*, the Venus of Divine Love. Certainly it is true that Venus asserts: 'Love is a spirit all compact of fire, /Not gross to sink, but light, and will aspire' (ll. 149–50). Even so, her description of love as a fiery 'spirit' receives little, if any, confirmation in the rest of the poem, the 'gross' physicality of her love for Adonis instead being stressed. And Adonis, just after he has associated her with *Venus Vulgaris* (l. 790), complains – accurately enough given his encounter with the goddess: '[L]ove to heaven is fled, /Since sweating lust on earth usurp'd his name' (ll. 793–4).[42] As far as the conventional, yet often refigured aspects of Shakespeare's Venus reveal, love in its manifold variety may be unstable, protean, incongruous and dangerous – insistent, self-demeaning and frequently comic, one could add – but it is not divine, though Venus is of course a goddess.

Although the different aspects of Shakespeare's Venus that are related, directly or otherwise, to the conventions of ancient religious practice or to those of mythography seem to form the major part of her characterization, there appears to be at least one further, important element in her portrayal: her personal discovery, as it were, of the way humans experience unrequited love – a greatly disorientating discovery for her, even though one necessarily limited by the fact that she is a goddess. That element of Venus' characterization often makes her look comic, adding to the ludic treatment of her throughout the tale. However the main point to be emphasized here is that, in partly discovering human experience of unrequited love, Venus also discovers, to a degree, the experience of love as otherness, as partly and disturbingly 'outside the system of normality or convention to which [she] belongs'.[43]

It was argued earlier in this discussion that Venus uses a predominantly male, in fact chiefly Petrarchan, language/rhetoric of love in order to seduce Adonis. She is given that form of erotic speech to involve her in simple (human) gender-reversal – to make her sexual assertiveness look clearly and oddly like male sexual assertiveness. Yet there is arguably another reason as well, namely, to suggest that in trying to seduce Adonis she comes personally to know how humans experience loving in vain. Venus' speech between ll. 187–216 provides brief, sample evidence of this. There Venus speaks to Adonis in what are obviously and mostly Petrarchan terms. ' "Thine eye darts forth the fire that burneth me . . . ," ' she says early on (l. 196), adding almost at once: ' "Art thou obdurate, flinty, hard as steel? /Nay more than flint, for stone at rain relenteth; /Art thou a woman's son and canst not feel/What 'tis to love, how want of love tormenteth?" ' (ll. 199–202). Those words suggest that the predominantly male form of erotic speech Venus uses can function not just to show her incongruously resembling 'a bold-fac'd [male] suitor' (l. 6) in her sexual aggressiveness but also, and simultaneously, to stress how human is her whole experience of loving Adonis in vain. To be more exact, those words suggest this: the Petrarchan language and rhetoric used so recurrently by Venus are able to involve her in (human) gender-reversal which is not merely a matter of narrowly limited analogy, for they at times function to confer on her many features of a primarily male, human, love psychology. Predictably, those features include angry, bewildered frustration and loss of self-control – the case in the passage quoted above – vulnerability, anguish, self-division, and so on, in keeping with the usual descriptions of male lovers in Petrarch-derived verse. And Venus' climactic words at this moment of the text, like her early ones, reveal that distinctly. A series of Petrarchan paradoxes recalls/anachronistically anticipates a multitude of fictional, male lovers' complaints to their disdainful beloveds: 'Fie, lifeless picture, cold and senseless stone, /Well-painted idol, image dull and dead, /Statue contenting but the eye alone . . .' (ll. 211–13). In short, the reader can see a more than superficial gender-reversal at work in some of Venus' speeches – but one working to make her appear recognizably (if *not* completely) human, rather than specifically male, in her experience of unrequited love.

The same process can sometimes be seen when Venus the would-be seducer is described in Petrarchan terms, whether or not she herself uses them. For example, just after Adonis has failed to recover his horse and has sat angrily down, Venus softly approaches him. The narrator remarks: 'O what a sight it was, wistly to view/How she came stealing to the wayward boy! /To note the fighting conflict of her hue, /How white and red each other did destroy!' (ll. 343–6). The Petrarchan images of 'white and red' imply Venus' alternating timidity and boldness or, as is also possible, bashfulness.[44] That emotional conflict is often ascribed in Petrarchan love poems (by means either of those images or of ones closely related to them) to a male lover cautiously approaching his disdainful beloved, as readers then and now would readily perceive. Venus' recurrent sexual assertiveness seems here to be modified by her knowledge that Adonis does not return her love. Consequently she draws near to him as might a wary human lover. Now it may be that her apparent wariness is merely a ploy to conceal her hitherto unsuccessful aggressiveness: that it is, in fact, a reinscription of her aggressiveness. Whatever the case, in the speech by her considered a moment ago she appears comically petulant in her human, sexual frustration; at this moment of the text, however, her human experience of unrequited love makes her appear comically hesitant but also pathetic, even if she may be falsely evoking pathos.

Much that is suggested by Venus' being repeatedly attributed with a Petrarchan love psychology seems to be summed up when the narrator compares her with Tantalus (see ll. 91–4 and 599–600). Those comparisons imply that her personal discovery of how humans experience unrequited love, even though limited, puts her in hell: for Venus, in effect, to feel how mortals experience loving in vain is to enter a hell of obsessive, frustrated desire. Her love for Adonis can therefore be seen as involving her in a second and simultaneous personal discovery, that of love as a new and alien experience.[45] The second discovery is limited because the first is also; nonetheless, it is significant because it means that, in loving Adonis, the goddess of love herself comes experientially to know something of love as otherness. She is led into human intensities of emotion: human yearning, frustration, misery and false hope.

A final point should be quickly added here. What might be called the Petrarchan humanizing of Venus contributes not only to the portrayal of her as would-be seducer but, as well, to the portrayal of her after Adonis has left (ll. 811ff.). In that latter part of the poem, nonetheless, it does not primarily indicate Venus' continued, personal discovery of how humans experience unrequited love; rather, it chiefly suggests her personal discovery of how humans experience separation from, and the death of, a beloved.[46] (Thus it also suggests development and intensification in her coming to know love as otherness.) For example, just after mentioning Adonis' departure from Venus, the narrator indicates her confusion, anxiety and misery by a series of motifs that recur throughout Petrarchan love verse (the lamenting lover's grief being echoed by nature, and so on; see ll. 823–46). Likewise, when he tells of her meeting with the boar (ll. 901–12) he describes her horrified response to the creature in Petrarchan terms (a sequence of paradoxes suggests her self-division and paralysis; see ll. 907–12). He accounts for her sudden change from belief to disbelief in Adonis' death by means of Petrarchan love psychology (there, too, the paradoxical is emphasized; see ll. 985–90). He partly describes her grieving for the dead Adonis, moreover, in Petrarchan terms (again, a paradoxical rhetoric indicates her self-division, as well as her confusion and loss of self-control; see, for example, ll. 1057–74). Unsurprisingly enough, for it was the case earlier in the poem, pathos is interwoven with comedy in those presentations of Venus humanized.[47]

A Venus humanized, even if only to a degree, is necessarily a Venus transformed. It was suggested above that self-transformation seems to be an enticement offered to Adonis when the goddess tries to seduce him. To repeat what was specifically suggested: in offering Adonis her love, Venus simultaneously offers him metamorphosis, a redefined subjectivity, in which self-perfection and safety will be supposedly gained but a loss of self will be inevitable. One instance of her putting that proposition to him has already been examined. In that particular instance, Venus implicitly promises Adonis self-perfection as a result of his sexual initiation. I want now to consider the most direct and elaborate offer of self-transformation that she makes to him (ll. 229–40), an offer in which she appears to envisage her own transformation.

At once embracing and imprisoning Adonis in her arms, Venus tells him: 'Within the circuit of this ivory pale [the fence, as it were, of her white arms]/I'll be a park, and thou shalt be my deer:/Feed where thou wilt . . .' (ll. 230–2). The goddess's serio-comic offer of transformation seems variously problematic. To begin with, her projected metamorphosis of her body into a site for Adonis to inhabit and enjoy, in fact, into a type of the 'ideal landscape', implies that to him she will be at once sentient and insentient, passive yet active, in her sexuality (active because, as she apparently sees it, she will in effect own Adonis: 'my deer/[dear]' she hopefully calls him in ll. 231–9).[48] More important, her projected metamorphosis of Adonis into her 'deer/[dear]' offers him a comprehensively redefined subjectivity – a new and ambiguous personal selfhood. Venus' 'deer' image suggests that, when sexually involved with her, he will be her beloved ('dear');

it also suggests, as she probably does not recognize, that in becoming her lover he will become less than human because merely concupiscent. His former role as someone committed to the active life will vanish. No longer a hunter, instead a captured creature of the hunt of love – the 'deer' image of course connecting with the motif of Venus as a predator – he will be both a new person and a lost one, safe from the consequences of his planned boar hunt (about which Venus does not yet know) but himself a hunter's prize. Venus' fantastic, sophisticated offer of metamorphosis to Adonis indicates that her desire for him necessitates his loss of self, his gaining a new, incongruously diminished selfhood. On the other hand, her imagined self-transformation does not so much imply change to her as it does change to his perception of her. Venus' disregard for Adonis' independent selfhood, which pervades her offer(s) of metamorphosis to him and indeed all her attempt to seduce him, is emblematized at the poem's end by her plucking the flower sprung from his blood and carrying it away.

The intricate portrayal of Shakespeare's Venus presents her as a diverse, unstable yet not incoherent characterization. If the goddess of love appears to be, for example, tender and callous, compassionate and predatory, sophisticated and naive, pathetic and comic, alluring but also at times repellent, her almost infinite variety is nonetheless held together by the force of her self-centred sexual desire. One Renaissance view of love, mentioned above, was that love's power draws into coherence the various and conflicting elements of the world, compelling them into an harmonious discord, or *discordia concors*. It seems reasonable to suggest that in *Venus and Adonis* the reader sees the goddess of love, and so erotic love itself, as *discordia concors*, centred upon desire's selfishness. The poem's representation of Venus implies love's often incongruous multiplicity. Her experience of love as otherness, co-existent with her humanized experience of love's frustration, implies human love's extremes of misery and of obsession (as well, momentarily, of elation) – a Petrarchan humanizing of the goddess being Shakespeare's recreation of Ovid's anthropomorphic refashioning ·of his divinities. Her offer of metamorphosis to Adonis indicates love's capacity to transform the lover and, chiefly, the unresponsive beloved should he (she) become in turn a lover. That transformation, it appears to be suggested, may involve uncertain gain but will involve unavoidable loss of self. Yet, as has just been proposed, the insistent egocentrism within the many aspects of Shakespeare's Venus seems to signal what remains constant amid her inconstancies, and thus those of human passion.

(IV) ADONIS THE RHETORICIAN. ADONIS, NARCISSUS
AND METAMORPHOSIS

Shakespeare's Adonis, like his Venus, has been primarily studied
either in terms of Renaissance thinking about myth and symbol or as
if a character in a play. Study in the first mode has connected Adonis
with the idea of beauty's transience, for example, a connection that
has been interestingly explored.[49] Study in the second mode has
closely traced his responses to Venus' sexual aggression, examining
his evasions, his defiances, and so on.[50] In what follows, and so in
parallel to my discussion of Venus, both familiar critical approaches
are used but new arguments about Adonis' characterization are put
forward. It is initially argued that, in response to Venus' assertive
(male) rhetoric of seduction, Adonis has at once an eloquent, silent,
female rhetoric of rejection and a Platonic, male rhetoric of love. He
also has, of course, an adolescent rhetoric of indignation and im-
patience at harassment. He has, that is to say, a rhetoric of chastity
through which to counter the goddess's *de facto* role as *Venus Mechanitis*.
Next it is argued that when Adonis refuses the goddess's seductive –
from her point of view – offer(s) of metamorphosis, he does not
thereby merely resemble Narcissus, with whom Venus scornfully
identifies him because of his unresponsiveness to her. On the contrary,
in some important respects he virtually becomes an antithesis to
Narcissus, almost an anti-Narcissus figure, and in this context self-
knowledge seems to be a central issue. Finally it is argued that not
Venus but Adonis appears to be foregrounded as the object of sexual
desire in Shakespeare's narrative. To be more specific, it is argued
that the narrator, particularly through his presentation of Venus, sets
up Adonis as the object of the male gaze.[51]

When confronting the unwelcome, mainly Petrarchan language and
rhetoric of seduction directed at him by Venus, and her bodily aggres-
sion, which often accompanies it, Adonis sometimes reacts with speech
whose terse, sullen anger seems appropriate to his years and his situation.
'"Fie, no more of love!/The sun doth burn my face, I must remove,"'
he cries when Venus tells him of his duty to breed or else become like
Narcissus (ll. 185–6; see ll. 157–74). At another moment, when Venus
forgets what she was talking about and asks, '"Where did I leave?"'
Adonis replies: '"No matter where . . . ,/Leave me, and then the story
aptly ends . . ."' (ll. 715–16). That adolescent rhetoric of indignation
and impatience has occasionally, moreover, a feminine tone to it, so
that it seems appropriate not only to Adonis' years and circumstances
but also to the poem's recurrent description of his beauty in female

terms – for example, in terms of perfect whiteness and redness, which immediately evoke the Petrarchan ideal of female beauty (as in l. 10). When Venus strokes Adonis' cheek then imprisons his hand, to cite one instance (ll. 352–64), he cries out: ' "For shame," . . . "let go, and let me go . . ." ' (l. 379; cf. l. 53).[52] The feminine tone that can be heard in such outbursts links them with a distinctly female rhetoric that Adonis at times uses, apparently not knowing that it is female.

Two episodes in the poem illustrate that clearly. In an early episode, Venus pushes Adonis to the ground (ll. 40–1) and he begins 'to chide' her (l. 46). She silences him, stopping his lips and warning that she will not let him speak in opposition to her (ll. 46–8). The narrator thereupon says: 'He [Adonis] burns with bashful shame, she [Venus] with her tears/Doth quench the maiden burning of his cheeks . . .' (ll. 49–50). One Renaissance commonplace about women was that they should be silent; often in early modern fictions they are simply voiceless, denied speech. It is odd, then, but not hard to understand, that in emblem books the ideal woman is sometimes figured by a tortoise. Like it she stays at home and is silent.[53] Forced into silence, like a woman but also by a female deity who pervasively uses a male, human language/rhetoric of love and seduction, Adonis responds with what is recognizable at once as part of a conventionally female – physical and silent – cultural rhetoric eloquent of sexual embarrassment and repudiation.[54] Later in the narrative, Venus warily approaches Adonis and, the narrator says, '[W]hat a war of looks was then between them!/Her eyes petitioners to his eyes suing,/His eyes saw her eyes, as they had not seen them,/Her eyes woo'd still, his eyes disdain'd the wooing . . .' (ll. 355–8). There are some clear differences between the earlier and later episodes. In the later one Adonis' silence is voluntary; further, he seems more vigorous in rejecting Venus. Nonetheless his rhetoric appears to be broadly the same in each. The later episode presents Venus, in her role as assertive lover, aggressing Adonis in his role as unwilling object of desire. Her role is conventionally male, his female; her role manifests a Petrarchized libertinism, his Petrarchism. Like a disdainful, Petrarchan lady he repudiates his suitor's insistent gaze, expressing himself physically, tacitly and eloquently.[55]

It was mentioned above that the other important and complementary element in what seems to be Adonis' rhetoric of chastity is a Platonic, male rhetoric of love. That rhetoric, while idealistic and combative, appears also to be problematic.[56] Just after Venus has again informed Adonis of his duty to breed (ll. 751–68) he makes the most substantial of his speeches (ll. 769–810). There – as unknowingly as when using a female rhetoric – he presents himself in the guise of an armed Petrarchan object of desire, firmly and cautiously resistant to Venus' seductive discourse (ll. 778–84). He unflatteringly identifies Venus as *Venus Vulgaris* trying to legitimize her desire by an appeal to her cognate function as *Venus Genetrix* (ll. 790–1).[57] Then he remarks, in asserting that Venus' love is actually lust: 'Call it not love, for love to heaven is fled,/Since sweating lust on earth usurp'd his name;/Under whose simple semblance he hath fed/Upon fresh beauty, blotting it with blame . . .' (ll. 793–6). Adonis distinguishes between a supplanted, original, absent Cupid of spiritual love (l. 793) and a usurping, parodic Cupid of sexual desire, now present on earth (l. 794). In doing so he deftly, if of course again unwittingly, evokes Pausanias' distinction in Plato's *Symposium* between two forms of love, each symbolized by a different Cupid and a different Venus: a Cupid and Venus of spiritual love (the latter being the heavenly Venus, or *Venus Urania*); a Cupid and Venus of sexual desire (the latter being the earthly Venus known as *Venus Pandemos/Venus Vulgaris*). Pausanias' distinction primarily concerns how adult males should, and should not, love adolescent males – hence it is aptly evoked, given that Venus woos the adolescent Adonis as might 'a bold-fac'd suitor'.

Adonis' Platonic allusion functions in a range of ways; however, a couple seem particularly relevant here. First, it indicates that, in opposition to Venus' male, Petrarchized, libertine discourse of se-duction, Adonis has a male, powerful, totalizing counter-discourse. On the other hand, Adonis uses that discourse only once at any length, and then some while after Venus has begun pursuing him. Next, it indicates that Adonis' view of spiritual love as having fled the earth is extreme (if not hard to understand, given his recent experience). Pausanius, in celebrating spiritual love, does not suggest that it cannot be achieved; he does not suggest that it cannot be found on earth. Adonis' Platonic rhetoric of love in this his major speech both forcefully counters Venus' discourse of seduction and reveals his intransigent belief that the world is loveless, that no human amatory experience is or will be spiritual. The male component of Adonis' rhetoric of chastity has, then, a problematic strength. Helping Adonis to demystify the sophistry of Venus, it nonetheless immerses him in an unrecognized sophistry of his own.

One of the best-known ploys in Venus' attempted seduction of Adonis is her telling him that his failure to love someone else, namely herself, may make him into another Narcissus.[58] Her use of Narcissus as an example of a dangerous indifference to others' desires, of the dangers attendant on self-love, seems narcissistic in its self-interestedness and indifference to Adonis' desires. Nonetheless, her comparison has some credibility insofar as Adonis, like Narcissus, resolutely rejects love and meets sexual advances with a hard unresponsiveness. Instances of the former can be seen in these lines: '"I know not love," quoth he, "nor will not know it . . ."' (l. 409); '"My love to love is love but to disgrace it . . ."' (l. 412). Instances of the latter can be seen when Venus calls Adonis a 'flint-hearted boy' and asks him if he is 'obdurate, flinty, hard as steel . . .' (parodies of the *domina petrosa* motif in ll. 95 and 199 respectively). In the *Metamorphoses*, Ovid's narrator says that '[m]any lads and many girls fell in love with him [Narcissus], but his soft young body housed a pride so unyielding that none . . . dared to touch him.'[59] Yet although Adonis may be seen to resemble Narcissus, he appears also to be significantly unlike him, in fact virtually to be his opposite.

One of the first things that Ovid's narrator relates about Narcissus is this. Just after he has been born and given a name, his mother asks the prophet Tiresias 'whether [the] boy [will] live to a ripe old age.' Tiresias' reported reply is: '"Yes, if he does not come to know himself."' Then the narrator says: 'For a long time this pronouncement seemed to be nothing but empty words: however it was justified by the outcome of events: the strange madness which afflicted the boy and the nature of his death proved its truth.'[60] Later in the tale, as Narcissus talks to his own, unrecognized image in the pool he suddenly makes the inevitable discovery and exclaims: 'Alas! I am myself the boy I see. I know it: my own reflection does not deceive me. I am on fire with love for my own self. It is I who kindle the flames which I must endure.'[61] Tiresias prophesied that if Narcissus were to gain self-knowledge his doing so would destroy him. Love brings the boy self-knowledge and with it comes a grief that hastens his death. The most significant dissimilarity between Ovid's Narcissus and Shakespeare's Adonis centres, I think, precisely on the issue of self-knowledge and its relation to love.

By way of explaining to Venus his refusal to love her, Adonis at one point declares: '"Fair queen, . . . if any love you owe me,/Measure my strangeness with my unripe years./Before I know myself, seek not to know me . . ."' (ll. 523–5). He adds: '"The mellow plum doth fall, the green sticks fast,/Or being early pluck'd, is sour to taste"' (ll. 527–8). Venus must well understand Adonis' argument, for much earlier in the tale she has remarked: '"The tender spring upon thy tempting lip/Shows thee unripe; yet mayst thou well be tasted"' (ll. 127–8). Subsequently, in the major speech where he asserts that true, spiritual love has fled the world, Adonis indirectly raises the 'unripeness' argument again: 'More I could tell, but more I dare not say:/The text is old, the orator too green' (ll. 805–6). It seems reasonable to propose that Adonis' insistences on his immaturity and on true love's having fled the world shape his main arguments for rejecting Venus' advances; as has just been indicated, both occur in his speech on the difference between true love and its counterfeit, lust. Be that as it may, however, the directly relevant point here is this. Whereas Narcissus self-destructively gains self-knowledge as a result of love, self-love though of course it is, Adonis wants to have self-knowledge prior to, and quite separately from, the experience of love. He apparently wishes to know himself – and so in effect to realize the ancient imperative '*nosce te ipsum*' ('know yourself') – without gaining sexual knowledge. The play on 'know' as cognition and sexual experience in his command/request, 'Before I know myself, seek not to know me' (l. 525), makes that much clear. Yet Adonis' wordplay there elides self-knowledge and sexual experience, implying (despite his wish) that they are actually connected, perhaps inseparable.

When Venus offers Adonis metamorphosis via sexual initiation (as I have argued above), she in fact offers him loss of self, insofar as he is someone committed to the active life, and the gain of a new, incongruously diminished selfhood as an aesthetic/sexual object and concupiscent prize of the hunt of love. In rejecting Venus' offers of lost and gained subjectivities, Adonis retains his self-definition as follower of the active life (hunter, servant of Diana), a self-definition that he obviously thinks either incomplete or as yet incompletely understood by himself, and refuses knowledge of his sexuality.[62] Thereby he repudiates not only Venus' proffered new subjectivities but also an extension of his self-knowledge: he deliberately limits his acquisition of self-knowledge by his stated decision to seek it prior to, separately from, sexual experience. Moreover, retaining his incomplete and asexual selfhood as follower of the active life, he therefore has his parodic sexual encounter with the boar, in which his very life is lost.[63] If self-knowledge in relation to love is a key issue in the characterizations of Shakespeare's Adonis and of Ovid's Narcissus, and the textual evidence seems to support the idea, then with respect to it the two figures are virtually antithetic. Venus' forceful, slightly accurate analogy between Adonis and Narcissus elucidates through its inaccuracy Adonis' presentation in the poem.

(V) ADONIS, THE NARRATOR AND THE MALE GAZE. MARLOWE'S *HERO AND LEANDER* AND DONNE'S 'ELEGY 19'

The final aspect of Adonis' characterization that I wish now to examine concerns the male gaze. As was suggested above, not Venus but Adonis appears to be emphasized as the object of sexual desire in Shakespeare's poem; in fact, the narrator, chiefly through his presentation of Venus, appears to set up Adonis as the object of the male gaze.[64] Perhaps the shortest way to start making that argument specific is by considering some of the poem's images of gluttony. Venus, in her role as *Venus Vulgaris*, seems appropriately (given the nature of that role) to think of Adonis as her 'banquet of sense'. For example, when concluding a celebration of how her senses do or would delight in Adonis, she says: '"But oh what banquet wert thou to the taste,/Being nurse and feeder to the other four!/Would they not wish the feast might ever last [?]"' (ll. 445–7). Seemingly mindful of Venus' eagerness to gourmandize on him, Adonis subsequently says in his major speech about the difference between love and lust: '"Love surfeits not, lust like a glutton dies"' (l. 803). But while his allusion to gluttony denigrates, deliberately or otherwise, her picture of him as her 'banquet of sense', it also echoes and condemns likewise a reference she has made to a sexual gluttony of the sight: 'Who sees his true-love in her naked bed,/Teaching the sheets a whiter hue than white,/But when his glutton eye so full hath fed,/His other agents aim at like delight?' (ll. 397–400).

Venus speaks those words when urging Adonis to follow the example of his horse, which has run off with '[a] breeding jennet' (l. 260), and 'learn to love' (l. 407; cf. ll. 385–408). Venus' words, that is to say, are designed to excite and to incite Adonis. They try to do so by putting before him an image of a desirable, available female subjected to a devouring, voyeuristic inspection – and of the male observer/lover's intent to follow that inspection by sexual action: she puts before him an image of the male gaze and of a consequent intent to enact its sexual power. Adonis is apparently meant to realize that he should more or less equate Venus with the desirable, available female figure in her description and that he should make himself approximate the male figure of sexual desire and power. The problem is, however, not only that Adonis does not want to become such a figure but that Venus in fact already resembles it. Adonis rather resembles the female figure in Venus' description, with the significant difference that he wishes to be neither an object of desire nor available.[65] While Venus is talking to him, uttering the words now being examined, she has him firmly by the hand and will not let him go, although he asks to be set free (see ll. 361–84, especially ll. 361–2 with their trope of imprisonment). More important, when Venus earlier tells Adonis about her victory over Mars (ll. 97–114) she also has the boy under physical restraint, but on that occasion

– in her role as assertive (male) lover – she proceeds to subject him to a version of the male gaze and to voice excitedly what that gaze reveals.[66] Yet Venus cannot, of course, enact the sexual power of her masculinized gaze; in that respect, as similarly in respect of gender-reversal, she diverges from the image of the male gaze and of its consequence which she puts before Adonis.

However if Adonis is subjected at some moments of the text to the masculinized gaze of Venus, he is pervasively and primarily subjected throughout it to the male gaze of the implied reader.[67] A main factor in that would seem to be the narrator's recurrent, emphatic devaluing in the poem of Venus, the goddess of love, as an object of desire. From the first stanza he treats her ludically, introducing her as '[s]ick-thoughted Venus' who 'like a bold-fac'd suitor 'gins to woo' Adonis (ll. 5–6). From the start she seems a figure of comedy and of pathos. Thereafter the narrator makes her appear not merely comic (as in ll. 463–8) or pathetic (as in ll. 1057–62) but grotesque as well – veering between the poles of comedy and of pathos: in her physical power (for example, when exercising force on Adonis; see ll. 29–35); in her unreasoning and excessive passion (see ll. 25–8, 61–6, 217–22, and so on). Those portrayals of her accord with the grotesqueness of much of her libertine rhetoric (cf. the excesses of pleading and of cajoling in ll. 187–98, for instance). The narrator stresses, too, the grotesqueness and (or) ferocity of her predatory desire (ll. 54–60, 67–8, 541–76, and so on). He treats her with condescension (as notably in ll. 607–10) and even celebrates her beauty only to heighten the reader's perception of Adonis' unique beauty (see, for example, ll. 352–64).[68] The repeated devaluing of Venus as an object of sexual desire, for all her beauty, helps in the placement of Adonis in that role; it facilitates, that is to say, the deflection of the implied reader's male gaze from the goddess of love to the adolescent boy.

The workings and results of that deflection can, I think, be briefly and representatively illustrated. When, to cite an early instance, Adonis has been pushed to the ground by Venus and is, in effect, restrained by her (ll. 40–2), her virtual imprisonment of the boy seems clearly to promote him as the implied (and male) reader's object of sexual focus. Venus 'stroke[s Adonis'] cheek' and begins to kiss him (ll. 45–8). His response to her doing so is represented in terms that feminize him (ll. 49–50, discussed above, and l. 53) – whereas, of course, her assertive sexual actions imply her masculinization. Moreover, the narrator then introduces a short, simple account of Venus' proceeding, again and again, to kiss Adonis' face (ll. 59–60), by vividly and at greater length comparing the impassioned goddess to an 'empty eagle' tearing at and devouring its prey (ll. 55–8). To that point in the episode, Venus has arguably been imaged as desiring rather than as desirable. Her beauty has been alluded to once (l. 51); her desire for Adonis has been indicated to be confining, insistent and fiercely predatory. On the other hand, and in contrast to the ultimately grotesque representation of Venus, the picture of Adonis has been that of a helpless, feminized victim of sexual violence. The reader sees a sexually devalued Venus and an Adonis whose sexual attract-iveness is emphasized at the goddess's cost.

In what immediately follows, the narrator uses that process of devaluing and emphasizing to set up Adonis as the object of the implied reader's male gaze. The immediately subsequent description of Adonis iterates his sexual distress: 'Panting he lies and breatheth in [Venus'] face' (l. 62). His distress may be made to look comic in its awkward physicality but, for all that, it is nonetheless distress. If the description again conveys something of Adonis' simplicity, it likewise implies his helplessness, his role as feminized victim of sexual violence. Whether or not Venus recognizes what Adonis' 'breath[ing] in her face' reveals about him, she responds to it with sexual excitement. 'She feedeth on the steam as on a prey,' the narrator says (l. 63). Inevitably, the narrator's word 'prey' in that line evokes his preced-ing representation of Venus as a sexual predator; and he alludes to it once more in ll. 67–8.[69] That continued process of devaluing and emphasizing, however, now functions differently from the way it did earlier in the episode. The narrator now uses it to focus on and to celebrate Adonis' beauty – actually, to put that beauty on display for inspection by the implied reader. Venus' excited praise of the boy's beauty is recounted (ll. 64–6); her virtually limitless pleasure in it is implied (ll. 77–84). And Venus' harassment of Adonis brings (the narrator relates with apparent pleasure) reactions from him which in fact heighten his feminized beauty (ll. 73–8).[70] The narrator's own appreciation of Adonis' physical appeal is expressed both there and at another moment of the text (l. 70). What seems to be happening here is a coercion of the female: a devaluation and (or) suppression of Venus' attractiveness, an emphasis on her obsessive desire for and delight in Adonis' beauty, so that her beauty can be pushed into the background of the episode and thereby help to emphasize his. Venus' desire for and delight in the boy's beauty, and the narrator's appre-ciation of it, merge in a cumulative and fairly long description – the results being that Adonis' beauty is elaborately displayed and that he is put forward as the (notional) object of sexual desire. Adonis' beauty appears to be held by the responsive narrator and by the sexually devalued goddess of love for appreciative inspection, for visual possession, by the (notionally male and not indifferent) reader. 'He' seems invited to view it with a 'glutton eye' (l. 399).

Although other instances in Shakespeare's poem could be examined, perhaps more revealing may be to make some comparisons between how Adonis is set up as an object of the male gaze and how the male gaze is exercised and (or) evoked in Marlowe's *Hero and Leander* and in Donne's 'Elegy 19 *To his Mistress Going to Bed*'.[71] In the former poem, the early and stylized descriptions of the soon-to-be lovers indicate that they are significantly alike. Hero, described in ll. 5–50, is supposedly an object of irresistible sexual fascination. She is wooed by Apollo for the beauty of her hair alone and worthy, in his opinion, to be yielded his throne so that all men can gaze on her (ll. 6–8). She is mistaken by Cupid for his mother Venus (ll. 39–44). Leander, described in ll. 51–90, supposedly complements her in attractiveness. Had his 'dangling tresses that were never shorn/ . . . been cut, and unto Colchos borne' (ll. 55–6) they would have inspired a second, but more compelling, quest for 'the Golden Fleece' (ll. 57–8); moreover, Cynthia – Apollo's sister – desires him (ll. 59–60). Yet the formal descriptions of Hero and of Leander indicate also that they are significantly unalike insofar as their supposed sexual allure is concerned.

The most important dissimilarity comes from the fact that whereas Marlowe's narrator describes Hero's clothing as well as her body, he subsequently pictures Leander's body but not his clothing. Such description as the narrator gives of Hero's body implies her impossible beauty; however, the account of her clothing suggests that her beauty – and the sexual desire that it can generate – is linked to violence and death. The depiction of the Venus and Adonis story on her sleeves (ll. 11–14), as well as the blood on her kirtle (ll. 15–16), suggests that and foreshadows Leander's fate. It is true that, when first describing Leander, the narrator foretells/reminds the reader of Leander's death (ll. 51–4). It is true, too, that some of the allusions to myth in the account of Leander's body have negative associations, linking beauty, sexual desire and death.[72] Nonetheless, even if the picture of Leander begins with a reference to his death, even if it links his beauty with sexual desire and death as does the account of Hero's clothing, it is startlingly appreciative and specific. Marlowe's narrator, seeming to delight in intimate celebration of the detail of Leander's body, puts him forward as an epitome of beauty taken too early from the world. In fact, the narrator's intimate celebration of Leander's beauty puts him forward, as an object of sexual desire, with an emotiveness and enthusiasm lacking in the description of Hero. Leander is celebrated and displayed by the narrator with delight and clearly for the pleasure of the implied reader's male gaze:

> His body was as straight as Circe's wand;
> Jove might have sipped out nectar from his hand.
> Even as delicious meat is to the taste,
> So was his neck in touching, and surpassed
> The white of Pelop's shoulder. I could tell ye
> How smooth his breast was, and how white his belly,
> And whose immortal fingers did imprint
> That heavenly path with many a curious dint
> That runs along his back. . . .
>
> (ll. 61–9)

Marlowe's narrator may describe Hero first and he may make Hero and Leander similar as creatures who are supposed to be sexually irresistible. For all that, Leander is foregrounded to Hero's cost, as Adonis is to that of Venus. Just as Shakespeare's narrator sexually devalues Venus, again and again, throughout *Venus and Adonis*, so Marlowe's narrator sexually devalues Hero throughout *Hero and Leander*. Her being fashioned as the blindly, paradoxically, vulnerably virginal priestess of *Venus Vulgaris* – 'Venus' nun' – makes her both comic and pathetic from the start; and there is the narrator's recurrent, ironic play with his characterization of her as at once beautiful and innocent.[73] The process of devaluing and emphasizing at work in Shakespeare's poem has a counterpart, though not an identical one, in Marlowe's. As has been argued above, the result of that process, in each poem, is the narrator's homoerotic celebration and display of the male protagonist for the male gaze.

In that context, Donne's Elegy 19 seems illuminatingly both like and unlike the poems by Shakespeare and by Marlowe. The main similarity lies in how Donne creates his persona and in how that persona apparently seeks to evoke and exercises the male gaze. The chief dissimilarity lies, of course, in the aggressive heterosexuality of Donne's poem. But the comparison and the contrast are more intricate than might be thought. Donne's persona in Elegy 19 recalls both the persona of Ovid's Elegies and, as it appears, Marlowe's recreation of that Ovidian persona in his translation of the Elegies.[74] Seeming to be wise in the ways of the world, of the flesh, and of letters, too sophisticated to take social or moral convention at face value, ingenious, ironic, fond of displaying his wit, self-assertive and self-centred, Donne's persona distinctly manifests his Ovidian and, very arguably, Marlovian lineage. He features, with varying emphases, in many of Donne's secular love poems; of necessity, given his lineage, he has much in common with the narrator of *Venus and Adonis* and with that of *Hero and Leander*.[75]

When Donne's persona commands his fictive mistress to undress, he celebrates both her body and her clothing: 'Off with that girdle, like heaven's zone glistering,/But a far fairer world encompassing' (ll. 5–6). His commands, as that example indicates, recreate the woman. In fact they, and almost everything else he says, reinvent and reinterpret her to the point where she becomes, from his angle of vision, his sexual/political colony, his private source of physical riches, his personal empire (see ll. 27–30). Donne's persona, that is to suggest, reinvents and reinterprets the woman to her face. The silent 'she' finds herself being refashioned by her lover as she stands before him. Her appearance is celebrated and made subject to the refashioning power of his male gaze. Moreover, in refashioning her before her own eyes (as it were) the persona holds his version of her on display for the appreciative male gaze of the implied reader – a twofold exercise of power. That exercise of power is also Donne's self-display, a display of rhetorical virtuosity to his mainly young, male audience containing fellow poets such as his friends the Brookes.[76] The fictional lady is, then, apparently put forward for appreciation yet actually devalued: made voiceless and refashioned. She is devalued in order that Donne's persona and hence Donne himself can be set on display for appreciation. One sees male display, even if not homoerotic display, at female expense; yet at the same time, that display also ironically indicates the dependence of male selfhood, in libertine discourse, on some conjectured notion of femaleness. So perhaps the assertive heterosexuality of Donne's poem may not very greatly distinguish it from *Venus and Adonis* or from *Hero and Leander*. The process of devaluation and emphasis, which is connected with the exercise and evocation of the male gaze by Ovidian speakers complicit, in their coercing of the female, with their implied readers, makes all three poems akin.

The calculated, flamboyant transgressiveness of Shakespeare's poem, of Marlowe's and of Donne's goes beyond issues such as the fashioning of narrators or of personae, and the representation of sexual politics, as one need hardly point out. Beyond them, though not separable from them, are issues such as how the relations among desire, ceremony, convention and anarchy are represented – and what the representations of them may imply. In Marlowe's poem, ceremony and anarchy co-exist: love is both ritual and disruption in a world seemingly centred on *Venus Vulgaris*. On the other hand, in Donne's poem the speaking self constructs a private world, centred on its all-subordinating desire, by means of literary and social conventions which at once shape the speaking self and allow it to reshape its surroundings.[77] Shakespeare's poem suggests love's often incongruous multiplicity and intense self-centredness, its ambiguous transformative power, each of which is indicated by the characterization of Venus. As in Marlowe's poem, yet not identically so, love is both ritual and disruption: ceremony and anarchy co-exist, but in a world where Venus has many aspects.[78] And the characterization of Adonis significantly complements that of Venus. His suggests, in counterpoint to hers, a link between chastity and self-ignorance, between sexual experience and self-knowledge. In rejecting sexual initiation Adonis may evade the insistence and egocentrism of sexual desire, and loss of his present, incomplete subjectivity for the gaining of a diminished, eroticised one, but he also evades self-knowledge, wilfully seeking to dissociate self-knowledge from sexual experience. Shakespeare's poem implies that if sexual desire is problematic in its diversity, self-centredness and disorderliness, so too can chastity be in its destructive frustration of self-knowledge. Moreover, whereas Venus in her role as *Venus Mechanitis* voices a failed rhetoric of desire, excessive desire marring the conventions of language designed to express desire, Adonis' characterization implies that chastity, desire's negation, may also flaw communication by having an intransigently idealizing, delusive rhetoric no less sophistic than that of desire. Adonis' characterization indicates as well, through its connection with a process of emphasis/devaluation and with the exercise/evocation of the male gaze, that love's multiplicity by no means excludes homoerotic desire. Shakespeare's first poem, inventively ludic, sceptical, emphatically various in its representations of sexuality, and meta-Ovidian in its sophisticated self-awareness rather than merely Ovidian, reveals how shrewdly he understood the rhetorical possibilities of the epyllion and, in doing so, its social possibilities as a means for displaying his virtuosity as a poet in the competition for patronage.

NOTES

1. All reference to the poem is from F. T. Prince (ed.), *William Shakespeare: The Poems* (1969; rpt. London: Methuen, 1976). My 'date' for the poem is in fact only a suggested boundary. See: Prince, *The Poems*, p. xxvi; S. Schoenbaum, *William Shakespeare: A Compact Documentary Life* (1977; rpt. New York: New American Library, 1986), pp. 159–70; R. Dutton, *William Shakespeare: A Literary Life* (London: Macmillan, 1989), pp. 35–40; R. Ellrodt, 'Shakespeare the Non-Dramatic Poet', in

S. Wells (ed.), *The Cambridge Companion to Shakespeare Studies* (1986; rpt. Cambridge: Cambridge University Press, 1989), pp. 35–48, at p. 45.

2. For an illuminating account of the 'plague years' and Shakespeare, see M. C. Bradbrook, *Shakespeare: The Poet in His World* (London: Weidenfeld & Nicolson, 1978), pp. 65–87.

3. That is, in any event, the conventional view.

4. See: G. P. V. Akrigg, *Shakespeare and the Earl of Southampton* (London: Hamish Hamilton, 1968), pp. 191–200; S. Schoenbaun (n.1), pp. 170–74; Charles Martindale and Colin Burrow, 'Clapham's *Narcissus*: A Pre-Text for Shakespeare's *Venus and Adonis?* (text, translation and commentary)', *English Literary Renaissance*, 22 (1992), 147–76.

5. For example, see Schoenbaum, pp. 173–4, and R. Dutton (n.1), p. 37.

6. See Bradbrook (n.2), pp. 70–8 and, more generally, also: G. F. Lytle and S. Orgel (eds), *Patronage in the Renaissance* (Princeton, N.J.: Princeton University Press, 1981); A. F. Marotti, *John Donne, Coterie Poet* (Madison: University of Wisconsin Press, 1986); Robert C. Evans, *Ben Jonson and the Poetics of Patronage* (Lewisburg: Bucknell University Press, 1989).

7. The term 'epyllion' has been controversial but, as it is also widely used, I use it throughout this chapter. The dating of Marlowe's poem is much debated, a point I discuss below. See S. Orgel (ed.), *Christopher Marlowe: The Complete Poems and Translations* (Harmondsworth: Penguin, 1971), pp. 9–10 and p. 219 (all further reference is to this edition); L. C. Martin (ed.), *Marlowe's Poems* (1931; rpt. New York: Gordian, 1966), pp. 1–8. However, I tend to agree with W. Keach, *Elizabethan Erotic Narratives: Irony and Pathos in the Ovidian Poetry of Shakespeare, Marlowe, and their Contemporaries* (New Brunswick, N.J.: Rutgers University Press, 1977), p. 85. See also: C. Hulse, *Metamorphic Verse: The Elizabethan Minor Epic* (Princeton, N.J.: Princeton University Press, 1981), p. 3. On the issue of genre in the English Renaissance, see especially A. Fowler, *Kinds of Literature* (1982; rpt. Oxford: Clarendon Press, 1985) and B. K. Lewalski (ed.), *Renaissance Genres: Essays on Theory, History and Interpretation* (Cambridge, Mass.: Harvard University Press, 1986).

8. Hulse, p. 23. Hulse provides other useful reasons but those are the most relevant here.

9. On the tradition of moralizing the *Metamorphoses*, see Douglas Bush, *Mythology and the Renaissance Tradition in English Poetry* (1932; rpt. New York: Norton, 1960), pp. 3–83. He discusses Lodge on pp. 83–8, emphasizing continuity with the past rather than novelty in *Scillaes Metamorphosis*.

10. For example, through his ingenious elaborations on it, especially his exaggerations, as can readily be seen in the version given in his *Metamorphoses*. Keach, at pp. 37–8, mentions Lodge's use of Ronsard. Reference to Lodge's poem is from E. S. Donno (ed.), *Elizabethan Minor Epics* (London: Routledge & Kegan Paul, 1963).

11. On the *primary* audience for Lodge's poem, see Keach, p. 40 and Schoenbaum, p. 173.

12. For the relevant moments in the poem where those traits are revealed, see respectively: stanzas 3, 8, and L'ENVOY; stanzas 84–8; stanzas 33 and 72; stanzas 90–4 – among many instances.

13. As E. S. Donno and N. Alexander have earlier noted, respectively in their editions, *Elizabethan Minor Epics*, pp. 6–7, and *Elizabethan Narrative Verse* (London: Arnold, 1967), pp. 9–10.

14. His humanity, for example, as a general trait doesn't count.

15. The poem is close in spirit, too, to Sackville's work and to Petrarch's love verse. Lodge's narrator is, therefore, also un-Ovidian in some obvious respects (one cannot tell, moreover, to what extent the design of the narrator is deliberate).

16. See, for example, Bush, p. 143.

17. Here, I follow Schoenbaum. See also Dutton, p. 38.

18. Perhaps because Shakespeare's role as a non-dramatic poet is new he calls *Venus and Adonis*, in the dedication, 'the first heir of my invention'.

19. It may be, too, that both Lodge and Shakespeare modelled their narrators on Marlowe's Ovidian narrator in *Hero and Leander*. However, given the difficulty of dating Marlowe's poem, and likewise given the distinct possibility that it was written closely in time to Shakespeare's (not before Lodge's), I prefer the account of relations between Lodge's and Shakespeare's narrators sketched above, which reflects acceptance of the notion that Lodge wrote the first English minor epic.

20. He is not, of course, in total control of the problems raised by what he pictures going on inside his imaginary world, especially insofar as those problems connect with everyday human problems which defy solution; the same is true of Ovid's narrator.

21. There has been general agreement, for example, about Venus' predatoriness, dishonesty, maternalism and so on – though with varying emphases. Among the commentaries on *Venus and Adonis*, see especially: D. N. Beauregard, '*Venus and Adonis*: Shakespeare's Representation of the Passions', *Shakespeare Studies*, 8 (1975), 83–98; W. A. Rebhorn, 'Mother Venus: Temptation in Shakespeare's *Venus and Adonis*', *Shakespeare Studies*, 11 (1978), 1–19; L. J. Daigle, '*Venus and Adonis*: Some Traditional Contexts', *Shakespeare Studies*, 13 (1980), 31–46; J. Doebles, 'The Many Faces of Love: Shakespeare's *Venus and Adonis*', *Shakespeare Studies*, 16 (1983), 33–43; H. Dubrow, *Captive Victors: Shakespeare's Narrative Poems and Sonnets* (Ithaca and London: Cornell University Press, 1987), pp. 21–79. See also: G. Sorelius, *Shakespeare's Early Comedies: Myth, Metamorphosis, Mannerism* (Uppsala: University of Uppsala Press, 1993), pp. 111–17; J. Bate, *Shakespeare and Ovid* (1993; rpt. Oxford: Clarendon Press, 1994), pp. 48–65; S. Wells, *Shakespeare: A Dramatic Life* (London: Sinclair-Stevenson, 1994), pp. 115–20; J. Bate, *The Genius of Shakespeare* (London: Picador, 1997), pp. 23–4.

22. See, for example: T. W. Baldwin, *On the Literary Genetics of Shakespeare's Poems and Sonnets* (Urbana: University of Illinois Press, 1950), pp. 1–93; D. C. Allen, *Image and Meaning: Metaphoric Traditions in Renaissance Poetry* (1960; rpt. Baltimore: Johns Hopkins Press, 1968), pp. 42–57; W. Keach, pp. 52–84; C. Hulse, pp. 141–75.

23. The mythographers drawn on in this discussion are chiefly Natalis Comes and Vincenzo Cartari, respectively in their *Mythologiae* (Venice: 1567) and *Le Imagini . . . Degli Dei* (Venice: 1571) – both in the Garland reprints of 1976, introduced by S. Orgel.

24. Whether or not other myths or tales depict or suggest that as having happened to the goddess prior to her loving Adonis, the discovery seems new to her in Shakespeare's narrative – as she indicates in her speech about Mars. See ll. 91–114. But were this not, in fact, her personal discovery, it would still be so forceful an experience of love as otherness that it almost completely disorientates the goddess of love herself.

25. Even if Venus has been previously obsessed with love for another divinity, love between immortals cannot be equated with love between mortals; hence the humanized experience of obsessive love she seems newly to undergo *in this tale* would have to be qualitatively different from any other experience she may have had of Love's power to preoccupy the consciousness.

26. See Cartari, *Le Imagini . . .* , p. 543.

27. The *Venus Vulgaris* that Shakespeare's Venus most closely resembles is that in the *Symposium*. See Pausanius' account of that Venus, and her celestial counterpart, in the *Symposium*, trans. W. H. D. Rouse (ed. E. H. Warmington and P. G. Rouse) in his *Great Dialogues of Plato* (New York: New American Library), pp. 78–82. See also: Comes, *Mythologiae*, 120(a); Pico, *Commento sopra una canzona de amore . . .* trans. Thomas Stanley, *A Platonick Discourse upon Love*, in *The Poems and Translations*, ed. G. M. Crump (Oxford: Clarendon Press, 1962), 2, 7–22. Filarete, *Treatise on Architecture*, trans. J. R. Spencer (New Haven and London: Yale University Press, 1965), Bk 18, fol. 148v. Insofar as Shakespeare's Venus resembles Pausanius' *Venus Vulgaris*, she aptly perceives Adonis as her 'banquet of sense'. That Venus is, however, a debased aspect of the *Venus Vulgaris* described by Pico and some others. They see *Venus Vulgaris* as having two aspects: one human, the other bestial. The former is concerned with sight and with the desire to reproduce beauty whereas the latter is concerned only with sexual satisfaction.

28. Heather Dubrow, in *Captive Victors*, notes that '*Venus and Adonis* is concerned with faulty or failed communication . . .' (p. 38), and I would wholly agree; however, her reading of Venus' opening speech and of its context differs significantly from my own (see pp. 31–7 of her study). My main point here is that Venus' speech subverts her role as *Venus Mechanitis*.

29. Again, images have immediately Petrarchan associations, though in fact they can be traced much further back. Cf. T. W. Baldwin, *On the Literary Genetics . . .* , pp. 9–10.

30. On parody of this in 'Damon the Mower', see my 'Marvell's "Upon Appleton House to my Lord Fairfax" and the Regaining of Paradise', in *The Political Identity of Andrew Marvell*, edited by C. Conden and myself (Aldershot: Scolar Press, 1990), 53–84, at p. 73.

31. On *varietà* and its link to *grazia*, see David Summers, *Michelangelo and the Language of Art* (Princeton, N.J.: Princeton University Press, 1981), pp. 82, 166, 172.

32. On *Venus Genetrix* see: Comes, *Mythologiae*, 122(a); Cartari, *Le Imagini . . .* , p. 530; Ficino, *Commentary on the Symposium*, 1, 5. It should be mentioned that, for Pico and others, *Venus Genetrix* is linked to the higher aspect of *Venus Vulgaris*.

33. Pico, *Commento*, trans. Stanley, 2, 20, 323. Ficino, in his *Commentary on the Symposium*, of course also calls such love 'bestial love'. See *Commentary on Plato's Symposium on Love*, trans. Sears Jayne (1985; rpt. Woodstock: Spring, 1994), 7, 3, 158. As mentioned earlier, 'bestial love' is the form of love associated by Pico with the lower aspect of *Venus Vulgaris*.

34. See, for instances: ll. 18–22, in her first speech, and especially ll. 445–50, 543–52.

35. On Adonis' supposed duty to breed, see ll. 163–74. I write 'primarily, at the very least', because Venus may also genuinely – if quite secondarily – want Adonis to reproduce his beauty through offspring.

36. That is, to make the point again, Venus' celebration of the generative impulse and her urging Adonis to breed are ploys in an attempt at seduction.

37. For further discussion of Venus' maternalism, see Rebhorn, 'Mother Venus . . .', cited in note 21.

38. On *Venus Apaturia*, see Comes' allusion in *Mythologiae*, 121(a). The goddess's role of *Venus Apaturia* naturally links to her role as *Venus Mechanitis*.

39. On Venus as *Magistra Divinandi*, see Comes, *Mythologiae*, 121(a).

40. Here I follow Edgar Wind, *Pagan Mysteries in the Renaissance*, rev. edn (1958; rpt. Harmondsworth: Penguin, 1967), pp. 91–6. Clark Hulse also discusses the motif, though differently. See his *Metamorphic Verse*, pp. 166–73.

41. There seems no need to give further examples, as they clearly tend the same way. It could be added, however, that if the *Venus Victrix* motif is dismantled, so too is that of *Venus Basilea* (Queen of Love).

42. In l. 791 he associates her with *Venus Genetrix*.

43. Jeremy Hawthorne, *A Concise Glossary of Contemporary Literary Theory* (London: Arnold, 1992), p. 124.

44. Cf. Ficino, *Commentary*, 1, 6.

45. Again, seemingly new and alien within the confines of the tale.

46. Of course, secondarily it *is* continued experience for Venus of how humans may experience unrequited love.

47. As regards the comic: exaggeration generates it – but then Venus actually is larger than human life, and Adonis, likewise, is perfect; the Petrarchan comedy, as it were, contributes to other comic elements – such as Venus' questioning the dogs and scolding the boar. As regards the pathetic: Venus' disorientation and misery are, despite all their comic features, nonetheless recognizably and familiarly human, evoking sympathy.

48. On the 'ideal landscape' see E. R. Curtius, *European Literature and the Latin Middle Ages* (1953; rpt. New York and Evanston: Harper & Row, 1963), pp. 183–202. Her self-description seems a recreation of Claudian's famous set-piece in his *Epithalamium de Nuptis Honorii Augusti*, ll. 49–96.

49. See, for example, C. Hulse, pp. 151–3. Sandys' note, 'Men of excellent beauties haue likely beene subiect to miserable destinies', has a topical relevance to Buckingham (*Ovid's Metamorphoses Englished*, p. 366).

50. See, for example, J. D. Jahn, 'The Lamb of Lust: The Role of Adonis in Shakespeare's *Venus and Adonis*', *Shakespeare Studies*, 6 (1970), 11–25.

51. On the gaze, and on the male gaze, see: Norman Bryson, *Vision and Painting: The Logic of the Gaze* (1983; rpt. London: Macmillan, 1985); Edward Snow, 'Theorizing the Male Gaze: Some Problems', *Representations*, 25 (1989), 30–41.

52. His cheek is 'tend'rer' than her hand, his hand rivals hers in whiteness, according to the narrator in ll. 352–4 and 362–4 respectively.

53. Valeriano, for example, makes that point. Greville's *A Letter to an Honorable Lady* interestingly reworks/revises it.

54. The narrator, having said that Adonis 'burns with bashful shame', goes on to specify the process as 'the maiden burning of his cheeks', emphasizing that Adonis' body language is a female, necessarily silent, expressive and conventional articulation of shamefastness.

55. Venus is voluble but, again, *male* in her volubility (she predominately uses, after all, a Petrarchan language and rhetoric of seduction).

56. The Platonic aspect of Adonis' rhetoric has been noted by others – but its problematic nature has not, as far as I am aware, been considered.

57. Again, an unknowing cultural specificity.

58. See ll. 157–62; cf. ll. 115–20.

59. Ovid, *Metamorphoses*, trans. M. Innes (1955; rpt. Harmondsworth: Penguin, 1968), 3, p. 83.

60. Ovid, trans. Innes, p. 83.

61. Ovid, trans. Innes, p. 86.

62. Again, see ll. 525–8.

63. Though in this he also *broadly* resembles Narcissus, because a refusal to love brings Narcissus to false love and death. The boar is clearly an antithesis to the horse: the former is unreasoning malevolence and

destructiveness, the latter, innate nobility; the former, a parodic pun-
ishment for sexuality avoided, whereas the latter is 'natural' sexuality
exampled.

64. In what follows, my thinking on the male gaze has especially taken
     into account Bryson and Snow.

65. *Venus* sees him as available, if not as her *willing* 'true-love'.

66. Lines 115–28; for an ironic counterpart see ll. 211–16.

67. The assumed readership for the poem would seem to be primarily
     male (in kind, much the same readership as for Lodge's epyllion), and
     hence the male gaze seems to be evoked. I do not wish to consider
     here the issue of the female gaze. Iser's notion of the 'implied reader'
     is interestingly elaborated on in S. Chatman's *Story and Discourse* (Ithaca,
     N.Y.: Cornell University Press, 1978).

68. Venus' beauty is not always praised or displayed, of course, only to set
     off that of Adonis. Venus' 'deer park' picture of her own body is an
     instance of her beauty being displayed for the implied reader's male
     gaze and in hope, on her part as it were, of evoking Adonis' male gaze.
     I am grateful to David Bevington for making me consider this point.

69. The picture of Adonis as her victim is evoked, in both cases, at the
     same time.

70. The Petrarchan red and white being iterated in description of Adonis
     and their hues being apparently heightened by his distress.

71. For examples of those other instances, see: ll. 241–52, 349–54, 427–
     52, 541–72; cf. ll. 595–606. There are not, as I read the poem, many
     instances at all of Venus' being displayed for the male gaze. Reference
     to Marlowe's poem is from Orgel's edition and reference to Donne's
     verse is from A. J. Smith's edition, *The Complete English Poems* (1971;
     rpt. London: Allen Lane, 1974). Subsequent reference to Donne's
     verse is from Smith.

72. Especially relevant here is the refiguring allusion to Narcissus, to whom
     Adonis seems a virtual antithesis.

73. For depiction of Hero as 'Venus' nun' (the phrase itself occurs at 1, 45)
     see 1, 131–66; for examples of the narrator's ironic play with his charac-
     terization of her as at once beautiful and innocent, see his comparison
     between her and Diana seeking to evade Actaeon (2, 260–2) and his
     comparison of her to a harpy (2, 270).

74. For similarities in rhetoric and language between Donne's persona
     (and the personae constructed throughout his Elegies as a whole) and
     Marlowe's Ovidian persona, see 3, 6 and 7 in Marlowe's translation.
     As S. Orgel remarks: 'Donne's elegies are full of a sense of Marlowe's
     language' (*Poems and Translations*, p. 233).

75. That is to say, with reference primarily to the narrator of *Venus and
     Adonis*, that the speaker(s) of Ovid's *Amores* has (have) features in com-
     mon with Ovid's speaker in *Metamorphoses*. Marlowe's *Hero and Leander*
     is certainly indebted to 'divine Musaeus' (1, 52) but the making of its

narrator is nonetheless indebted to Ovid's fashioning of his speaker(s) in his earlier erotic verse.

76. See R. C. Bald, *John Donne: A Life* (Oxford: Clarendon Press, 1970), pp. 35–79.
77. The conventions of libertinism both shape and free (in some respects) the self, helping it to create a private world of desire that subordinates all to it: the woman; politics; God, and so on.
78. Thus to identify one of the differences between the world of *Venus and Adonis* and that of *Hero and Leander.*

Chapter 2

Lucrece

(I) VERSIONS OF THE LUCRETIA STORY BY OVID, LIVY, BOCCACCIO, CHAUCER AND GOWER

Shakespeare's second narrative poem was printed not long after his first, in 1594, and like its predecessor it was dedicated to the Earl of Southampton.[1] As has been often suggested, the dedication preceding *Lucrece* seems to address Southampton more intimately than does that preceding *Venus and Adonis*.[2] The initial words of the dedication certainly appear to indicate something more than a distant respect: 'The love I dedicate to your Lordship is without end. . . .' So too do these: 'What I have done is yours, what I have to do is yours, being part in all I have devoted yours.'[3] Such words have led some commentators to a further suggestion, namely, that the apparently more intimate style of the later dedication implies Shakespeare's pursuit of the Earl's patronage to have been not without success.[4] That may well be true; nonetheless, what Shakespeare gained from offering Southampton *Lucrece* remains as unclear as what he gained from offering him *Venus and Adonis*.

Just as the dedications of Shakespeare's narrative poems are markedly different, so of course are the poems themselves. They are virtually opposites: *Venus and Adonis* tells of a young male's sexual harassment by a female (who has authority because she is a goddess); *Lucrece* tells of a married female's rape by a male (who has authority because he is a king's son). Further, the earlier poem is comic – though its comedy is mingled with pathos – whereas the later is tragic.[5] Despite those differences, however, there seem also to be important continuities between the poems. It is not just that both are narrative poems and dedicated to the same person. Both examine sexuality in relation to self-knowledge, subjectivity and death. Both, moreover, are Ovidian, though *Venus and Adonis* has affinities with the *Metamorphoses* (and the *Elegies*, indirectly) whereas *Lucrece* has affinities with the *Fasti* (and, arguably, the *Heroides*). Finally, at this point, it should be mentioned that both are sceptical in their interpretations of human experience; the scepticism of *Lucrece* appears, however, to be more complex than that of *Venus and Adonis*. Perhaps the most useful way to begin considering those continuities in detail is to look, first, at the intertextual relations between *Lucrece* and Ovid's *Fasti*, then at the relations between Shakespeare's poem and other versions of the Lucretia story written before his – versions that were available to him and that he may have used when rewriting one of the oldest narratives in western culture.

Ovid's *Fasti*

It has long been accepted that Ovid's account of Lucretia's (or Lucrece's) rape and its aftermath, given in *Fasti* 2, 685–852, strongly influenced Shakespeare's.[6] If Ovid's version is read against that unfolded by Shakespeare's poem in conjunction with the 'Argument' preceding it, then one sees that the sequence of basic events, those immediately leading to, concerning, and following the rape, is much the same in each. But neither the similarities nor the discrepancies of plot are directly relevant here. All the forms of the Lucretia story now to be looked at, those usually thought significantly related to Shakespeare's, put forward much the same plot. To consider other, more revealing similarities and differences of emphasis between Ovid's version and Shakespeare's will start to illuminate those elements of *Lucrece*, mentioned above, which it shares with *Venus and Adonis*.

Ovid emphasizes at the start of his narrative the violence and treachery of Tarquin's father then, next, the treachery and violence of Tarquin himself (ll. 685–710). In the 'Argument' Shakespeare stresses the treacherous violence of Tarquin's father (ll. 1–6) then subsequently Tarquin's own treachery and violence (ll. 17–23). Ovid foregrounds Tarquin as betrayer and as murderer, his narrator telling how Tarquin betrayed – with a treachery completed through mass murder – the city of Gabii into the hands of his besieging countrymen or, more precisely, those of his father (ll. 691–710). At a later and crucial moment of Ovid's tale, when the narrator recounts Tarquin's voicing determination to rape Lucretia (ll. 781–3), Tarquin directly compares his forthcoming assault on her to his capture of Gabii, eliding her with the city. Images of cities besieged and betrayed recur throughout Shakespeare's poem. There, for example, the narrator describes the initial physical violence of Tarquin's rape of Lucrece as if it were an episode in the siege of a city (ll. 463–9); much later, moreover,

Lucrece pictures herself as a betrayed city and Tarquin as the traitor to her/it (ll. 1541–7). Shakespeare seems to have developed not merely the general characterization of his Tarquin but a specific, dominant motif in the characterizations of both his Tarquin and his Lucrece from Ovid.[7]

His doing the latter may be even more specific than has been suggested. When, near the start of Ovid's tale, the narrator relates the capture of Gabii he thereby highlights Tarquin's similarity to his father (see especially l. 691). Yet Tarquin is shown to have betrayed the city of Gabii by a trick resembling that said to have been used by Sinon in his betrayal of Troy: explicitly Tarquin's actions reveal his likeness to his father; implicitly and distantly, they make him an analogue to Sinon. In Shakespeare's poem Tarquin at first implicitly evokes Sinon (ll. 92–119, 440–69); thereafter, Lucrece explicitly identifies him with Sinon and herself with Troy (ll. 1541–7). What is merely connoted by Ovid's preliminary representation of Tarquin comes to the fore in Shakespeare's poem as an aspect of the cities-besieged-and-betrayed imagery that helps characterize Tarquin and his victim. As will be argued below, it contributes to the association of Tarquin with Satan and to the portrayal of him as comprehensively a violator. As will also be argued, it contributes likewise to the representation of Lucrece as a victim of the male gaze and as a tragic figure acting in a foundational moment of history.

Not all the other important similarities and dissimilarities of emphasis between Ovid's text and Shakespeare's can be discussed here; nonetheless, some of the more striking ones need to be considered. For a start, after Ovid's narrator has first shown Tarquin in action, he then puts before the reader a concise picture of 'the prudent Brutus' in action.[8] The reader is shown Tarquin's tyrant father, Tarquin's close and unpleasant likeness to his father, and subsequently the 'prudent' Brutus, who interprets a divine oracle as enigmatically signalling the possibility of his overthrowing the tyrant and the tyrant's clan. The figure of Brutus the liberator thus precedes and follows that of Lucretia: his story encloses hers, framing it; his implies hers to be essentially of political significance. Shakespeare's Brutus, of course, abruptly appears near the end of *Lucrece*. His story only follows hers. More to the point, Lucrece herself identifies the political significance of her story, and in doing so she identifies the political as one strand of significance implicated with various others, concerning cognition, sexuality, violation, subjectivity and history. It is arguable, too, that in Shakespeare's narrative Brutus steals Lucrece's selfhood, by rewriting it, in order to re-establish his own.[9]

Major differences of emphasis between Ovid's tale and Shakespeare's seem, however, to be outnumbered by similarities.[10] Shakespeare, for example, like Ovid stresses the male dispute that exposes Lucrece/ Lucretia to the gaze, desire and imagination of Tarquin.[11] Shakespeare's Lucrece, like Ovid's Lucretia, is implied to be a type of the chaste Roman matron. And Shakespeare, too, emphasizes the pathos of his heroine. The pathos of Lucretia is indicated initially by a speech that she makes to her handmaids. She is given a speech which, through its elaborately stylized artlessness, naivety and spontaneity, highlights the selfless love, unquestioning fidelity and worried admiration that she has for her husband (ll. 745–54). Ovid's narrator then heightens the pathos of Lucretia by relating that her speech ended in tears, and with her burying her face in her lap (ll. 755–6). Both her action and her tears were 'becoming' ('appropriate') he adds approvingly ('*decuit . . . decuere*', l. 757).[12] Ovid's narrator later suggests the pathos of Lucretia, just before Tarquin rapes her, by comparing her to 'a little lamb that, caught straying from the fold, lies low under a ravening wolf' (ll. 799–800). In *Lucrece*, the pathos of Shakespeare's heroine is emphasized in much the same ways. The narrator says, as the rape of Lucrece begins: 'The wolf hath seiz'd his prey, the poor lamb cries,/ Till with her own white fleece her voice controll'd/ Entombs her outcry in her lips' sweet fold' (ll. 677–9; cf. ll. 165–8). The images of wolf and of lamb distinctly recall those of Ovid, forming part of the imagery of predatoriness used to describe Lucrece as Tarquin's pathetic victim.[13] Further, Lucrece's speech to ward off Tarquin's assault seems clearly designed to present her as figure of pathos, as even more obviously do her three lamenting speeches of reproach, after the rape, directed against night, opportunity and time.[14] Shakespeare seems again to be elaborating on, and perhaps trying to overgo, his Ovidian pre-text.

It could reasonably be proposed, I think, that Shakespeare reworks those elements of Lucretia's representation in the *Fasti* by drawing on the rhetoric of the *Heroides*: that he uses one Ovidian work as a means of rewriting another. For the time being, however, discussion has to stay more directly focused on Ovid's version of the Lucretia story and on Shakespeare's revisioning it. Therefore, in addition to the aspects of *Fasti* 2, ll. 685–852 that have been looked at in some detail, a few others that are also immediately relevant, if less important, have at the least to be mentioned. Shakespeare iterates Ovid's emphasis on Tarquin as a victim of desire, roused not only by Lucretia's beauty but also by her chastity.[15] Shakespeare, as does Ovid, represents Tarquin as a victim of his own imagination (cf. ll. 769–78 of Ovid's text). Ovid has Tarquin appeal for help to 'God and fortune' (l. 782); Shakespeare takes that prayer and shrewdly reworks it (ll. 341–57). Moreover, Lucretia struggles three times to tell of her violation; Lucrece also struggles three times to voice it. Lucrece refuses to 'acquit' herself (l. 1706), Lucretia to 'pardon' herself (l. 830) – though neither is blamed by others. The political conclusion to Ovid's narrative is abrupt; Shakespeare's, likewise, is a striking instance of *brevitas*. Having concluded his account of the Lucretia story, Ovid then follows it with two couplets in which he alludes to the myth of Procne, another tale of rape. Shakespeare memorably weaves that myth into his narrative (ll. 1128–48).

Livy's *History of Rome*

Although Livy's formulation of the Lucretia story, in his history of Rome, Book 1, Chapters 57–60, was also used by Shakespeare, for the most part it seems to have been less significantly used than Ovid's.[16] Livy's version clearly shares several emphases with the versions of both Ovid and Shakespeare. His narrator stresses the intensity of the male dispute about who has the best wife (1, 57, 6–8); he indicates that Lucretia is a type of the chaste Roman matron (1, 57, 9); he points not only to her beauty but also to her chastity as exciting Tarquin's desire (1, 57, 10).[17] His narrator makes a number of emphases, of course, not made by Ovid's or by Shakespeare's. In Livy's tale, for example, Lucretia has no hesitancy in telling her husband what has happened to her: she immediately and forcefully relates her misfortune (1, 58, 7–8). More interesting and revealing are the emphases made by Livy's narrator and by Shakespeare's but not by Ovid's. A particularly important instance concerns the overpowering sense of history that Livy's Lucretia and Shakespeare's Lucrece have in common. Just after the former has been cleared from any imputation of guilt by those who have been listening to her, she says: '[N]ot in time to come shall ever unchaste woman live through the example of Lucretia' (1, 58, 10).[18] Thereupon she commits suicide. Shakespeare's heroine says: '[N]o dame hereafter living/ By my excuse shall claim excuse's giving' (ll. 1714–15). She then names Tarquin, identifies him as the cause of what she is about to do, and kills herself. It seems that from Livy's narrative Shakespeare developed Lucrece's profound sense of herself as a type or exemplar of absolute chastity, and of exemplarity as a chief means of perceiving and establishing meaning, value and subjectivity in the flux of history.[19]

Boccaccio, Chaucer, Gower and the Lucretia story

Among the accounts of the Lucretia story that were written closer in time to Shakespeare's, those respectively by Boccaccio, Chaucer and Gower appear to be here the most directly relevant. Boccaccio's narrative starts by emphasizing that Lucretia is a 'model', or exemplar, of chastity: 'Lucretia, the outstanding model of Roman chastity and sacred glory of ancient virtue, was the daughter of Spurius Lucretius Tricipitinus.'[20] In fact the opening of Boccaccio's narrative chiefly identifies Lucretia's subjectivity in terms of exemplarity. Her exemplarity, furthermore, enables the ethical interpretation, or illumination, of a moment in Roman political history: the transition of Rome from monarchic to republican government. Just after denouncing Tarquin to her relatives, as Boccaccio's version has it, she echoes the last words of Livy's heroine, saying: '[I]n the future no woman will live dishonorably because of Lucretia's example' (p. 102). Boccaccio's story, then, makes explicit the implicit emphasis in Livy's (as in Ovid's) on Lucretia as an exemplar; more important, Boccaccio's Lucretia repeats the words spoken by Livy's heroine that imply exemplarity is a means of interpreting history. Yet if Boccaccio's tale announces Lucretia's role as an exemplar, and indirectly identifies her subjectivity with that role, Shakespeare's narrative goes a step further. His narrator indicates that Lucrece is chastity's exemplar (ll. 7–8) and suggests that her very face reveals it (ll. 52–73); in addition, however, Lucrece herself signals her conscious role as an exemplar and elides her subjectivity with it.[21] Moreover, whereas in Livy's and in Boccaccio's narratives Lucretia implicitly, briefly and memorably emphasizes exemplarity as a means of interpreting history, Shakespeare's Lucrece, as has been mentioned above, has a deep, pervasive sense of exemplarity as a means of clarifying and stabilizing historical process, as a means of defining subjectivity within it. Later in this chapter I shall argue that Lucrece's concern with exemplarity as a form of selfhood ties in with her apparent notion that her own subjectivity has been imposed, and can be defiled or deleted, from without.

The last versions of the Lucretia story, prior to Shakespeare's, that will now be considered are Chaucer's in *The Legend of Good Women* and Gower's in *Confessio Amantis*.[22] Chaucer's narrator, acknowledging Ovid and Livy to have provided the material of his tale (l. 1683), claims that a desire to celebrate 'Lucresse' (ll. 1684–6) impels him, rather than a wish to relate 'th'exilynge of kynges/ Of Rome, for her horrible doynges' (ll. 1680–1). He suggests that he is interested in focusing on Lucresse's moral stature rather than on the political implications of her story. For all that, like Shakespeare's narrator he pays close attention to the political aspects of his tale as well as to its heroine. Several emphases in Chaucer's tale correspond to those made in Shakespeare's – and that is not always because both writers draw on Ovid and on Livy. Nor do all those emphases bear directly on the characterization of Shakespeare's Lucrece. Like the narrators of Ovid, Livy, Boccaccio and, of course, Shakespeare, Chaucer's narrator stresses the male dispute over who has the best wife. Yet in doing so he emphasizes something that only Shakespeare's narrator also highlights, if more distinctly: Collatine, through his boasting, in effect initiates the violation of both his domestic space and his wife. According to Chaucer's narrator, Collatine says: ' "I have a wife . . . that, as I trowe,/ Is holden good of al that ever hir knowe./ Go we tonight to Rome, and we shul se" ' (ll. 1708–10). Then, the narrator relates: 'Tarquynius answerde, "That lyketh me."/ To Rome be they come, and faste hem dighte/ To Colatynes hous, and doun they lyghte,/ Tarquynius and eke this Colatyne' (ll. 1711–14). In the other versions of the Lucretia story looked at so far, Collatine does indeed also boast and invite his fellow contestants to compare Lucretia with their own wives. In the other versions, however, Collatine's boasting and invitation are described in ways obviously differing from the way they are described in Chaucer's narrative.

Ovid's version has Tarquin begin the dispute over who has the best wife, but Collatinus suggest that the competition be resolved by a sudden visit to Rome (ll. 725–37). Collatinus is seen to make, unwittingly, a fatal mistake; even so, his suggestion surely seems impulsive, unconsidered, and little more. According to Livy's version, no one in particular initiates the dispute; it just begins. Then Collatinus suggests the visit to Rome, boasting that thereby his competitors will 'know, in a few hours' time' (1, 57, 7) the superiority of his wife. Collatinus' suggestion, as in Ovid's narrative, seems rash, unconsidered and unconsciously dangerous; in addition, though, Collatinus' words also provocatively draw his competitors' attention to Lucretia, who is named. Thus he focuses Tarquin on her. Livy's Collatinus therefore resembles Ovid's yet seems to be more directly inviting disaster than does his counterpart in the *Fasti*. But in Boccaccio's account of the dispute Collatinus figures less culpably – in fact, less culpably than he does even in Ovid's version. As Boccaccio's narrator tells it, both the dispute and the decision to visit Rome come from the group of 'royal youths, among whom was Collatinus' (p. 101). The *group* makes a mistake. Chaucer's narrator, in the passage quoted above, tells the tale otherwise; so too does the narrator of *Lucrece*.

Chaucer's narrator conveys the personal aggressiveness of Colatyne's boasting ('"I have a wife, ... that, as I trowe ..."') and also its imprudence, for Colatyne puts his wife on display, he exposes her to the male gaze of his competitors ('"Go we tonight to Rome, and we shul se"'). Then the narrator conveys Tarquin's immediate, abrupt and sinisterly ambiguous response, '"That lyketh me"', which suggests his willingness – perhaps even eagerness – to view Lucresse. In his blind pride Colatyne becomes complicit in making his wife Tarquin's victim. His complicity is affirmed when the narrator reports: 'To Rome be they come, and faste hem dighte/ To Colatynes hous' (ll. 1712–13). Colatyne in effect hurries his wife's enemy and his own into his home. The guilt of Colatyne is likewise that of Collatine in *Lucrece*, with the difference that the latter seems more, and more directly, guilty than does the former. Shakespeare's narrator says, very early in the poem: 'Collatine unwisely did not let/ To praise the clear unmatched red and white/ Which truimph'd in that sky of his delight' (ll. 10–12). He proceeds to elaborate:

For he the night before, in Tarquin's tent
Unlock'd the treasure of his happy state:
What priceless wealth the heavens had him lent,
In the possession of his beauteous mate;
Reck'ning his fortune at such high proud rate
    That kings might be espoused to more fame,
    But king nor peer to such a peerless dame.

(ll. 15–21)

... [W]hy is Collatine the publisher
    Of that rich jewel he should keep unknown
    From thievish ears, because it is his own?

Perchance his boast of Lucrece' sov'reignty
Suggested this proud issue of a king. ...

(ll. 33–7)

The indirect emphasis on the guilt of Colatyne in Chaucer's poem clearly has a more direct and insistent counterpart in *Lucrece*.

One further similarity of emphasis between Chaucer's *Legend of Lucrece* and Shakespeare's poem might be mentioned before discussion turns to relations between Gower's and Shakespeare's versions of the Lucretia story. Chaucer's narrative, as is often the case in his writings, calculatedly mingles pagan and Christian world views or perspectives. For example, when Lucresse pleads with Tarquin not to rape her, and 'axeth grace, and seith al that she kan' (l. 1804), Tarquin replies:

'Ne wolt thou nat, . . . / As wisly Jupiter my soule save,/ As I shal in the stable slee thy knave,/ And lay him in thy bed . . .' (ll. 1805–8).[23] A major result of the two world views' interaction in Chaucer's tale is that through it his narrator offers, deliberately or otherwise, an implicit defence of Lucresse's reputation against St Augustine's attack on her for having committed suicide.[24] At the story's end, Chaucer's narrator says of Lucresse: 'And she was holden there [Rome]/ A seynt, and ever hir day yhalwed dere/ As in her lawe' (ll. 1870–72). He adds:

> [S]he was of love so trewe,
> Ne in hir wille she chaunged for no newe,
> And for the stable herte, sadde and kynde,
> That in these wymmen man may alday fynde.
> Ther as they kaste her hert, ther hit duelleth.
> For wel I wot that Crist himselve telleth
> That in Israel, as wyde as is the londe,
> That so gret feythe in al the lond he ne fonde
> As in a woman, and this is no lye.

> (ll. 1874–82)

Far from being ultimately, if not merely, a self-murderer as St Augustine had argued, Chaucer's Lucresse is a type of conjugal fidelity who, said to have been given saintly status in ancient Rome, is carefully, obliquely linked to the figure of Christ.

As was suggested above, Shakespeare's *Lucrece* also seems to inter-play pagan and Christian views of the world. Lucrece herself seems often to have a double vision of experience, two voices as it were. To take a slight example, when pleading with Tarquin she says: 'To all the host of heaven I complain me' (l. 598). The Roman matron's complaint is addressed to the inhabitants of the Christian heaven. Likewise, a little later she says to Tarquin: 'Hast thou command? by him [God] that gave it thee,/ From a pure heart command thy rebel will' (ll. 624–5). Lucrece's words indicate that Tarquin's will to violate offends against both pagan and Christian values; but is it that, unknowingly, she voices two world views in two languages, or is it that, at privileged or maybe particular moments, she perhaps knowingly has or reveals a syncretic, appositional consciousness?

The question becomes more difficult to answer and more import-ant when Lucrece reproaches opportunity (ll. 876ff.).[25] In doing so, Lucrece examines the problem of causation in natural process and in human action. She blames opportunity –'[T]hy guilt is great!' (l. 876) – for facilitating, and even directly causing, destruction in the one, evil in the other: 'Thou sets the wolf where he the lamb may get;/

Whoever plots the sin, thou poinst the season./ 'Tis thou that spurn'st at right, at law, at reason' (ll. 878–80). The terms of Lucrece's reproach bring together the pagan and the Christian: 'opportunity' is the Roman *occasio*, part of the mythology of Time and Fortune; 'sin', while not of course an exclusively Christian term or concept, is presented by her in recognizably Christian form.[26] Here again, then, Lucrece seems to have a twofold vision, to speak with two voices: however, the pagan does not fully accord with the Christian in her account of opportunity's responsibility for facilitating or causing destruction and evil. Lucrece's blaming opportunity/*occasio* for destruction of particular kinds in the natural world may not be irreconcilable with some pagan, or with some sixteenth-century Christian, views of 'mischance' or 'misfortune' in nature. Nor may her blaming it for facilitating or causing human evil be irreconcilable, at some points of her speech, with the Christian notion that 'the occasion of sin is death'. But her blaming it for causing human evil seems clearly irreconcilable with Christian concepts of sin when she says, for example: ' "Thou [opportunity] mak'st the vestal violate her oath" ' (l. 883; cf. ll. 905–8). The complementarity and conflict between her two visions, her two registers, would apparently indicate either that she unknowingly mingles the pagan with the Christian, or that her perhaps knowingly syncretic, appositional consciousness fails to harmonize fully the pagan with the Christian. It is not possible, I think, for the reader to know the conscious range of Lucrece's ethical and religious perceptions, the degree to which they are anachronistic, especially in relation to some of her more complex and crucial attitudes and decisions.

The last of the pre-Shakespearean versions of the Lucretia story to be considered here, that by Gower in his *Confessio Amantis*, has many of the emphases that are made also in the others. For example, there is emphasis on the astuteness of Brutus (especially in ll. 4741–5), on the male competition about wives (ll. 4763–85), and on Lucrece/Lucretia as a figure of pathos (as in ll. 4809–41). Yet there are, as well, emphases not made in the other versions. The most important of them is arguably an insistent association of tyranny with lust, of lechery with tyranny's violating the rule of law. Gower's narrator remarks, when initially describing the Tarquins:

> [They] token hiede of no justice,
> Which due was to here office
> Upon the reule of governance
> Bot al that evere was plesance
> Unto the fleisshes lust thi toke.

(ll. 4603–7)

Later the narrator says of 'Arrons' (for the rape is attributed to another of the elder Tarquin's sons) that '[H]e . . ./ With melled love and tirannie,/ Hath founde upon his tricherie/ A weie which he thenkth to holde' (ll. 4898–901). Near the tale's close, 'al the toun' (l. 5117) is reported as crying: '"Awey, awey the tirannie/ Of lecherie and covoitise!"' (ll. 5118–19). That emphatic, recurrent association of lust with tyranny and its violating the rule of law appear likewise in *Lucrece*.[27] Shakespeare almost certainly insists on that association in order to align his Tarquin with a conventional Renaissance image of the tyrant derived from Plato's *Republic*, but nonetheless Shakespeare's tyrant figure may be indebted to the simpler one fashioned by Gower.[28]

(II) GENRES

Some of the pre-texts to *Lucrece* having been discussed, there remains one further preliminary to consideration of the poem itself and its links to *Venus and Adonis*: discussion of the genre to which *Lucrece* belongs and of its significant affinities with other genres. Like *Venus and Adonis*, though with the differences noted in the second paragraph of this chapter, *Lucrece* can be seen as a minor epic. Clark Hulse's account of that genre could be cited again as offering reason enough. Unlike *Venus and Adonis*, however, *Lucrece* highlights the epic no less than the erotic. Shakespeare's second minor epic, in imaging Tarquin's erotic pursuit of Lucrece and its consequences, metonymically suggests to the reader the heroic prospect of early Roman history. The poem juxtaposes two mythologized, supposedly foundational moments in Roman history, the rape of Lucrece and the fall of Troy. It thus brings together respectively the notional moment of the republic's beginning and, likewise, that of Rome's origin. Shakespeare's violently erotic narrative, through the heroic and tragic female figure at its centre, is causally linked to or symbolically recreates originary, epic episodes in the story of Rome.

It has been often pointed out by commentators that *Lucrece* in particular, and minor epics in general, have affinities with tragedy and with the complaint.[29] Certainly those two genres seem to be the ones with which Shakespeare's poem has its most significant affinities. But to what form or forms of tragedy is it connected? How is it associated with the complaint? Answers to the first question vary; here, I should like to put forward a couple. First, *Lucrece* can be seen as akin to the medieval *de casibus* tragedy or tragic narrative: a tale of an illustrious person's fall from high estate to low, from felicity to misery, at the turn of Fortune's wheel.[30] When Lydgate wrote his version of the Lucretia story in his *Fall of Princes*, he shaped it as a *de casibus* tragic narrative.[31] So his narrator tells of 'Lucrece, exaumple off wifli trouthe', and 'How yonge Tarquyn hir falsli dede oppresse,/ And afftir that, which was to gret a routhe,/ How she hirsilff[e] slouh for heuynesse' (2, 974–7). Second, it can be also suggested that *Lucrece* is related to the tyrant play: a form of tragedy examining the excesses, the violence – including self-violence – of tyrannic rule.[32] The characterization of Tarquin, as was mentioned above, accords with a conventional Renaissance image of the tyrant derived from Plato's *Republic*. When Tarquin assaults Lucrece he is not yet, of course, Rome's king. She, then understanding him too late, perceives the king he will likely become: an horrifically parodic king, a tyrant. She asks him: ' "How will thy shame be seeded in thine age,/ When thus thy vices bud before thy spring?/ If in thy hope thou dar'st do such outrage,/ What dar'st thou not when once thou art a king?" ' (ll. 603–6).[33] Tarquin looks as if he will become a tyrant because his actions now reveal him as a proto-tyrant. It is by no means always the case in tyrant plays that a tyrant's victim effects both revenge on him and his overthrow. In Shakespeare's minor epic, Lucrece manages to achieve rather more, for in effecting revenge on a proto-tyrant she causes the overthrow of a tyrannic dynasty.

Tyrant tragedies sometimes contain complaints: verse monologues mingling reproach with lament. So do *de casibus* tragedies, while *de casibus* tragic narratives often unfold as complaints.[34] It is not surprising, then, that in having significant affinities with tragedy *Lucrece* has them with the complaint as well. The *Mirror for Magistrates*, a long-influential collection of *de casibus* tragic narratives presented as complaints, was first published in 1559. All the complaints in the first edition of the *Mirror* are spoken by men; however, in the 'parts added' to the *Mirror* by John Higgins and by Thomas Blenerhasset (in 1574 and 1578 respectively) some complaints are spoken by women, such as 'Cordila' or Cordelia. Insofar as recent critical commentary has focused on the complaint genre, particular attention has been given to Samuel Daniel's *The Complaint of Rosamond* (1592), for it has been reconsidered as the later Elizabethan poem conventionally understood to have renewed the complaint genre and to have been in effect a prelude to *Lucrece*.

Hallett Smith, in his pioneering *Elizabethan Poetry* (1952), wrote that during the 1590s there occurred 'a revival of the complaint form, with new emphasis and character' in which 'the *Mirror* tradition has interesting connections with the pastoral convention, with the Petrarchan love tradition, and with Ovidian-mythological poetry'.[35]

A main element of the new complaint, he argued, was the recurrence of female speakers concerned with the preservation of chastity (pp. 103–26). And, he pointed out: 'The vogue of the new complaint poem was started by Samuel Daniel with *The Complaint of Rosamond* in 1592. What *Hero and Leander* was for the Ovidian poem, *Rosamond* was for the complaint' (p. 104). Among the poems that he discussed in his account of the renewed complaint was *Lucrece* (pp. 104, 108, 113–15). One might demur at so close an association of Shakespeare's poem with the neo-complaint; nonetheless, Smith's discussion valuably suggested affinities between *Lucrece* and *Rosamond*, between Shakespeare's second poem and the complaint genre's recent transformation.

An important refining of Hallett Smith's thesis came with Heather Dubrow's essay 'A Mirror for Complaints: Shakespeare's *Lucrece* and Generic Tradition' (1986).[36] Dubrow suggested that the generic context for *Lucrece* was not exactly as specified by Smith. She argued that *Lucrece* belongs to a subgenre of the complaint which includes 'certain of the works' named by Smith 'and a number of others as well' (p. 401). 'In some poems of this [latter] type', she continued, 'the heroine . . . retain[s] her chastity, but in others she surrenders it. And, significantly enough, she is threatened by a ruler, a situation that invites speculations on the uses and abuses of power' (*ibid.*). Dubrow proceeded to argue that the subgenre of the complaint identified by her contained at least seven poems published 'within the brief span of [the] years [1592–4]' (*ibid.*), among them *Rosamond* and *Lucrece*. Linking the seven poems, she proposed, are such things as 'allus[ion] to the perils of praise . . . and of . . . flattery', repeated focus on 'the moral ambiguities involved in the process of persuasion', and 'concern for the political implications of what Lucrece herself terms "private pleasure"' (pp. 401–2). What distinguish Shakespeare's poem from its companions, she subsequently argued, are its design (it 'incorporates [Lucrece's complaints within] a larger narrative') and, more important, its 'render[ing] the values and assumptions of the complaint problematical, generally by directing our attention to the psychological implications behind issues treated more uncritically and straightforwardly in those other complaints and in *A Mirror for Magistrates* itself' (p. 404).[37] One might want to suggest that the 'larger narrative' which 'incorporates' Lucrece's complaints in fact distinguishes Shakespeare's poem from its notional companions by making it a minor epic. On the other hand, one could only agree with Dubrow's account of the elements, mentioned above, that link *Lucrece* with those other poems. It seems hard, too, not to agree with the attractive notion that *Lucrece* is a 'problem complaint' (p. 417). One might want nonetheless to argue that, in its richness, Shakespeare's poem renders far more than the complaint genre problematic.[38] But the scope of Shakespeare's poem is not directly relevant here; more relevant and revealing are, first, that *Lucrece* has close connections with the complaint, second, that Daniel's *Rosamond* is its influential, immediate predecessor – the relations between the two poems therefore needing to be examined.

Lucrece seems not so much to resemble *Rosamond* as to contradict it, to be written against the grain of the earlier poem. No one would want to deny that the poems do indeed have similarities much as described by Smith and by Dubrow. For example, in each the chastity of the main female figure is attacked by a ruthless political superior. But in fact there are other similarities as well. Both Rosamond and Lucrece are associated with Eve; in connection with that and with the motif of aggressed chastity, both are described through flower imagery; both complain against night and fortune/*occasio*; both are betrayed; both commit suicide. The differences between the poems seem, however, to be more revealing. Their structures differ, as Dubrow observed – a difference that, in my view, generically distinguishes the poems. Their fictional worlds differ, too. It is not simply that one is medieval and English, the other ancient and Roman. The fictional world of *Rosamond* is a Christian one paganized, in terms not unfamiliar from earlier complaints.[39] That of *Lucrece*, as has been discussed briefly above, is a pagan one variously Christianized. Moreover, whereas Rosamond is and feels guilty because ultimately responsible for her loss of chastity (see, for example, ll. 64–98), Lucrece is innocent, because a rape victim, but nonetheless feels guilty (see, for example, ll. 1700–15). Rosamond complains, from the very start of Daniel's poem, at her loss of honour; almost from the moment when first assaulted by Tarquin, Lucrece seems no less concerned for her husband's honour than for her own. Certainly, Shakespeare's poem has a complexity, a richness beyond Daniel's. In particular, Shakespeare characterizes Lucrece more complexly than Daniel characterizes Rosamond, which is not at all to depreciate Daniel's writing. The point being put forward here, nonetheless, is that *Lucrece* seems calculatedly to rework and to overgo its predecessor. It is as if Shakespeare's poem were designed both to acknowledge and to transcend Daniel's, to acknowledge the renewal of the complaint genre but to transcend the genre itself.

The accounts offered above of *Lucrece* in relation to some pre-texts and to some genres have made several suggestions about how Shakespeare reworked the Lucretia story and about his poem's generic affinities. For a start, it has been suggested that Ovid's emphasis on Tarquin's violence and treachery was developed by Shakespeare into a dominant motif in the characterizations of both his Tarquin and his Lucrece – the imagery of cities besieged and betrayed – which is linked in Shakespeare's poem to the identification of Tarquin with Sinon and to the representation of Lucrece as at once a victim of the male gaze and as someone caught in an originary historical moment. Then, too, it has been suggested that whereas Ovid's Brutus reveals Lucretia's story as being essentially of political significance, Shakespeare's Lucrece reveals the political significance of her story and, as mentioned above, indicates the political to be one strand of significance implicated with various others. It has been proposed, moreover, that Shakespeare's Brutus rewrites Lucrece's subjectivity in order to re-establish his own.

Comparison between Livy's version of the Lucretia story and that by Shakespeare, on the other hand, raised the likelihood of Shakespeare's having developed Lucrece's deep sense of herself as an exemplar of chastity, and of exemplarity as crucial to stabilizing the flux of history, from the narrative by the Roman historian. A glance at Boccaccio's *Concerning Famous Women* suggested that his version of the Lucretia story links her subjectivity with exemplarity and iterates the implicit emphasis by Livy's heroine on exemplarity as a means of interpreting history. It was then suggested that Chaucer's stress on Collatine as being ultimately responsible for his wife's sufferings is affirmed and developed in *Lucrece* – deliberately or otherwise – and that, likewise, in Shakespeare's narrative as in Chaucer's there occurs an ambiguous mingling of pagan with Christian perspectives. Finally, it was proposed that Gower's association of political tyranny with lust in his retelling of the Lucretia story harmonizes with Shakespeare's probably Platonic representation of Tarquin as tyrant.

Broadly summarized, those are some of the main suggestions made in the preceding pages as to how Shakespeare reworked various pre-texts to *Lucrece*. The main suggestions made about his poem's generic affinities can be summarized as follows. *Lucrece* is a minor epic, with more emphasis on the epic aspect of the genre than can be seen in *Venus and Adonis*. It is related to both *de casibus* and tyrant tragedy. It is also related to the complaint; in particular, it seems associated with the complaint as renewed by Daniel's *Rosamond*. Shakespeare's poem, however, appears to be written in contradiction to Daniel's, as if designed to acknowledge and to overgo it, to acknowledge and to transcend the genre it revitalized. Having indicated something of how Shakespeare reformulated the Lucretia story and generically positioned his version of it, one now needs to turn to *Lucrece* itself.

(III) TARQUIN, LUCRECE AND COLLATINE

As might be expected, much of the more recent commentary on *Lucrece* has focused on the interrelated matters of politics, gender and subjectivity. The poem's representation of the Roman world and its politics, especially its sexual/gender politics, has been studied; how *Lucrece* emerges from the variously political discourses of later Elizabethan society, and its negotiations with them, have been considered; the poem's representations of subjectivity in relation to patriarchy and to rape — and their connections — have been widely discussed.[40] In focusing on those matters, most commentary has inevitably centred on the characterization of Lucrece herself. But as a result the mutually defining nature of characterization in the poem has received insufficient attention.[41] Here I want to propose that by examining the reciprocal formation of consciousness and of role among Shakespeare's Tarquin, Collatine and Lucrece as far as the beginnings of his poem's rape scene (that is, approximately from lines 1 to 441) one sees that the characterizations established early in *Lucrece* are more complex in their discursive relations than has been acknowledged. Recognition of their being so helps to illuminate not merely subsequent happenings in the poem, such as Lucrece's insistent denial of her own innocence and her decision to commit suicide, but also crucial concerns of the poem, such as the sceptical interrogation of exemplarity, the interaction between exemplarity and historical process.

In particular, I shall argue here that while Tarquin is a tyrant figure, and distinctly a Platonic type of the tyrant, he is as well a demonic parody of the Petrarchan lover insofar as he pursues a lady, Lucrece, who is portrayed as at once an exemplar of the chaste Roman matron and an incarnation of the Petrarchan mistress. Violating her, Shakespeare's Tarquin sexually heightens and violates the Petrarchan discourse of love. Yet it is not Lucrece's primary misfortune that, in her guise as Petrarchan mistress, she attracts a tyrant figure (in fact, a proto-tyrant) who defines himself specifically, as a tyrant, in relation to her via the role of grimly parodic Petrarchan lover. Rather, as is argued here, it seems that Lucrece's primary misfortune lies in the hubris of her husband, Collatine. When part of the Roman army besieging Ardea, Collatine tries to gain a personal victory over the king's son, his superior and kinsman: Collatine's boastful vying with the proto-tyrant redirects Tarquin's violence and desire from the enemy/foreign/public to the kindred/Roman/private. The poem registers that redirection of Tarquin's violence and desire not only in terms of Petrarchan discourse but also in terms of the myths of the

Golden Age and of Eden. Tarquin becomes an analogue to Satan; Lucrece, indicated as embodying both Tarquin's and Collatine's notions of the absolute good on earth, becomes an analogue to the earthly paradise and (an incorruptible) Eve; Collatine thus figures as a self-betraying Adam, who brings the serpent to Eden and tempts the serpent into violating his (unwilling) Eve.

When the intricate interactions among Tarquin, Collatine and Lucrece in the early part of Shakespeare's poem are seen especially as expressed through those Platonic, Petrarchan and Golden Age/Edenic discourses, then the immediately relevant consequences are as follows. Tarquin's mutually intensifying, interconnected roles, read in conjunction with the also mutually intensifying and interconnected roles of Lucrece, which are antithetic to his, clarify her comprehensive sense of violation and contamination. Thus clarified, too, is her deep sense of defacement, of her innermost self's having been stolen; both clarifications, in turn, help to illuminate her decision to commit suicide. Light is shed, moreover, on the sceptical questioning of exemplarity and on other of the poem's concerns. The final consequence, then, appears to be that a new perspective is offered on the poem as a whole: important happenings can be viewed from a revealingly un-familiar angle; things not previously observed, such as the sceptical questioning of exemplarity, come sharply into view.

The easiest way to start specifying what has been outlined above is probably by looking at the characterization of Tarquin, for with him the poem itself begins. Tarquin's historical role as proto-tyrant seems to be his basic one in the poem. Shakespeare's narrator may also picture Tarquin in the roles of parodic Petrarchan lover and of Satan, but it is indicated that they are Tarquin's expressions of his tyrannic role in relation to Lucrece. At the beginning of the 'Argu-ment', the narrator signals that Tarquin's immediate role model is his father, whose pride, treachery, violence and violations − of family bonds, of laws and of custom − manifest his will to power, his will to tyranny (ll. 1−6). The poem reveals, of course more thoroughly than does the 'Argument', that Tarquin is certainly his father's son.[42]

The opening of *Lucrece* predominantly characterizes Tarquin in terms of desire. The 'Argument' emphasizes his underlying role to be that of proto-tyrant, the opening stanzas do so as well; but as proto-tyrant he is initially and chiefly characterized in the poem by the 'desire' (l. 2) which informs the expressions of his tyrannic role in relation to Lucrece.[43] The narrator implies several things about the nature of that desire: its treachery ('trustless' and 'false', in l. 2, suggest that it betrays Tarquin while impelling him to betray Collatine and

Lucrece); its possession of Tarquin (he becomes '[l]ust-breathed', the narrator says in l. 3); its sinister, even demonic, energy (ll. 4–7); its violence which displaces the military violence directed by Tarquin against Ardea. Desire, treachery and violence are, according to Plato's *Republic*, marks of the tyrannic character.[44] In fact, desire and the need to gratify it tyrannize over the tyrant. He becomes driven by a 'master passion' in whose service he will violate even domestic sanctities (9, 572–5). The characterization of Tarquin as proto-tyrant accords in those respects, then, with Plato's type of the tyrant in his *Republic*.[45] And it does so in others as well. According to Plato's text, desire possesses the tyrant but he is vulnerable also to fears: 'He is naturally a prey to fears and passions of every sort' (9, 579b). Tarquin's soliloquy in his chamber dramatizes the compelling force of his desire in conflict with the constraining power of his fears (ll. 190–280).[46] Further, Plato describes the tyrant as bestial and, more specifically, as a wolf to his fellow citizens (8, 569b and 565d–566a). Shakespeare's narrator compares Tarquin, just before the rape of Lucrece, to a 'cockatrice' (l. 540), a 'gripe' (l. 543; that is, to a vulture or an eagle) and to a 'foul night-waking cat' (l. 554). Tarquin is thereafter compared to a 'wolf' when he rapes Lucrece (ll. 676–7). Subsequently he is figured as a 'full-fed hound or gorged hawk' (l. 694) and 'thievish dog' (l. 736). In his primary role as proto-tyrant, Tarquin seems deliberately represented in accord with Plato's account of the tyrannic character. He may be, as Ovid had indicated and Shakespeare apparently accepted from Ovid, truly his father's son but he is also more than a reincarnation of his tyrannic father.

How much more than that he is can be seen from his relations to Lucrece. The ways in which Tarquin perceives Lucrece and defines himself in response to his understanding of her express, of course, his desire for her and thus his role as Platonic tyrant figure in relation to her. As has been foreshadowed above, one such expression of his role as tyrant in relation to her is his role as parodic Petrarchan lover. When first the narrator describes Tarquin, characterizing him predominantly in terms of desire, it seems that '[l]ust-breathed' Tarquin (l. 3) is as a man possessed. What tyrannizes over the proto-tyrant is desire for a woman pictured to him, by her husband, in a way that anachronistically celebrates her as a type of the Petrarchan lady: 'Collatine unwisely did not let/ To praise the clear unmatched red and white/ Which triumph'd in that sky of his delight' (ll. 10–12). The narrator confirms that image of Lucrece by adding to his report of Collatine's imprudent eulogy. He praises Lucrece's eyes, identifying them with the stars. They are, he says, '[M]ortal stars as bright as

heaven's beauties' (l. 13). Reworking the Petrarchan motif of the
lady's eyes being, or resembling, stars, Shakespeare's narrator con-
firms what his report of Lucrece's public celebration by Collatine has
previously, and likewise metonymically, indicated through Petrarchan
allusion ('red and white', l. 11): Lucrece's role as Petrarchan object
of desire. So Tarquin, the Platonic tyrant figure tyrannized by desire
for a woman imaged to him as virtually prefiguring Laura, becomes
in relation to her a counterpart to the Petrarchan lover.[47] But the
differences between Tarquin and, say, Petrarch's speaker in '*Passa la
nave . . .*' are more important than the similarities. In particular, the
latter's desire for his lady seems ambivalent. Tarquin's desire for
Lucrece is, however, solely unspiritual, a 'lightless fire' (l. 4) con-
cerned only with the body and with violation: 'lurk[ing] to aspire,/
And girdle with embracing flames the waist/ Of Collatine's fair love,
Lucrece the chaste' (ll. 5–7). Expressing his will to tyranny, his proto-
tyrannic role, Tarquin's desire makes him a brutal parody of the
Petrarchan lover as a species; it makes his pursuit of Lucrece a sexual
heightening and violation of the Petrarchan discourse of love. As
might be expected, Shakespeare's narrator implies that very distinctly
and emphatically in his account of Lucrece's rape.

The interaction between that parodic role and Tarquin's other
main roles in relation to Lucrece is intriguing; nonetheless, before it
can be looked at those roles through which her subjectivity is chiefly
fashioned in the poem must be considered. Lucrece's initial and
main role in the poem is, almost inevitably, that of chaste Roman
matron: the narrator first identifies her as 'Collatine's fair love, Lucrece
the chaste' (l. 7). Her subsequently established guise of Petrarchan lady
complements her initial one by heightening the reader's sense of both
her chastity and her beauty (see especially ll. 12–14). The two roles
also have a less obvious harmony, for they can be seen – though in
different ways – as imposed. Lucrece's initial role gives her selfhood
in terms of a conventional category of the female in her society. In
that sense the basic role given to her in the poem, which concurs
with her own notion of who she basically is, appears to be culturally
imposed. And not only does Lucrece acknowledge the role of chaste
Roman matron to be in fact essential to her idea of who she is; she
acknowledges, too, her feeling or consciousness of its being imposed
from without (by implication, socially). Her most explicit acknow-
ledgement occurs, I think, just after her three long complaints, when
she is pondering suicide: 'I was a loyal wife:/ So am I now, – O no,
that cannot be!/ Of that true type hath Tarquin rifled me' (ll. 1048–
50).[48] The reader may not agree with Lucrece's refusal to accept her

own innocence but, that aside, it would seem clear that she thinks of herself as being primarily a chaste Roman matron and as having received that role from without – of her basic selfhood as therefore ultimately able to be erased from without.

Lucrece's externalized sense of her ultimate self thus appears to be inseparable from, and to clarify, at once her profound consciousness of herself as an exemplar of chastity and her profound fear of becoming an exemplar of unchastity. She recognizes that others have established her as the former and that they can turn her into the latter: she recognizes her vulnerability as an exemplar, how indifferent to her inner life and beyond her control that aspect of her selfhood is (see ll. 519–39 and 806–40). Her consciousness of herself as exemplar seems to clarify, in turn, her sense of being immersed in historical process. Rape impels Lucrece to look anxiously to the future and also anxiously to the past, as well it might.[49] But for her, as exemplar, there is a special reason for its doing so. Exemplarity, in her world as of course in Shakespeare's, is a means of illuminating and stabilizing historical process, of defining subjectivity within it. Anticipating misrepresentation of her role as exemplar, its unjustly parodic inversion, Lucrece simultaneously anticipates the falsification of history (see, for example, ll. 813–26). To preserve her existence as an exemplar of chastity is likewise, for her, significantly if partly to save the present from future misinterpretation, to protect history from false tradition. The case is alike yet interestingly different when she turns to the past. Looking to a picture of the Trojan past for comfort, she seeks consolation in discovering an exemplar of misery (ll. 1443–56), not merely in order that she may find a companion in her distress but, as well, that she may find another self – one whom she may vindicate and so, through whom, amend history (ll. 1457–98).

Lucrece's preoccupation with her exemplarity and with control of meaning and of subjectivity in interpretation of the past will be examined again below. For the moment, discussion must focus on what seem to be her other main roles in the poem. Those other roles are, much like the ones previously considered, imposed from without. That is to say, although they are revealed by the narrator as consonant with personal appearance and impulse in Lucrece, they are also revealed by him as in effect deriving from Collatine's devotion to her and from Tarquin's perception of her via the celebratory picture drawn by her husband. They connect with, as well as complement, her roles as chaste Roman matron and Petrarchan lady, just as they evoke from Tarquin roles linked to his guises of Platonic tyrant figure and parodic Petrarchan lover. They are, moreover, syncretic and in part anachronistic: as was indicated earlier, they figure Lucrece as a type of the earthly paradise and (an incorruptible) Eve; Tarquin therefore comes to figure as a type of Satan (later, of course, he becomes an analogue to Sinon); Collatine thence comes to figure as a self-betraying Adam, who unwittingly tempts the serpent to violate, to steal. It is a powerful mingling of discourses – Platonic, Petrarchan, Golden Age/Edenic – that combines with what is chiefly an Ovidian historical discourse to characterize the three main actors in Shakespeare's narrative and thereby re-present the rape of Lucrece.

The representation of Lucrece in terms of Golden Age/Edenic discourse begins with the initial picturing of her as an ideal Petrarchan lady. When Shakespeare's narrator first mentions Collatine's unwary celebration of Lucrece, he affirms her husband's reported and summarized speech by describing her face as the 'sky of [Collatine's] delight;/ Where mortal stars as bright as heaven's beauties,/ With pure aspects did him peculiar duties' (ll. 12–14). The Petrarchan allusions in those lines have already been discussed; what I wish to emphasize here is that the Petrarchan imagery suggests Lucrece to be Collatine's heaven on earth ('lent' to him by 'the heavens', as the narrator subsequently remarks in another context).[50] With the initial use of Petrarchan discourse in the poem, then, another discourse also emerges, the Golden Age/Edenic: from that signifying of Lucrece to be Collatine's heaven on earth follows imaging of her as the earthly paradise and as Eve. In fact Lucrece's face, 'that sky of [Collatine's] delight' (l. 12), is soon after described twice by the narrator as a 'fair field' (l. 58; 'her fair face's field', l. 72).[51] The elaborate, conventional trope seems important for several reasons. First, it suggests that Lucrece's face is an ideal landscape and so it complements the preceding image of her face as Collatine's 'sky of . . . delight' (l. 12). Further, the trope forms part of a compressed allegory that, in emphasizing the fusion of beauty and virtue in Lucrece, indicates her to be a Golden Age innocent living in a world far removed from the 'world's minority' (l. 67; see ll. 52–73). Then, too, it pictures Lucrece so attractively (and as so vulnerable) at the moment when she is welcoming Tarquin into her home. Finally, the trope derives from Petrarchan tradition, as ll. 71–2 signal, and thus hints at the extent to which Golden Age/Edenic discourse in the poem is generated by Petrarchan discourse.[52] The latter also initiates the former, as it happens, in what is the last identification of Lucrece as an earthly paradise before she is raped.

That moment of identification, which deserves closer attention than it is often given, occurs in the report of Tarquin's long, intense gazing on the sleeping Lucrece (see ll. 365–71, 386–420), the visual assault that precedes his more directly physical one. The narrator starts his account as follows:

> Her lily hand her rosy cheek lies under,
> Coz'ning the pillow of a lawful kiss;
> Who therefore angry, seems to part in sunder,
> Swelling on either side to want his bliss:
> Between whose hills her head entombed is,
>> Where like a virtuous monument she lies,
>> To be admir'd of lewd unhallowed eyes.
>
> Without the bed her other fair hand was,
> On the green coverlet; whose perfect white
> Show'd like an April daisy on the grass,
> With pearly sweat resembling dew of night.
> Her eyes like marigolds had sheath'd their light,
>> And canopied in darkness sweetly lay,
>> Till they might open to adorn the day.
>
> (ll. 386–99)

Petrarchan images of 'lily' and of 'ros[e]' (l. 386), used recurrently to describe Lucrece, introduce the passage. They serve immediately to eroticise the picture of the sleeping woman in terms of propriety and of impropriety ('Coz'ning', 'lawful' in l. 387). The '[c]oz'ning'/ 'lawful' conceits, in themselves, obliquely contrast the playfully imagined, innocent, frustrated desire of the 'pillow', which may rightfully 'kiss' Lucrece, to Tarquin's unlawful, violent and as yet unfulfilled desire to possess her physically. However, insofar as those conceits are at once suggestive of conflict (the mock conflict between 'hand' and 'pillow') and linked to Petrarchan imagery, they serve also to remind the reader that it is especially the Petrarchan images used to describe Lucrece throughout the poem that tend to identify her as a site of conflict. The first instance of Petrarchan imagery, for example, identifies her as the embodiment of perfect beauty through whom Collatine can vaunt his superiority over Tarquin, but through whom, likewise, Tarquin will assert his tyrannic will and role over Collatine (see ll. 7–14). According to the narrator, moreover, a struggle between 'beauty and virtue' (l. 52) as to which 'should underprop [Lucrece's] fame' (l. 53) can be seen in the 'silent war of lilies and of roses' (l. 71) occurring 'in her fair face's field' (l. 72). It is interesting and significant, too, that the Petrarchan images beginning the passage lead subsequently to the notion of Lucrece as monument, a notion connecting with her sense of herself as an exemplar of chastity (see ll. 390–2). But it seems most interesting and most significant that then, only after associating her with conflict and emphasizing her role as exemplar (an emphasis with overtones of death), the Petrarchan images introduce the picture of her as an earthly paradise.

There is a striking contrast between the playful, ominous, reverential prelude to that picture and the picture itself. An unspoiled, tranquil, natural richness is suggested by the picture's vivid detail: the 'perfect[ly] white' hand (l. 394) lying on 'the green coverlet' (l. 394), which is likened to an 'April daisy on the grass' (l. 395); the 'pearly sweat resembling dew of night' (l. 396); the 'eyes like marigolds' that have 'sheath'd their light' (l. 397). Metonymically that detail associates the inviolate, perfectly beautiful Lucrece with an inviolate, perfectly beautiful nature. And one sees Petrarchan images both introducing that picture of Lucrece and helping to create it. Lucrece's 'other fair hand', like the one beneath her head, is of 'perfect' whiteness; further, the narrator celebrates the splendour of her eyes in terms that form a counterpart to those used by him near the poem's beginning.[53] Lucrece thus appears as both an earthly paradise and a Golden Age innocent; but those representations of her do not alone imply her role as a type of Eve. Her husband and Tarquin chiefly impose that on her.

Like Chaucer's narrator in *The Legend of Good Women*, Shakespeare's narrator emphasizes Collatine's responsibility for exciting the interest of Tarquin in Lucrece. Although he speculates on a number of specific possibilities – that Lucrece's very chastity aroused Tarquin (ll. 8–9), that Collatine's vaunting her 'sov'reignty' provoked the king's son (ll. 36–7) or that Tarquin's own 'envy' and pride did so (ll. 39–42) – the narrator emphatically blames Collatine's imprudence for causing Lucrece's misery. 'Collatine unwisely did not let/ To praise' his wife in Tarquin's hearing, the narrator says (ll. 10–11).[54] '[I]n Tarquin's tent,' he adds by way of elaboration, Collatine '[u]nlock'd the treasure of his happy state:/ What priceless wealth the heavens had him lent,/ In the possession of his beauteous mate' (ll. 15–18). '[W]hy is Collatine the publisher/ Of that rich jewel he should keep unknown/ From thievish ears, because it is his own?' he asks (ll. 33–5). Yet it is not merely Collatine's imprudence that the narrator stresses. He emphasizes, too, the hubris that makes Collatine fatally incautious. In his account of Collatine's 'boast of Lucrece' sov'reignty' (l. 36), the narrator tells of him '[r]eck'ning his fortune at such high proud rate/ That kings might be espoused to more fame,/ But king nor peer to such a peerless dame' (ll. 19–21). In a moment when military conflict with a foreign enemy is deferred, Collatine uses his wife as a means of seeking personal victory over his superior and kinsman; the result of his hubris is that he redirects Tarquin's violence and desire from the enemy/foreign/public to the kindred/Roman/private.[55] His over-reaching pride – an aggressive, patriarchal vanity that firmly links him with the otherwise dissimilar Tarquin – leads him to flaunt the wife who is his heaven on earth, his earthly paradise and, in effect, an innocent from the Golden Age, before the proto-tyrant. The latter, then perceiving her as 'the heaven of his [own] thought' (l. 338), quickly resolves to dispossess him. So, as has been suggested earlier, Collatine unknowingly tempts Tarquin to violate and thus to steal the woman represented by the narrator as an embodiment of Golden Age/Edenic discourses. In doing that, he also unwittingly refigures both himself as a self-betraying Adam (an Adam who falls through pride) and Lucrece as an innocent, unfallen Eve. Simultaneously and appropriately, of course, he thereby helps to refigure Tarquin as a type of Satan, Tarquin's subsequent actions reinforcing his own role and that imposed on Lucrece.

The process of characterization outlined above results, then, not merely from some trivial, male rivalry. It derives from Collatine's attempt to impose over Tarquin's will to illegitimate power – as proto-tyrant and son of a tyrant – his own will to illicit power, functioning within and expressed through the notionally unthreatening and not to be threatened sphere of the domestic.[56] In that attempt, of course, Lucrece is objectified and so Tarquin perceives her; on the other hand, the end of the poem suggests that Lucrece has always been objectified by her husband and by her father.[57] Tarquin, moreover, could arguably never have perceived her except as 'an *object* of consciousness', although he may not have seen or particularly considered her at all had not Collatine set her image compellingly before him.[58] The end of that struggle between wills to illicit power, between domestic and public regimes (respectively Collatine's and Tarquin's), seems immediately to be the mutual defining of subjectivity for its participants, including Lucrece as an unknowing participant. The struggle of wills generates, in short, refigured subjectivities for each participant and thence a comprehensively refigured myth of the Fall.

One can now consider, I suggest, Tarquin's role as a type of Satan. That role seems implicit from virtually the moment he enters Lucrece's home. The narrator says, referring initially to Lucrece and subsequently to Tarquin:

This earthly saint adored by this devil,
Little suspecteth the false worshipper;
For unstain'd thoughts do seldom dream on evil,
Birds never lim'd no secret bushes fear:
So guiltless she securely gives good cheer
    And reverend welcome to her princely guest,
    Whose inward ill no outward harm express'd.

For that he colour'd with his high estate,
Hiding base sin in pleats of majesty,
That nothing in him seem'd inordinate,
Save sometime too much wonder of his eye. . . .

(ll. 85–95)

The allusion to Lucrece as '[t]his earthly saint' (l. 85) evokes her connected roles as chastity's exemplar and Petrarchan lady; it harmonizes,
too, with the notion that she is Collatine's heaven on earth. More to
the point, however, the trope allows the narrator to characterize
Tarquin antithetically to her as a 'devil' (l. 85), a 'false worshipper'
(l. 86) and agent of 'evil' (l. 87), who conceals from her his 'inward
ill' (l. 91), his 'base sin' (l. 93). That insistently demonic representation
of Tarquin is elaborated on by the narrator's subsequent references
to his 'parling looks' (l. 100), which are likened to 'baits' and 'hooks'
(l. 103). But it is specifically an emphasis on innocence in the characterization of Lucrece, and allusion to her as an embodiment of the
earthly paradise, that indicate Tarquin to be Satanic rather than
merely demonic, here and subsequently in the narrative.

As has been argued above, the opening description of Lucrece as
'[t]his earthly saint' develops into a representation of her as someone
naturally innocent. '[U]nstain'd thoughts do seldom dream on evil,/
Birds never lim'd no secret bushes fear . . . ,' the narrator says (ll. 87–
8), explaining her 'guiltless' (l. 89) and unsuspecting reception of her
visitor.[59] The images initiating perception of Lucrece as naturally
innocent point back to the image of 'her fair face's field' (l. 72), with
its connotations of an ideal landscape and of Golden Age virtue, and
forward to the description of her, just prior to Tarquin's assault, as a
type of the earthly paradise, of uncontaminated nature (ll. 386–99).
And it is precisely her natural innocence which the narrator proceeds
to emphasize in describing how she responds to the intense, erotic
gaze of Tarquin – the 'inordinate' stare (l. 94) that she necessarily
notices but cannot decipher. According to the narrator:

. . . [S]he that never cop'd with stranger eyes,
Could pick no meaning from their parling looks,

Nor read the subtle shining secrecies
Writ in the glassy margents of such books;
She touch'd no unknown baits, nor fear'd no hooks:
 Nor could she moralize his wanton sight,
 More than his eyes were open'd to the light.

(ll. 99–105)

Unable to read, much less to interpret, the language of seduction in
Tarquin's eyes, Lucrece perceives no harm in his gaze. In being
unaware of the artifice of seduction, she is like a fish that neither
recognizes enticement nor fears to be snared (l. 103): an allusion to a
familiar Petrarchan motif. Thus Lucrece, represented predominantly
in terms that both suggest her natural innocence and evoke her
recurrent presentation as a type of the earthly paradise (which thereby
refigures her as Eve), is unwittingly betrayed by her husband (in
effect, an overreaching Adam) to temptation by the demonized
(Satanized) Tarquin. He, moreover, disguised as his apparent self,
knowingly falls from high estate in pursuing her.[60] The poem's nar-
rator puts before the reader a Romanized, Petrarchized, re-visioned
story of the Fall – and in doing so arguably generates much of the
intellectual intricacy, as well as emotive power, in Shakespeare's
version of the Lucretia story.

Lucrece seems to be no simple Eve figure; certainly, she becomes
a quite complex one as the poem progresses. Lucrece/Eve fights
back, so to speak, and makes Tarquin/Satan experience not just a fall
from the dignity of high estate, from the honour code of the Roman
aristocracy, but a fall from high estate itself in Rome. Tarquin,
likewise, appears not to be simply refigured as, and refiguring, Satan.
For a start, his nocturnal soliloquy on whether or not to rape Lucrece
shows him pondering in effect whether to abandon or to deepen his
Satanic role.[61] What seems particularly relevant at this point, how-
ever, is that the Petrarchan discourse used recurrently throughout
the earlier part of the poem to fashion Tarquin's subjectivity appears
strikingly at the end of his speech, to signal his consciously imperfect
resolution of his inner conflict. Near the very end of his soliloquy,
he declares:

Affection is my captain, and he leadeth;
 And when his gaudy banner is display'd,
 The coward fights, and will not be dismay'd.

(ll. 271–3)

And the final words of his speech are:

Desire my pilot is, beauty my prize;
Then who fears sinking where such treasure lies?

(ll. 279–80)

The lines first quoted evoke Petrarch's sonnet '*Amor, che nel penser mio vivo e regna*', translated by Wyatt and by Surrey; Tarquin's words offer a desperately pugnacious reworking of the love-as-warfare allegory in Petrarch's poem. Tarquin's concluding words perhaps likewise evoke a sonnet by Petrarch, '*Passa la nave mia colma d'oblio*'; if so, they offer an aggressive reworking of the love-as-a-perilous-sea-voyage allegory in that poem.[62] There is a Petrarchan finale, as it were, to Tarquin's soliloquy – and appropriately so. Tarquin's acute self-consciousness in his soliloquy can be seen in his sensitivity to history: paradoxically enough, like Lucrece he is all too aware of how he may be officially represented, of how his existence may be constructed (but not in his case misconstrued), in years to come (see ll. 202–10, 223–4). Exemplarity is a concern for him as it is for Lucrece. His acute self-consciousness can also be seen in his sensitivity to his own speechmaking, in his politician's sense of the rhetorical nature, the theatricality, of his moment of decision (see ll. 225–7, 267–8). A Petrarchan finale certainly befits such a speech but it seems especially suitable because Petrarchan discourse acknowledges, notionally with regret, reason's incapacity to govern desire.[63] Petrarchan discourse can be used, therefore, to legitimize one's denial of constraint by reason. So, in effect, it is used here by Tarquin. The proto-tyrant making up his mind to commit rape is shown *de facto* to misappropriate and, likewise, desperately to rework Petrarchan discourse.[64] He is thus represented in order for the reader to perceive the dishonesty of his characterizing himself as the warrior compelled now to fight in the service of passion, the lover overwhelmed by desire.[65] The Petrarchan ending to the soliloquy signals his consciously specious resolution of his dilemma.

That ending signals, of course, other things as well. It confirms how thoroughly parodic a Petrarchan lover Tarquin is. Yet arguably, too, it confirms something about Tarquin as a Platonic tyrant figure and type of Satan: he can possess, and then momentarily, 'the heaven of his thought' (l. 338) only by violation, which he knows to be also self-violation because violation of the aristocratic Roman code of conduct by which he, at any rate, thinks his existence primarily defined.[66] Moreover Tarquin's final, mock-Petrarchan characterization of himself as love's warrior leads to what can be perceived, after his piously inaccurate remark about the gods' abhorrence of rape (ll. 349–50), as his committing a rape which distantly parodies the myth of

Mars' rape of Rhea Silvia. Certainly, the rape of Lucrece does seem an ironic counterpart to that myth. The ancient myth tells of a rape which is an originary event for Rome: the chaste Rhea Silvia, raped by the god of war, conceives Romulus and Remus. The rape of Lucrece is, likewise, an originary event for Rome, but in a significantly different way: the Roman Republic is unwittingly and indirectly engendered by a warrior/parodic 'warrior of love', a self-confessed enemy to the gods (ll. 344–57), who in doing so initiates the overthrow of the monarchy and hence his own downfall.

What might now, and finally, be considered here is the means through which Tarquin primarily expresses himself as a Platonic tyrant figure, a parodic Petrarchan lover, and a type of Satan in relation to Lucrece before he expresses those roles through directly physical sexual violence. It seems that he does so through the male gaze. The pervasiveness of the male gaze in his relating to her can be readily shown. When Tarquin first sees Lucrece, the narrator refers to his 'traitor eye' (l. 73): traitorous to the 'beauty and virtue' displayed in her face (l. 52), and ultimately to himself as well. That 'traitor eye' initially succumbs to the purity of what it perceives (l. 73); it is initially intimidated, and Tarquin looks at Lucrece with the 'silent wonder of still-gazing eyes' (l. 84). The innocent Lucrece, of course not recognizing Tarquin for what he is (at that moment, a Satan figure), nonetheless remarks the 'sometime too much wonder of his eye' (l. 95). She stands vulnerable to 'his wanton sight' (l. 104).

But Tarquin himself falls victim to the gaze in imposing it on Lucrece. At the end of his soliloquy he announces: 'My heart shall never countermand mine eye' (l. 276). The gaze imposed on Lucrece subdues the man imposing it, a phenomenon interestingly linked with Tarquin's role as parodic Petrarchan lover at that moment of the narrative. Not much later, Tarquin notes with approval that, because it is night, he is free from the divine gaze: 'The eye of heaven is out, and misty night/ Covers the shame that follows sweet delight' (ll. 356–7). Imposing the gaze, and victim of his imposing it, he is also subject to a cosmic and sacred form of it. Lucrece would escape his infliction of it if she could (ll. 540–6); he seems relieved to have escaped the divine, transcendent gaze antithetic to his own.

Feeling liberated from the divine gaze, he then tyrannically indulges his: the male gaze thence expressing, in particular, his roles of Platonic tyrant figure, and type of Satan, in relation to Lucrece. When, according to the narrator, '[i]nto [Lucrece's] chamber wickedly he stalks' (l. 365), Tarquin 'gazeth on her yet unstained bed[;]/ The curtains being close, about he walks,/ Rolling his greedy eyeballs in his head' (ll. 366–8). 'By their [his eyes'] high treason is his heart misled', adds the narrator (l. 369).[67] The proto-tyrant's compulsion and betrayal by desire are metonymically indicated by means of the gaze, which thereby signals his role as a Platonic tyrant figure. Thereafter, at the moment of symbolic violation when Tarquin opens the curtain to Lucrece's bed (ll. 372–8), the narrator describes Tarquin's gaze in cautiously Petrarchan terms which lead to representation of him as Satan. Viewing Lucrece, Tarquin is dazzled: '[T]he curtain drawn, his eyes begun/ To wink, being blinded with a greater light' (ll. 374–5). The narrator suggests that the brightness blinding Tarquin – and so negating the gaze – may be the light reflected from Lucrece herself (ll. 376–7), a plausible suggestion given his previous and subsequent praise of her skin's whiteness. That being the case, then *by itself* the innocent beauty of the Petrarchan lady repels the gaze: a Petrarchan convention. Even if it is not the case (l. 377), then, nonetheless, in imposing the gaze Tarquin is blinded like any less transgressive Petrarchan lover looking too rashly or too long at a chaste and resplendent lady. If only the power of the gaze had at that moment been broken, the narrator laments (ll. 379–85). But of course it is not; on the contrary, having been temporarily blinded as if some merely rash or insistent Petrarchan lover, Tarquin again imposes the gaze (ll. 414–17) and in doing so figures as a type of Satan (ll. 386–99, discussed above). His unchecked gaze, the narrator remarks, both 'slak[es]' his lust and stimulates it to more directly physical sexual violence (ll. 425 and 427).

To trace Tarquin's imposition of the gaze on Lucrece is to demonstrate its pervasiveness, and necessarily to suggest its prime importance, as a means through which he in his various guises relates to her. A more precise account of that importance requires, however, some further discussion of Tarquin and the gaze. I should like briefly to consider three things: the aesthetics of the gaze; the power of Tarquin's male gaze; the reader's implication in and distancing from Tarquin's imposition of the gaze on Lucrece. When Tarquin first imposes his 'traitor eye' (l. 73) on Lucrece and his gaze is overpowered, the narrator says: 'Therefore that praise which Collatine doth owe [to Lucrece's beauty]/ Enchanted Tarquin answers with surmise,/ In silent wonder of still-gazing eyes' (ll. 82–4). The words 'Enchanted', 'wonder' and 'still-gazing' seem allusions to, but certainly evoke, the then current, and linked, aesthetic categories of *meraviglia* (wonder) and *stupore* (astonishment or amazement).[68] That Lucrece should be perceived by Tarquin as marvellous and so fill him with wonder, stupefy him with amazement, is not itself wonderful given her role as ideal Petrarchan lady. Yet that is not the immediately relevant point. Venus, in Shakespeare's earlier narrative poem, would perfect Adonis as an aesthetic and erotic object (see l. 21 of that poem, for example); here, Tarquin's initial response to Lucrece objectifies her in aesthetic and erotic terms. At the same time, however, Lucrece's unique combination of beauty and virtue both overcomes and elevates his male gaze: rendered relatively passive, raised from the solely carnal to an aestheticized eroticism, Tarquin's male gaze ascends for an instant beyond unrefined *curiositas* (lust of the eyes) and simple concupiscence. At the moment when Tarquin is about to be assigned his Satanic role, he views Lucrece much as Milton's Satan momentarily views Eve: '[T]he evil one abstracted stood/ From his own evil, and for the time remained/ Stupidly good . . .' (9, 463–5).[69] Subsequently, of course, his gaze resumes its power.

As the narrator recounts what Tarquin could see of the sleeping Lucrece (ll. 386–420), he says:

> Her breasts like ivory globes circled with blue,
> A pair of maiden worlds unconquered;
> Save of their lord, no bearing yoke they knew,
> And him by oath they truly honoured.
> These worlds in Tarquin new ambition bred;
>   Who like a foul usurper went about,
>   From this fair throne to heave the owner out.
>
>   (ll. 407–13)

To Tarquin's male gaze, the narrator suggests, Lucrece's breasts are so much new, sexual geography: 'maiden worlds' (l. 408) for him to conquer as if he were an Alexander the Great of sex (l. 411). The implicit emphasis on the colonizing impulse in Tarquin's gaze thus emphasizes, too, Tarquin's characterization as proto-tyrant and as Platonic tyrant figure. Further, it contributes to his identification as a type of Satan, one who ejects a self-betraying Adam (Collatine) from possession of his earthly paradise/Eve.[70] Demonized though Tarquin's male and colonizing gaze affirms him to be, however, it does not in itself distinguish him from other personae fashioned in verse by Shakespeare's contemporaries or successors. For example, the persona in Donne's Elegy 19 says to the lady supposedly subordinated to his male gaze: 'O my America, my new found land,/ My kingdom, safeliest when with one man manned' (ll. 27–8). A more complex example is the persona in 'The Sun Rising'. Using the languages and categories of the world beyond the walls of his and his lady's bedroom, he constructs the fiction that he and his lady inhabit a private utopia

of love, one which variously refigures, subsumes and displaces the
outer world – transcending time and space, class and riches. Yet in
his alternative world, the 'good place' that is also 'no place' but in his
fiction, he reinscribes patriarchal, Jacobean rule. With reference to
his lady, he orders the sun: 'Look, and tomorrow late, tell me,/
Whether both th'Indias of spice and mine/ Be where thou left'st
them, or lie here with me' (ll. 16–18). Again with reference to his
lady, he announces: 'She'is all states, and all princes, I' (l. 21). The
beloved on whom the persona focuses his gaze (ll. 13–14) is not
merely objectified. She is colonized: in his eyes she becomes a body
of claimed territory that, as he tells it, lies subject to his autocratic
rule. Shakespeare's Tarquin and the Donne personae discussed above
may be different in ways that are many and clear; nonetheless, they
are not insignificantly alike.[71]

To have explored the power of the gaze is necessarily to have
raised questions about resistance and implication. For example, how
and where in the narrative is the gaze resisted? Is the reader never
implicated in Tarquin's imposition of it on Lucrece? Perhaps those
questions, and some others, can be usefully if partly answered by
one's returning to the episode in which the narrator describes Lucrece
as she lies asleep (ll. 385–420). His description of her is at once
stylized, vivid and intimate. Its being so seems to make it curiously
ambiguous. Allowing the reader to see what Tarquin sees when he
gazes on Lucrece, the description offers a celebration of and com-
mentary on her beauty; it ends with emphasis on the vehemence of
Tarquin's response to that beauty. Thus it offers shared visions, min-
gled gazes. At once praising Lucrece's body in fairly intimate detail
and commenting on the innocence and vulnerability of her beauty,
the description implicitly sets the narrator's moralized male gaze in
opposition to the male and colonizing gaze of Tarquin. For all that,
the self-indulgent intimacy and ludic elaboration of the description
(as in ll. 386–9 and 401) indicate the narrator's gaze to be indeed a
moralized *male* gaze which, though certainly resisting and condemn-
ing Tarquin's, does not merely allow the reader to see what, and
something of how, Tarquin saw, but also implicates the narrator and
the implied male reader in Tarquin's violating gaze. There is an irony,
then, in the narrator's questions, 'What could he [Tarquin] see but
mightily he noted?/ What did he note but strongly he desired?'
(ll. 414–15). Tarquin's is not the only 'wilful eye' (l. 417).[72]

From that concluding discussion of Tarquin and the gaze, one
might now turn to consider what studying the reciprocal formation of
consciousness and of role among Tarquin, Lucrece and Collatine can

be said to reveal about the establishing of characterization in Shakespeare's second narrative poem. For a start, doing so strongly suggests that the characterizations established early in *Lucrece* are more complex in their discursive relations than has been acknowledged. The three main figures in the poem are not merely translated from the pages of Ovid: they are at once Ovidian and comprehensively transformed. In particular, they become actors in a Romanized, Petrarchized, re-visioned myth of the Fall – a version in which the type of Eve is innocent and betrayed, not betraying (a version, too, in which she ultimately gains her revenge on the counterpart to Satan).

Moreover, thus perceiving the characterizations of Tarquin, Lucrece and Collatine early in the poem seems to illuminate both subsequent happenings in it and some of its main concerns. When one recognizes that Tarquin's sexual assault involves his forcing on Lucrece his mutually intensifying, connected roles, which are antithetic to hers, then the scope of his violence can be seen more clearly: his assault appears to involve unusually comprehensive psychic violence in conjunction with extreme physical violence. Lucrece's profound sense of contamination seems, therefore, even more understandable. So too does her decision to commit suicide. Yet if those later occurrences in the poem are illuminated, what are arguably among its main concerns appear as well to have new light shed on them. The mutually defining nature of characterization early in the poem indicates that Lucrece's interactive roles are variously imposed on her from without and, further, that she well knows her basic role as chaste Roman matron to have been externally imposed and to be removable. Recognizing the externality of Lucrece's selfhood, and her partial awareness of its being so, perhaps first clarifies yet more distinctly her feeling of contamination and her decision to commit suicide: one comes to see that she thinks of Tarquin's assault as having stolen her main role in her world. And Lucrece's sense that her role as chaste Roman matron derives from without seems at the same time to shed light, too, on her insistent denial of her innocence. To her mind, apparently, Tarquin's assault has erased her basic self and thus she is no longer chaste and hence not completely innocent. Those matters aside, however, the externality and imposition of Lucrece's selfhood arguably have more important implications.

Lucrece's awareness of her basic role's imposition from without is firmly linked to her consciousness of herself as an exemplar of chastity. That link raises questions about exemplarity in, and beyond, the poem. Well aware that her role of exemplar, like her one as chaste Roman matron, derives from without, Lucrece believes that her rape immediately deletes the latter but also that it will subsequently make ambiguous or delete the former. To regain the one, to preserve the other, she resolves upon suicide. Her perception of who she ultimately is, and the self-negating decision that results from it (to lose herself in order to save herself), seem to raise several major questions about exemplarity. First, if one's role as exemplar is imposed from without, in light of external circumstance and with no, or little, precise knowledge of one's inner life, then how reliable can exemplarity be as a means of defining subjectivity, of identifying an incarnation of an ideal? Further, how can exemplarity therefore be regarded as a reliable means of interpreting history, of clarifying and stabilizing it? That question has a special relevance, I think, because the intertextual relations of Shakespeare's narrative suggest how often and how variously Lucrece's role as exemplar has been reconstructed: continuity, variation and contradiction all mark its descent. Moreover, what does it indicate about exemplarity if Lucrece has to kill herself to preserve its/her integrity and hence the integrity of historical tradition? Lucrece successfully preserves her exemplarity, preserves historical tradition, and seemingly reveals the hermeneutic limitations or incapacity of exemplarity. There are of course other questions implicitly raised; nonetheless, my main point here is as follows. Exemplarity appears not merely to be subverted in the poem, though aspects of it certainly are; rather, it is subjected to close and sceptical examination.[73] Shakespeare's narrative suggests that exemplarity is reliable and unreliable as a means of defining subjectivity and interpreting history: it is more or less simply accurate in Tarquin's case, for instance; however, because of its dependence upon externals and contamination by opinion, it has to be made accurate in the case of Lucrece. It works and it does not. Perhaps in some of Montaigne's essays, rather than in contemporary English writings, one finds the counterpart to Shakespeare's sceptical treatment of exemplarity in *Lucrece*.[74]

Just as exemplarity is sceptically examined in the poem, so too is neoplatonism. Although an account of the poems' sceptical inquiry into neoplatonism cannot be offered without *Lucrece* having been considered as a whole, some things can nonetheless be suggested now in connection with the poem's establishing of characterization. Lucrece tends, unknowingly, to read human subjectivity in neoplatonic terms. In so reading Tarquin she makes a tragic mistake, as she soon discovers and in effect acknowledges (ll. 1527–61): his soul is not to be read in his appearance. Yet hers is, as Tarquin sees at once when he meets her. That contradiction, for all its bluntness, has more subtlety than might at first be thought. It seems primarily to indicate that a neoplatonic reading of human subjectivity, like a reading of subjectivity and of history by means of exemplarity, can be seen as unreliable and as reliable: sometimes not working, sometimes working well. Yet the contradiction seems also to imply that Lucrece, chaste matron of early Rome and *mulier economica* (woman in the role of household manager), necessarily lacks the education and experience required for her to understand the problems inherent in the neoplatonic scheme of reading – outlined for Shakespeare's contemporaries by Castiglione, among others. His outline of those problems, however, arguably heightens rather than resolves the contradiction, for the words he has Bembo speak on the matter do not help one to recognize when, or not, appearance can be read as truly indicative of the soul.[75]

Finally, here, a few remarks need to be made about the gaze and the counter-gaze in the earlier episodes of *Lucrece*. It might be mentioned again that more than one gaze is alluded to in those episodes. There, to be sure, the narrator indicates that Tarquin most vigorously imposes it but Tarquin himself draws the reader's attention to the divine gaze: that of '[t]he eye of heaven' (l. 356). His allusion to the divine gaze, particularly to its being 'out' (l. 356), evokes and queries the notion of divine providence, which Lucrece in effect considers when lamenting her misfortune (ll. 764–1015, for example). It might be mentioned again, likewise, that if the divine gaze is suggested by Tarquin to be in contradiction to his own, a counter-gaze is also implicitly exercised by the narrator (especially in ll. 386–420). As has been argued above, however, gaze and counter-gaze elide – if not always, then nonetheless often enough and significantly, as at the crucial moment when Tarquin surveys the sleeping Lucrece (ll. 386–420). The counter-gaze seems either to be absent or treacherously to merge with the thing it should oppose. To study the establishing of characterization in *Lucrece* leads one to encounter a use of the gaze, a transformation of myth, a scepticism, more complex than can be seen in *Venus and Adonis*.

(IV) THE RAPE OF LUCRECE

To have examined the establishing and the discursive relations of characterization early in the poem illuminates, it will now be argued, how Shakespeare re-presents the story of Tarquin's directly physical assault on Lucrece.[76] Briefly put, that argument is as follows. Shakespeare chiefly re-presents the rape, at first, by having the Platonic discourse of tyranny appropriate and violate, so to speak, Petrarchan discourse. That is to say, Shakespeare's narrator at first chiefly re-presents the rape as a perverse epiphany in which Tarquin's early physical and verbal transgressions of Petrarchan discourse are succeeded by his subsuming it, by his comprehensive violation of it. Within Shakespeare's Platonic and Petrarchan reworking of the story of the rape, both an implicit portrayal of Tarquin as a type of Satan and an implicit portrayal of Lucrece as a type of the earthly paradise and of Eve appear again. Tarquin, moreover, in his dialogue again evokes the matter of exemplarity; Lucrece, in hers, likewise evokes the matter of reading human subjectivity in neoplatonic terms. Yet to those, and to other, continuing elements of the poem important new ones are added – political ones, in particular. A notion of pre-civil society is foregrounded that seems to connect with a powerful, Ciceronian political myth. Then, also, there are allusion to and apparent subversion of the notion of the just, Christian prince. That argument suggests Shakespeare's re-presentation of the rape of Lucrece to be, as one might expect from his poem's preceding lines, intricate and sceptical rather than merely elaborate.

The appropriation and violation of Petrarchan by Platonic discourse is signalled at the very beginning of the poem's rape scene. Lucrece's role as Petrarchan lady is suggested earlier in the narrative by various means, one of which is conventionally Petrarchan celebration of her eyes; the rape scene begins, however, with that celebration of her eyes being deftly and brutally parodied. When Tarquin has placed '[h]is hand . . . [o]n her bare breast' (ll. 437 and 439), Lucrece confusedly awakes and 'much amaz'd, breaks ope her lock'd-up eyes,/ Who peeping forth this tumult to behold,/ Are by his flaming torch dimm'd and controll'd' (ll. 446–8). Moreover,

> She dares not look, yet winking there appears
> Quick-shifting antics, ugly in her eyes.
> Such shadows are the weak brain's forgeries;
>   Who, angry that the eyes fly from their lights,
>   In darkness daunts them with more dreadful sights.
>
> (ll. 458–62)

Tarquin's physical assault on Lucrece viciously parodies the Petrarchan 'warrior of love' trope and so reveals him in the role of parodic Petrarchan lover – a role that obviously expresses his anterior one as a type of the desire-possessed, Platonic tyrant.[77] It also clearly indicates how effectively, if of course unwittingly, Collatine has redirected and misdirected Tarquin's military violence from the siege of Ardea. The main point here is, however, that Tarquin's assault abruptly transforms Lucrece's appearance from being that of a woman whose eyes are 'mortal stars bright as heaven's beauties' (l. 13) to being that of a woman whose eyes manifest her terror and confusion: from that of a Petrarchan lady to that of a female victim. The description of Lucrece's eyes reveals Tarquin, as a type of the Platonic tyrant and thence parodic Petrarchan lover, appropriating and distorting Petrarchan discourse, initiating physical violation of Lucrece and hence that discourse's comprehensive violation.

The motif that perhaps most distinctly implies his doing so refigures the Petrarchan trope of the lady as an invincible embodiment of virtue, warred against in vain.[78] The military images used by the narrator to communicate the uncontrollable physical violence of Tarquin at this point in the poem, especially the images of pillage and of siege, culminate in his objectifying Lucrece as 'this sweet city'.[79] Both by itself and in its immediate context – 'To make the breach and enter this sweet city' – the 'sweet city' metaphor suggests the narrator's complicity with Tarquin's desire. The metaphor also anticipates a counterpart in Tarquin's words to Lucrece: 'I come to scale/ Thy never-conquer'd fort' (ll. 481–2). The figuring of Lucrece's genitalia as her 'never conquer'd fort' is, of course unknowingly by Tarquin, a reduction of the Petrarchan trope of the lady as honour's or chastity's invincible embodiment. Now it is apparent that the 'fort' image further implicates the narrator with Tarquin; but, more important, in conjunction with the 'city' metaphor it emphatically suggests that Tarquin, when physically assaulting Lucrece, does indeed manifest himself as a Platonic tyrant figure appropriating and comprehensively violating Petrarchan discourse. Simultaneously it would seem to foreshadow Lucrece's identification of herself as a second Troy and of Tarquin as a second Sinon (see ll. 1541–7).

As might be expected, with the Platonic and Petrarchan elements of characterization at this moment of the rape scene can be discerned others from earlier in the poem. Tarquin, for example, seems once again to be associated with Satan. In his initial speech to Lucrece he says: 'I see what crosses my attempt will bring,/ I know what thorns the growing rose defends' (ll. 491–2). There he portrays himself, in unselfconscious parody, as the Petrarchan 'martyr to love'.[80] In doing that, however, he seems also to portray himself as something more. The images of 'crosses' and of 'thorns' suggest that he is not merely love's martyr but its man of sorrows: an anti-Christ of love. In his self-dramatizing, deeply duplicitous, intimidating first speech to Lucrece he reveals his true self far more accurately and thoroughly than he is aware, though he is obviously aware of revealing the secret of his obsessive desire. And just as Tarquin there appears again, perhaps climactically, to be associated with Satan, so he proceeds likewise to reveal his self-division: what could be called his Ovidian conscience. He says: 'I have debated even in my soul,/ What wrong, what shame, what sorrow I shall breed;/ But nothing can affection's course control' (ll. 498–500). He adds: 'I know repentant tears ensue the deed,/ Reproach, disdain and deadly enmity;/ Yet strive I to embrace mine infamy' (ll. 502–4). The experience he describes there could be summed up in Medea's words from *Metamorphoses* 7: '[D]esire sways me one way, reason another. I see which is the better course, and I approve it; but still I follow the worse.'[81] But his account of his self-division has unmistakably Christian overtones, too ('I have debated even in my soul'; 'repentant tears'), which for Protestant readers would have harmonized with the Calvinist notion of the 'inordinate' desire, the 'viciousness' of heart, or concupiscence, at work in the fallen human soul.[82]

It is in fact the Christian rather than the Ovidian overtones of those words that are finally amplified in the rape scene. When the narrator describes Tarquin's guilty departure from Lucrece's home, he says: 'O deeper sin than bottomless conceit/ Can comprehend in still imagination!' (ll. 701–2). Soon after he adds: 'The flesh being proud, desire doth fight with grace;/ For there it revels, and when that decays,/ The guilty rebel for remission prays' (ll. 712–14). Then he unfolds the forceful allegory of Tarquin's soul as the 'princess' infected ('spotted') with mortal sin.[83] That religious allegory clearly indicates the personal irony of Tarquin's assault on Lucrece. For a start, it feminizes Tarquin by drawing on the conventional gendering of the human soul as female (Donne's 'Batter my heart . . .' offers an obvious but interesting comparison), and implies that his physical assault on Lucrece has both offended against his own body and contaminated, almost violated, his spiritual and 'female' self. Rape has almost been self-rape. The narrator's earlier imaging of Lucrece as a 'sweet city' which Tarquin wants '[t]o . . . breach' then to 'enter' (l. 469) thus has a counterpart – a Christian one – in his later images of Tarquin's soul as a 'fair temple' whose 'consecrated wall' has been 'batter'd down' by the violence of desire (l. 723). If, for Tarquin, penetration signals at once power exercised triumphantly over Lucrece and victory over the presumptuous Collatine, to the reader it is additionally made to signal Tarquin's self-violence and his unknowing yet still culpable breaking of Christian law. Lucrece reminds him, of course, that to assault her is to violate the Roman aristocracy's code of honour; but then virtually his first words to her suggest his keen awareness of that.[84]

While Tarquin is implicitly portrayed in the rape scene as a type of Satan, seemingly as an anti-Christ of love, Lucrece is implicitly portrayed as a type of the earthly paradise and of Eve. Once again, those latter roles are introduced by Petrarchan imagery. Tarquin replies to Lucrece's very reasonable question as to '[u]nder what colour he commits this ill' (l. 476), with: 'The colour in thy face,/ That even for anger makes the lily pale/ And the red rose blush at her own disgrace,/ Shall plead for me and tell my loving tale' (ll. 477–80). The conventionally Petrarchan images of lily and of rose, already much used in the poem and here grotesquely used against the very woman whom they celebrate, associate Lucrece with perfect natural beauty. Soon after, in words that again reveal the Platonic tyrant figure behind the parodic Petrarchan lover, Tarquin says to his victim: '[T]hou with patience must my will abide,/ My will that marks thee for my earth's delight;/ Which I to conquer sought with all my might' (ll. 486–8). There one sees the proto-tyrant in his roles as parodic 'warrior of love' and as colonizer; however, one also sees his identifying Lucrece as his chosen earthly bliss ('my earth's delight', l. 487). His emphatic 'earth's delight' trope, moreover, ironically parallels the narrator's much earlier imaging of Lucrece's face as the 'sky of [Collatine's] delight' (l. 12), which initially indicated Lucrece to be her husband's heaven on earth. Finally, brief mention might be made of Tarquin's admission: 'I know what thorns the growing rose defends;/ I think the honey guarded with a sting' (ll. 492–3). The 'rose' and 'honey' images, especially of course the former, associate Lucrece with an eroticized natural beauty and sweetness. Very early in the rape scene Shakespeare's narrator reminds the reader that Lucrece incarnates a transcendent, uncontaminated, natural beauty and innocence. It is indicated once more that she refigures both the earthly paradise and Eve.

As was suggested initially, however, there are also other continuities between the narrative preceding the rape scene and that scene itself. Exemplarity is again considered sceptically; so, too, is the reading of human identity in neoplatonic terms. When threatening to disgrace Lucrece if she does not consent to have sex with him (ll. 512–39), Tarquin says:

> 'So thy surviving husband shall remain
> The scornful mark of every open eye;
> Thy kinsmen hang their heads at this disdain,
> Thy issue blurr'd with nameless bastardy.
> And thou, the author of their obloquy,
>> Shalt have thy trespass cited up in rhymes
>> And sung by children in succeeding times.

(ll. 519–25)

The main terms of Tarquin's threat are quite clear, as he means them to be. Collatine will be publicly dishonoured; Lucrece's extended family will as well; the legitimacy of her children will be put in question; she will become an exemplar of unchastity, a type of wifely infidelity. Nonetheless, Tarquin's threat mingles bluntness with cunning. First, he appeals paradoxically to her love for and loyalty to her husband: will she agree to have sex with another man in order to protect Collatine's honour? Then Tarquin appeals in much the same way to her loyalty to her extended family. That appeal, nonetheless, seems more cunning than the first. One of the virtues conventionally identified in the sixteenth century as needful in women is willingness to place family interests before her own.[85] Tarquin implicitly demands that Lucrece behave virtuously and sleep with him. Finally, and again paradoxically, he appeals to the power of exemplarity and thus to her sense of self. It was argued in the previous section of this discussion that Lucrece has an externalized sense of her basic selfhood – as chaste Roman matron – which appears to be inseparable from her profound consciousness of herself as an exemplar of married chastity. She recognizes that, just as her basic selfhood has been given from without and can be erased from without, so others have established her as an exemplar and can disestablish her: she recognizes her vulnerability as an exemplar, how indifferent to her inner life and beyond her control that aspect of her subjectivity also is. In the climactic last lines of the stanza quoted above, Tarquin first imposes those recognitions on her. He confronts her with his power to erase her basic selfhood and to invert her role as exemplar. Thus he reveals to her, at the same time, his power to falsify history. Yet he also reveals more than that to her. Easily undermining the integrity and interpretative authority of exemplarity by laying bare its dependence upon externals, its contamination by opinion and its indifference to one's inner life, Tarquin reveals exemplarity's limitations as a means of illuminating and stabilizing historical process, of defining subjectivity within it. He does so, nonetheless, while turning himself into a true exemplar of tyrannic lawlessness. Undermining exemplarity, he simultaneously affirms it.

The sceptical perspective on exemplarity disclosed by Tarquin's words, although apparent to the reader, remains of course unseen by Lucrece: she cannot know that Tarquin is becoming an exemplar even as he undermines exemplarity. In fact she seems either to reject the wider implications of Tarquin's threat or not to see, in her fear and confusion, the incongruity between his threat and her subsequent warning to him, for she proceeds in effect to warn him that he is on the way to becoming an exemplar of tyranny (ll. 603–23). Nor, moreover, does she see the sceptical perspective that her reply to Tarquin opens on the reading of subjectivity in neoplatonic terms. Near the middle of that reply, she says:

> 'In Tarquin's likeness I did entertain thee:
> Hast thou put on his shape to do him shame?
> To all the host of heaven I complain me,
> Thou wrong'st his honour, wound'st his princely name;
> Thou art not what thou seem'st, and if the same,
>   Thou seem'st not what thou art, a god, a king:
> For kings like gods should govern everything.
>
> (ll. 596–602)

Lucrece's words imply that Tarquin has compelled her to recognize or, at least, to acknowledge the lack of necessary congruence between personal appearance and the inner self. Yet the difference between Tarquin's kingly appearance and his (proto) tyrannic role does not merely undermine the neoplatonic reading of subjectivity, disconcerted though Lucrece is to discover, in effect, its fallibility. If Tarquin's looks do not reveal what he is, Lucrece's certainly reveal what she is. The horror in Lucrece's words arguably springs in part from the untroubled continuity between appearance and role in her own existence. As the narrator has repeatedly emphasized, she is exceptional; for all that, the neoplatonic reading of subjectivity seems in the poem to be both denied and affirmed.

Lucrece's painful recognition that people may be not at all what they seem is linked, as the quotation above suggests, to a distinction that she draws in her speech between true kingship and tyranny: more specifically, between the just, Christian prince and the lawless, God-defying tyrant. That distinction introduces into the rape scene an element both new and important. Throughout the poem there has been an almost continuous (Platonic) representation of tyranny but no focus on true kingship as its opposite. Now, Lucrece confronts Tarquin with an ideal of true kingship and, in doing so, evokes a powerful ideal of kingship belonging to other times, other cultures. Thus she opposes to the Platonic discourse of tyranny, which gives Tarquin his basic role, a forceful counter-discourse: that of the just, Christian prince. In presenting it, however, she seems at the same time unknowingly to subvert it. Tarquin, moreover, interrupts her speech then rapes her. The notion of the just, Christian prince is introduced, therefore, at a crucial moment in the narrative and its treatment deserves scrutiny; however, before it is closely considered another new and not unimportant element introduced into the poem needs to be looked at. That, as was foreshadowed above, is a notion of pre-civil society which seems to connect with a widely influential, Ciceronian political myth.

Earlier in the rape scene, when Tarquin has just delivered his threats to Lucrece (ll. 477–539), the narrator says:

> Here with a cockatrice' dead-killing eye
> He rouseth up himself, and makes a pause;
> While she, the picture of pure piety,
> Like a white hind under the gripe's sharp claws,
> Pleads in a wilderness where are no laws,
>   To the rough beast that knows no gentle right,
>   Nor aught obeys but his foul appetite.
>
> (ll. 540–6)

The description has many interesting aspects. For example, there are the various animal images used to figure Tarquin and, linked to them, the climactic insistence on his being driven by desire, all of which signal the tyrannic role about to be expressed in the rape of Lucrece. Then, too, there is the Petrarchan imaging of Lucrece herself as a 'white hind'.[86] However, in the allegory which follows from that comparison there is also the likening of Lucrece's home – specifically, her private chamber – to 'a wilderness where are no laws' (l. 544). Tarquin's assault on Lucrece, that is, a type of the Platonic tyrant in his assault on a type of the Petrarchan lady, initially violates at once the laws of hospitality and the site of domestic pieties – the latter's code of the sacred being of course implicated with that of the state. Thus the narrator aptly suggests that Tarquin's assault in effect makes Lucrece's home 'a wilderness where are no laws': a site where no civilized law exists, where only desire is law (ll. 545–6), of *natura naturans*. Desire engenders anarchy, first in Tarquin himself (ll. 424–34), then in Lucrece's home; finally, it engenders revolution.

The notion that violent, egocentric desire does not merely dehumanize the individual subject but, if unrestrained, negates civil order is formulated by Cicero in a myth about the origins of rhetoric and of society. Much alluded to or imitated in sixteenth-century English texts, that myth is unfolded by Cicero in his early rhetorical treatise *De Inventione*.[87] It need not and could not be argued that here Shakespeare alludes to Cicero's text; but it can be suggested that Cicero's widely influential text illuminates Shakespeare's narrative at this point. According to the Ciceronian narrator:

[T]here was a time when men wandered at large in the fields like animals and lived on wild fare; they did nothing by the guidance of reason, but relied chiefly on physical strength; there was as yet no ordered system of religious worship nor of social duties; no one had seen legitimate marriage nor had anyone looked upon children whom he knew to be his own; nor had they learned the advantages of an equitable code of law. And so through their ignorance and error blind and unreasoning passion satisfied itself by misuse of bodily strength, which is a very dangerous servant.

(1, 2, 2)

There are important similarities between that description of pre-civil human life and the account of Tarquin quoted above. In that account, the narrator alludes to Tarquin's being ruled by 'his foul appetite' (l. 546), an aspect of his characterization which has been emphasized from the poem's start. Cicero's myth identifies 'blind and unreasoning passion' as directing pre-civil human life.[88] Moreover, Cicero's myth relates that uncivilized humanity's compelling desire 'satisfied itself by misuse of bodily strength'; so now Tarquin's seeks satisfaction. And for him, 'bodily strength' will indeed prove 'a very dangerous servant' because his 'misuse' of physical force against Lucrece will be turned against him and his family. The Ciceronian myth also suggests that, in pre-civil times, no one 'had looked upon children whom he knew to be his own'. Bringing the legitimacy of Lucrece's children into doubt forms part of Tarquin's threat to her (see ll. 519–21).

But despite all those similarities there is, of course, a crucial dissimilarity. Pre-civil humanity, according to Cicero's myth, had 'as yet no ordered system of religious worship nor of social duties', neither had it 'learned the advantages of an equitable code of law'. Tarquin has. The point is, however, that earlier in the poem he has quite deliberately repudiated his society's 'ordered system of religious worship'. Having prayed to the gods for help with his intended rape of Lucrece, then having decided – in apparent forgetfulness of Rhea Silvia, for a start – that the gods 'abhor' rape, he declares: 'Then love and fortune be my gods, my guide!'[89] Like other tyrant figures in early modern writings, Tarquin has to reject his society's 'ordered system of religious worship' so that he can seek the fulfilment of his anarchic desire (Greville's Alaham is an interesting analogue).[90] Further, Tarquin knows only too well that his assault on Lucrece violates both his society's 'ordered system of . . . social duties' and its 'equitable code of law'.[91] Even if he had, as it were, forgotten both, Lucrece distinctly reminds him (as in ll. 568–76, for example). Thus Cicero's political myth suggests the scope of that allegory where Tarquin appears as a predator in 'a wilderness where are no laws' (l. 544). It illuminates

the extent to which Tarquin's obsessive desire makes him regress to
a pre-civil existence, the condition of which he imposes on Lucrece
in the otherwise quiet, civilized order of her home.[92] His willed
regression, in effect, to pre-civil life indicates where tyranny (at least,
as conceived by Plato) leads and what it is.

Cicero's myth illuminates, however, not merely the characterization
of Tarquin in the rape scene but also that of Lucrece. After describing
early humankind's anarchic existence, Cicero's myth then suggests
how that existence became transformed into civil life. The first orator
appeared, says the Ciceronian narrator, and he

> assembled and gathered [people together] in accordance with a plan; he
> introduced them to every useful and honourable occupation, though they
> cried out against it at first because of its novelty, and then when through
> reason and eloquence they had listened with greater attention, he trans-
> formed them from wild savages into a kind and gentle folk.   (1, 2, 2)

Early humankind, although directed by 'blind and unreasoning passion',
can nonetheless − and necessarily − be reasoned with, according to
Cicero's myth. The first orator's 'reason and eloquence' transform
human life. Yet if Cicero's mythic orator succeeds in civilizing his
desire-disordered contemporaries, Lucrece fails of course to civilize the
desire-disordered Tarquin through her use of 'reason and eloquence'.
It is true, certainly, that whereas Cicero's narrator represents the first
orator as 'a man − great and wise I am sure' (1, 2, 2), Shakespeare's
narrator describes Lucrece as a victimized woman whose fear, distress
and misery mar her speech, at least initially. But the failure of Lucrece's
oratory cannot be attributed solely to her suffering.

Lucrece's oratory fails to civilize and so to deter Tarquin, it seems
fair to suggest, because of failings in the basic role culturally imposed
upon her. A brief way to illustrate that notion would be by considering
one of the narrator's remarks about Lucrece's response to Tarquin's
gaze. When the proto-tyrant enters Lucrece's home and starts to
subject her to his gaze, the narrator says:

> . . . [S]he that never cop'd with stranger eyes,
> Could pick no meaning from their parling looks,
> Nor read the subtle shining secrecies
> Writ in the glassy margents of such books;
> She touch'd no unknown baits, nor fear'd no hooks:
>   Nor could she moralize his wanton sight,
>   More than his eyes were open'd to the light.

(ll. 99–105)

Embodying the Roman cultural ideal of the chaste matron and, by extension, that of *mulier economica* Lucrece has centered her life on her home.[93] Consequently she lacks the benefit of 'practical knowledge' – that is to say, of prudence (*prudentia*) – to guide her in dealing with Tarquin. She is innocent, to be sure, but not merely that. Rather, she is imprudent: her basic role in Roman society has deprived her of just that 'practical knowledge of things to be sought for and of things to be avoided' identified by Cicero as the more important of the forms of wisdom.[94] Moreover, as Victoria Kahn has noted, '[i]n Cicero's view . . . the faculty of prudence is inseparable from the ideal practice of the orator', a connection which seems to lead to the heart of the matter.[95] Lucrece cannot see the futility of elaborately warning Tarquin against becoming a tyrant because she cannot recognize that he already possesses a tyrant's psychology. For that reason, too, she cannot see the futility of setting before Tarquin a celebration of the ideal ruler. Her lack of prudence misdirects her rhetoric. But her role as chaste Roman matron (and *mulier economica*) has arguably another failing which also mars her speech.

When Shakespeare's narrator summarizes, or perhaps reports the beginning of, Lucrece's plea to Tarquin (ll. 568–74), her chief mode of persuasion seems to be an appeal to the moral structure of the world as she understands it. She appeals to the authority of 'high almighty Jove' (l. 568), to that of the allied aristocratic codes of honour and of male friendship (l. 569), to her misery as an unjustly victimized woman and to her lawful spouse's love for her (l. 570).[96] She appeals as well to the authority of the marriage bond (l. 571) and to all the moral force informing 'heaven and earth' (l. 572). A major part of her moralizing oratory is, as has been mentioned above, her setting before Tarquin a dispraise of tyranny and a celebration of the ideal ruler, that is to say, of the just, Christian prince. In her celebration of the latter she alludes distinctly to the notion of the divine right of kings (ll. 601–2).[97] Lucrece's speech, then, notionally situates both her and Tarquin in the context of an unchanging and ultimately unchallengeable moral hierarchy; but her speech's attempt to do that seems, at the least, problematic. To begin with, Lucrece's speech denounces tyranny but Tarquin's father is a tyrant who has murdered his way to power and extended his power by means of assassination, as Lucrece seems unaware or to ignore.[98] Further, as 'The Argument' and the opening stanzas of the poem have made clear (not to mention the penumbral Gabii episode), Tarquin is very much his father's son. It would hardly be in Lucrece's interest, of course, to make either point in pleading with Tarquin; in any event, she has not recognized him for what he is. But the facts that Tarquinius Superbus is a tyrant and that his son is a proto-tyrant, possessor of a tyrannic cast of mind, make startlingly ironic her reproach to Tarquin: 'Thou seem'st not what thou art, a god, a king:/ For kings like gods should govern everything' (ll. 601–2). More important, through her husband she is implicated in the Tarquin clan's tyrannic rule – if innocently yet also unquestioningly. Setting before Tarquin the notion of the ideal king, she is nonetheless implicated in government by that ruler's parodic counterpart, the tyrant. Her role as chaste Roman matron – and that of *mulier economica* – has bound her, through her husband, to the form of government which now afflicts her and which she now denounces. Her oratory seems to express no cognizance of either her world's political realities or of her relations to them.

As a result, her anachronistic celebration of the ideal king as the just, Christian prince appears to be doubly inapposite. But the ideal itself seems to be subverted. The poem vividly elaborates on Lucrece's description of the tyrant, attesting to the terrible force of desire as expressed in the tyrannic personality, as variously informing the will to tyranny, whereas her image of the ideal king/just, Christian prince seems far removed from the poem's representations of the political: an abstraction signifying moderation, self-control, beyond the capacities of men. The characterization of Tarquin is not alone in implying that; so, too, do the characterizations of Collatine and of Brutus. The sexually violent proto-tyrant, the ambitious husband, the shrewdly manipulative politician all indicate the remoteness of that ideal.

(V) LUCRECE, TROY AND BRUTUS

It was suggested above that Lucrece's consciousness of especially her basic selfhood as having been imposed from without causes her, after the rape, to have a comprehensive sense of violation and also a sense of defacement. The last part of Shakespeare's narrative insists again and again on the power and contradictoriness of those aspects of her post-rape experience. So profound is her sense of violation, for example, that she believes herself guilty of an offence against marital chastity, and hence her husband, even though she simultaneously knows herself to be innocent. Tarquin's assault has deprived her at once of her chastity and of her ultimate role, as she seems to see it in her anguish: no longer completely chaste, she is no longer wholly innocent – and yet she knows that she is innocent.[99] Moreover she accepts both the impossibility of her having physically resisted Tarquin and the notion that she should have done so (ll. 1044–7, 1639–52). It is not, for all that, primarily on Lucrece's sense of violation or of effaced subjectivity that the final section of this chapter will now focus. Her understanding of what ultimately caused her basic role's erasure, and of how that role can be re-established, will instead receive closer consideration. Thus the poem's representation of Lucrece's thinking, after she has been raped, about what makes things happen in the world – and about how one can intervene in or change them – will be examined, particular attention being given to what she says in her three long complaints, what she sees and what she says when looking at the picture of Troy's fall, and Brutus' response to her suicide. The final section of this chapter examines, then, outcomes of the mutually defining characterization in Lucrece; in doing so, it examines the poem's last and evasive dealings with such concerns as subjectivity, history, exemplarity, and neoplatonism.

When pleading with Tarquin not to assault her, Lucrece appeals to the authority of her orthodox, if syncretic, model of a divinely ordered reality. As the narrator relates:

> She conjures him [Tarquin] by high almighty Jove,
> By knighthood, gentry, and sweet friendship's oath,
> By her untimely tears, her husband's love,
> By holy human law and common troth,
> By heaven and earth, and all the power of both . . .
>
> (ll. 568–72)

After the rape, when lamenting her wretchedness and seeking to define the ultimate cause of her basic role's erasure (ll. 764–966), she neither calls upon nor blames the Olympian gods.[100] Further, she presents an account of how the world works which differs markedly from the one that she put before Tarquin. She describes the world and human affairs not as divinely ordered, as governed by a hierarchy of divine, then of human, powers and a network of laws, but rather as chiefly directed by forces either hostile to order in human life and in physical nature or ambiguous in themselves and ambivalent in their actions. Those forces, she says, are ultimately to be blamed for Tarquin's theft of her selfhood. She does not say how those forces relate to the gods; however they may do so to her mind – if the reader is to think that she has any distinct view on the matter – the gods themselves are absent from her account of the workings of the world.

That the first of Lucrece's three complaints should be against night seems appropriate for a number of reasons. Tarquin assaulted her at night: its 'unseen secrecy' (l. 763), as she is necessarily aware, immediately enabled his attack on her. In addition, when speaking to Lucrece during the assault Tarquin significantly associates himself with night (for example, in ll. 485 and 512); the narrator, too, associates him with it during the assault, having conventionally demonized it much earlier in the poem.[101] Furthermore Lucrece herself closely associates Tarquin with night: she figures him as 'night's child' (l. 785) and so makes night, rather than his human and tyrannic father, responsible for him and his assault.

All those reasons suggest why Lucrece should complain first against night; however, in looking at her complaint one can see another reason as well, namely, that night seems to become for her not merely something she is able to blame for her misery but also a symbol of her predicament. Lucrece's complaint implies that night is a primeval force which has conspired to ruin her: 'Vast sin-concealing Chaos,/ nurse of blame!/ Blind muffled bawd, dark harbour for defame,/ Grim cave of death, whisp'ring conspirator/ With close-tongued treason and the ravisher!' (ll. 767–70). Trying to characterize that force she reveals, as the lines just quoted indicate, its amorphousness. She interprets night as a site of hostile and dispersed meanings. She confronts an abyss, the '[v]ast . . . Chaos', where single and positive meaning is dissolved. Her *mise en abyme* interpretation of night reflects, then, her sense of lost meaning and subjectivity in her own life: her sense of having been cast by Tarquin, the 'child' of the '[v]ast . . . Chaos', into an abyss where the primary, positive meaning of her life – that is to say, her basic role as chaste Roman matron – has been erased and she has become part of a universal process of negation (ll. 848–75). Moreover, the force against which Lucrece complains is female. Deflecting blame from Tarquin's tyrannic father to what she constructs as the proto-tyrant's symbolic mother, she chooses to identify a terrible, female other as the source of her betrayal and pain. Lucrece's complaint implies the continuity as well as the inevitable discontinuity between what she now experiences and her experience of having been, as it were, cast into 'a wilderness where are no laws' (l. 544) when Tarquin began his assault.

In suggesting that rape has cast her into an abyss, Lucrece's complaint suggests several other things as well. For example it indicates that, despite the obvious affinities between *Lucrece* and *Titus Andronicus*, the characterization of Lucrece herself at this crucial moment of the poem both resembles and tellingly contrasts with that of Lear, when the king wanders in the wilderness and curses the world. Lucrece's complaint begins with denunciation of night and then proceeds to express a transference of guilt: from Tarquin to herself; from Tarquin and herself to night (l. 772). She is not, of course, exculpating Tarquin; rather, she is implying that he has made her, too, guilty (of marital unchastity) and asserting that night must bear ultimate responsibility for his guilt because he is, as she fables in l. 785, 'night's child'. What seems most important about that quite elaborate process of transference is Lucrece's attempt to invoke night's aid – because of its final responsibility for her own supposed guilt – to conceal her 'disgrace' (l. 802) from the light of day (ll. 772–826).

So that she may remain hidden from sight, Lucrece asks night to attack and to overthrow the natural order of things (l. 774). Hers is an apocalyptic vision not unlike Lear's, for he likewise asks that the natural order be undone: 'And thou, all-shaking thunder,/ Strike flat the thick rotundity o' th' world!/ Crack Nature's moulds' (3, 2, 6– 8). Displaced and lost, Lear invokes the world's end because of his personal suffering; Lucrece, herself displaced and lost although still within her own home, invokes the world's confusion because of her pain. In fact she asks for an end to growth in physical nature and thus to life on earth, but the reader is probably to infer that she does not perceive that as an implication of her request or demand. The immediate difference between her pain and Lear's, and hence between her invocation and his, can hardly be overstated, of course. Lear's wretchedness and, finally, his madness come from his living out his egocentric view of reality. Convinced of his innate centrality to his world, he abandons the political position which defines him, which gives meaning to the title 'king' and thus his selfhood. Lear displaces himself; he loses his way as a consequence of his personalizing and enacting, in effect, the conventional notions that humankind is central to the world and that humankind is the measure of all things. But Tarquin displaces Lucrece, he makes her lose the direction of her life – he and, at the last, his symbolic mother, as Lucrece would fable it. There is a shared, self-centred ferocity, nonetheless, in the speeches of Lear and of Lucrece. He wishes for a second Great Flood, for the world returned to chaos; she for night to war upon and to overthrow the light forever, or '[w]ith rotten damps [to] *ravish* the morning air' (my emphasis) and so poison the male god of light, hence returning the world to the primeval (and life-denying) dark.[102]

Self-centred as Lucrece's grief and anger are interestingly and unpejoratively shown to be in the earlier part of her complaint, later in it they are shown as well to be profoundly selfless. It is true that, when reflecting on the false selfhood which mistaken tradition, cor-rupted exemplarity, will confer on her (ll. 799–847), Lucrece thinks initially of herself (ll. 799–808). It is also true that she then considers at length how Tarquin's assault on her has wronged Collatine (ll. 809–47). Her doing so makes her characterization conform to an early modern code of virtue for aristocratic women: her preoccupations with conjugal fidelity and with placing the family's interests above her own clearly attest to that.[103] More important, her doing so reveals that her desire at first to preserve and, subsequently, to re-establish her basic selfhood is for Collatine's sake as well as for her own. As she says, with regard to preserving her role as chaste Roman matron: 'Let my good name, that senseless reputation,/ For Collatine's dear love be kept unspotted' (ll. 820–1). Lucrece at one moment, furthermore, represents her rape as a secret, dishonourable victory gained by Tarquin over her husband:

> O unseen shame, invisible disgrace!
> O unfelt sore, crest-wounding private scar!
> Reproach is stamp'd in Collatinus' face,
> And Tarquin's eye may read the mot afar,
> How he in peace is wounded, not in war.
>
> (ll. 827–31)

Unknowingly she alludes in those words to the competition between the two men which led to Tarquin's assault on her, the rivalry displaced from the spheres of the military and of the political into the sphere of the domestic. But while her words suggest that, and also her keen awareness of the threat Tarquin delivered before attacking her, they anticipate one of the main, altruistic reasons for the suicide which will establish her again – as she sees it – in the role of exemplarily chaste wife: to deny Tarquin victory over her husband and her family; to defeat the apparent conqueror (see ll. 1058–78).

Lucrece's second object of blame and complaint is, like her first, female. Ultimate responsibility for her misery is again transferred from a male agent to a female cause or facilitator (ll. 876–924). On the other hand, although Lucrece does indeed transfer guilt from Tarquin to 'opportunity' without exculpating the rapist himself (opportunity being denounced in l. 888, for example, as a 'ravisher' and 'traitor'), the ambiguity of opportunity as a force directing life seems to differ from that attributed to night. Lucrece appears to think of night as both a cause of her ill and a possible, albeit partial, remedy for it; she claims, by way of contrast, that opportunity withholds its help from those who need it (ll. 896–917). However, as was argued earlier in this chapter, she seems to view opportunity, to interpret it, from a perspective simultaneously pagan and Christian, making ambiguous opportunity's role as a cause or facilitator of harm and evil.[104] The

suggestion might even be made that Lucrece tends to represent oppor-
tunity as the occasion of sin rather than as *occasio*. Be that as it may,
the directly relevant issue here would seem to be that in Lucrece's
complaint against opportunity, as at various moments in the poem,
she seems to have a twofold vision, to speak as it were with two voices,
and the reader cannot know the conscious range of her ethical and
religious perceptions. There is in her complaint a slippage between
the notions of *occasio* and of the occasion of sin: the pagan does not
fully accord with the Christian in her account of opportunity's re-
sponsibility for facilitating or causing destruction or evil. As a result,
her attribution of blame to opportunity neither merely concurs with
the mythology of *occasio* nor is conventionally Christian. Her vision
of opportunity as a culpable force affecting her life and the lives of
others is elusive, confused and confusing, as seems appropriate to the
dramatization of her profoundly distressed consciousness.

The last of Lucrece's complaints, that against time (ll. 925–1015),
resembles her complaint against night perhaps especially for two
reasons: she constructs for herself an account of time which denies it
a single, predominant meaning; she represents time as able to heal as
well as to harm (see, for example, ll. 936–45). Yet there are obvious,
important differences between her depictions of night and of time.
Time is culpable (l. 931) but male not female; further, Lucrece asks
night to conceal her perceived 'disgrace' whereas she asks time to
take her life – her declared intention to commit suicide being clearly
anticipated (*ibid.*); most important, although she transfers blame from
herself to time she also asks time to destroy Tarquin (ll. 967–1001).
It should probably be mentioned, before her request is looked at,
that from her third complaint a kind of world view emerges, accord-
ing to which night and time are 'copesmate[s]' (l. 925) and oppor-
tunity is time's malefic 'servant' (l. 932). The role of the gods in that
world view remains indeterminate – they are absent from her com-
plaints, after all – and Lucrece may be inventing her view of things
as she speaks. Whatever the case, her curse against Tarquin interest-
ingly reveals once more her preoccupation with transference. Her
curse seems to consist mostly in her asking time to transfer her
misery to Tarquin: she asks, in effect, that just as she has been made
an outcast, so may he likewise become one (see, for example, ll.
984–9); just as she has been made to enter a new reality which is
hellish, so too may he (see, for example, ll. 971–3, 998–9). She does
not know, of course, that he already has, nor could she know that
his decision to assault her involved his consciously abandoning, in
the first place, the gods and their laws, the conventional order of

Roman life, for a private reality.[105] And it is interesting that, given the intimation of suicide in her complaint against time, she wishes the impulse to suicide on Tarquin (l. 998). However the final question is surely whether her curse works or whether her suicide makes it work.

That question can be usefully considered in the light of Lucrece's immediate repudiation of her complaints and her curse – and also of her decision to commit suicide. 'Out idle words, servants to shallow fools,/ Unprofitable sounds, weak arbitrators!' she bursts out, rejecting words with words, in fact, her rhetoric of complaint with that same rhetoric now directed against words themselves (ll. 1016–17). Part of her reason for repudiating what she has just said at length is '[s]ince [her] case is past the help of law' (l. 1022). Tarquin's tyranny has at once wronged her and deprived her of access to legal redress; he has both obscenely subjected her and, as she sees it, taken away her selfhood and rights as an individual/political subject. Therefore, as she goes on to say: 'This helpless smoke of words doth me no right' (l. 1027). Lucrece's placing her rape in that political context, something she also does very specifically and elaborately before Tarquin's assault on her, justifies her impatient rejection of her own anguished words, cathartic as they are and even though they imply that she has gained a victim's understanding of tyranny.[106] In short, the political nature and context of Tarquin's assault being acknowledged by the reader as they are by Lucrece herself, her private complaints and her curse can hardly be seen as other than words spoken '[i]n vain' (ll. 1023–6): emptily. It could be suggested, nonetheless, that her complaints and her curse form part of a process in which first she redefines the workings of her world and then she determines how to regain what she thinks she can of her subjectivity.

Having redefined how her world works and subsequently determined that her redefinition actually effects nothing, Lucrece proceeds from an affective but politically powerless rhetoric of language to what she forecasts will be, as it were, an affective and effective rhetoric of action.[107] Suicide is for Lucrece the way to re-establish something of the basic role taken from her and, apparently, the way to gain or to achieve other things at the same time. It will be a physical 'remedy' (l. 1028) ridding her of 'foul defiled blood' (l. 1029): Lucrece's sense of physical contamination will thus be relieved. Collatine and the other men to whom she later tells the story of her misfortune do not agree. According to them, she is indeed physically contaminated but '[h]er body's stain her mind untainted clears' (l. 1710) and therefore suicide is unnecessary. The narrator, however, seems implicitly yet thoroughly to agree with Lucrece's notion that suicide will purge her 'defiled blood', as his aetiological mythmaking indicates.[108]

Suicide's action as a purgative will also enable it, as Lucrece thinks, to deny Tarquin a sexual and familial victory over Collatine because it denies Tarquin secret fatherhood in Collatine's family (ll. 1062–8). More important, suicide confirms to Lucrece that she is 'the mistress of [her] fate' (l. 1069) and, as such, able not merely to deny Tarquin victory over her husband and family but to gain victory over him via Collatine's revenge (ll. 1177–83). Subsequently she implies that suicide will save her from being turned into and misused as an exemplar of marital unchastity (ll. 1714–15). Her suicide will thus save exemplarity itself from misuse – preserving its interpretative authority while revealing its vulnerability – and so history from false tradition. And she seems well aware that her death will help to preserve the integrity of exemplarity and of historical tradition. Nonetheless the main and final achievement of Lucrece's suicide will be, she makes clear, the regaining of her 'honour' and so the regaining of her selfhood. Lucrece believes that rape erased her basic role and that suicide will erase in turn her 'shame' (l. 1190) to re-establish her in the role of chaste Roman matron, all but giving her back the selfhood of which she has been deprived. As she says: 'For in my death I murder shameful scorn:/ My shame so dead, mine honour is new born.'[109] Suicide will re-establish her status in the cultural system that has so comprehensively fashioned her sense of self. The reader sees, then, that the Roman emphasis in her reflections upon suicide ultimately displaces the anachronistically Christian emphasis recurring throughout them, although another way to make the point might be to suggest an uneasy reconciliation between the Roman and the Christian elements of her reflections, a reconciliation in which the Christian are ultimately subsumed by the Roman.

The issues of subjectivity, exemplarity and history evoked by Lucrece's decision to commit suicide seem likewise to be evoked by the picture of Troy's fall on which she gazes when seeking diversion from the grief and anxiety attendant upon her decision.[110] There, as in Lucrece's process of self-determination, the issues are interwoven, problematic and connected as well to issues of empowerment and of knowledge. Perhaps the way to begin clarifying what I mean is to suggest that the picture lets Lucrece both imaginarily enter and have a synoptic view of a foundational moment of Roman history. Entering and yet encompassing the recreated moment of origin, she at once confirms and adds to the re-establishing of her role as chaste Roman matron – and thus of her subjectivity; doing that, she helps confirm the shape of the originary moment in which she herself unwittingly is an agent. Her interaction with an image of the moment in which lies the origin of Rome helps to plot the moment in which lies the origin of the Republic.

Lucrece's first impulse in looking at the picture of Troy's fall is to find a representation of extreme grief (ll. 1443–56), yet she seeks more than an imaginary companion in misery. Certainly she scans the picture in order to find just such a figure: one into whose misery, into whose world, she can enter. She additionally does so, however, both as a way of re-examining her own misery – looking at it in the mirror of another life – and as a strategy of self-empowerment. That Hecuba's suffering becomes a mirror in which to reconsider her own is evinced by the anger which Lucrece focuses on Paris, to whom she refers in words that suggest her anger at Tarquin: 'Thy heat of lust, fond Paris, did incur/ This load of wrath' (ll. 1473–4). And: 'Why should the private pleasure of some one/ Become the public plague of many moe?' (ll. 1478–9). Again, with Tarquin in view: '[O]ne man's lust these many lives confounds' (l. 1489). Her resentment of Helen, the beautiful but unfaithful wife, is no less revealing: 'Show me the strumpet that began this stir,/ That with my nails her beauty I may tear!' (ll. 1471–2). As has been indicated above, however, Lucrece's involvement with the image of Hecuba and of Troy's fall does not mean merely that she reconsiders her own misery; as the lines referring to Helen suggest, that involvement implies, too, Lucrece's desire for and impulse to self-empowerment. Reconsidering her anguish, Lucrece wants among other things to assert control over her selfhood and her own life. She indirectly signals that by her wish to act as a *dea ex machina* intervening imaginarily in the fall of Troy, seeking symbolically to amend the (originary) moment of history with which she has already closely identified herself via the image of Hecuba and with which she will later explicitly identify herself and her rape (see ll. 1541–7). She says, for example, that she wishes to 'drop sweet balm in Priam's painted wound,/ And rail on Pyrrhus that hath done him wrong,/ And with [her] tears quench Troy that burns so long' (ll. 1466–8). Lucrece's wish to act as a *dea ex machina* accords with her earlier assertion that she is 'the mistress of [her] fate' (l. 1069): her will to regain power over her life, her selfhood, is expressed directly by her determination to commit suicide and, here, indirectly by her wish to amend symbolically the injustice inflicted upon Hecuba at the fall of Troy. Thus her interaction with the picture of Troy's destruction confirms the re-establishing of her selfhood; but it also significantly adds to that process.

What chiefly adds to the process is, of course, the moment of recognition when Lucrece identifies Sinon with Tarquin.[111] Her identifying Sinon with Tarquin interestingly develops the poem's earlier presentation of the proto-tyrant as a type of Satan. A Satan-like betrayer of Lucrece as a type of Eve and of the earthly paradise, Tarquin becomes in relation to her a type of the treacherous Sinon when she refigures herself as a second Troy. In that moment of recognition Lucrece effectually perceives the fallibility of her neoplatonic way of reading subjectivity: '"It cannot be," quoth she, "that so much guile," – / She would have said, – "can lurk in such a look."/ But Tarquin's shape came in her mind the while,/ And from her tongue "can lurk" from "cannot" took' (ll. 1534–7). Yet here, as before in the poem, the reader sees a sceptical rather than a merely subversive perspective opened onto the neoplatonic mode of interpreting subjectivity in terms of appearance. Sinon both can and cannot be read in terms of his looks: within the Troy narrative, so to speak, he cannot be thus read; from outside it, he can. On the other hand, most of the other figures in the picture can directly and straightforwardly be read in terms of their appearances; still, that is only because they have been depicted, characterized, so that their appearances immediately identify them – that is, in a way which harmonizes both with the neoplatonic mode of interpreting the internal via the external and with traditional exemplarity. One can accurately read Lucrece, then, by means of her looks but not everybody can be so read. Lucrece has now learned to reject, as the moment of recognition distinctly implies, belief in the universal truth of her neoplatonic reading of subjectivity. Like Eve she has gained knowledge – self-knowledge, in her case – at a terrible price; unlike Eve, she has not fallen in gaining it.[112] Tarquin has fallen. In *Venus and Adonis*, Adonis rejects the winning of self-knowledge through sexual experience. Lucrece gains self-knowledge by the tyrannic imposition on her of sexual violence.

The implicitly sceptical treatment of neoplatonism in the picture of Troy episode has clear connections with the likewise implicitly sceptical treatment of exemplarity in that episode and throughout the poem. But perhaps more important, at this point, than the poem's continuingly sceptical perspective on exemplarity is what seems to be suggested about the issue of history's having, or not having, a design. Taken as an originary moment, the fall of Troy can be seen to indicate that history has a design, a providential shape. It is interesting if not surprising that Lucrece, when she looks at the picture of Troy's ruin, does not appear to think of the picture's positive implication. She sees misery and destruction, not the origins of Rome.

Just so, when she considers her own, immediate anguish she does
not appear to think of that anguish as being part of some providential
design; on the contrary, she seems rather to think of her history, of
current events, as having no true design and meaning without the
shaping intervention of her suicide. The picture of Troy can be seen,
even if not by Lucrece, as an icon of the providential ordering of
human experience down through time. Lucrece's resolve to commit
suicide, in her capacity as 'the mistress of [her] fate', suggests that she
is oblivious of or beyond reliance on the notion of history as having
a providential order. Indeed, looking at the picture of Troy confirms
Lucrece's determination to order the present and the future by her
own action (see ll. 1567–8). And that sceptical balance of opposites is
complicated by the role of Brutus at the poem's end.

The competitive objectifying of Lucrece by her father and by her
husband at the poem's end has been variously commented on; what
seems of greater significance, however, than the macabre rivalry of
those two men is Brutus' manipulation, even theft, of Lucrece's re-
established subjectivity in order to reinstate his own. By her suicide
Lucrece directly initiates the moment for Brutus to reveal his for-
merly disguised subjectivity: he manifests himself by means of her
and thus indirectly she gives Rome a new political identity.[113] Collatine
and Lucretius are of course the two men present at Lucrece's suicide
who should decide what happens next. Revenge, as the narrator
relates, is in Collatine's mind but grief paralyses him as it does
Lucrece's father.[114] In deciding what happens next and leading the
way, Brutus indicates both his capacity to seize the moment posit-
ively – in contrast to Tarquin, Collatine, Lucretius and to Lucrece's
insistently negative view of opportunity/*occasio* – and his prudence, a
virtue possessed by none of the poem's other main characters.[115] For
all that, what Brutus does and how he leads the way seem linked to
political expedience rather than to the demands of justice, to callous
cunning rather than to virtue.

The mutually defining characterization at the poem's end suggests,
as has been foreshadowed above, that by her death Lucrece allows
Brutus to reveal his previously masked subjectivity (see especially
ll. 1810–16). Yet he appears to do so through politic theft, then
reconstruction, of hers. In revealing his long-concealed selfhood and
exhorting Collatine to follow his lead, Brutus says:

> 'Is it revenge to give thyself a blow
> For his foul act by whom thy fair wife bleeds?
> Such childish humour from weak minds proceeds;

Thy wretched wife mistook the matter so,
To slay herself that should have slain her foe.'

(ll. 1823–7)

Brutus does not deny Lucrece's re-established role as an exemplarily chaste Roman matron; nor, of course, does he wish to appropriate that or something like it to himself. His words perpetrate theft of a kind, nonetheless. Through them he denies, for his immediate convenience only, the heroic virtue and status of Lucrece's suicide. Doing so, he appropriates heroic virtue and status to himself as things that he can confer – for example, on Collatine – and he steals, too, the transformative power of her suicide. He will not, at the moment, allow Lucrece's death to make her into an heroic icon of married chastity: chastity's martyr.[116] Rather, he uses her death in order to effect a moment of personal political theatre, the transformation of himself from being the fool at large to being the leader of opposition to Tarquin. Subsequently in his speech he goes on to monumentalize Lucrece as chastity's martyr (ll. 1835–41): an ironic fulfilment of the monumentalizing process begun by the narrator yet always in accord with Lucrece's self-representation. He monumentalizes her so as to make himself pre-eminent in a foundational act, the expulsion of Tarquin and hence of the tyrant/king's proto-tyrannic heir. And that treatment of Lucrece's subjectivity by Brutus is arguably a manipulation or recreation of it, for he now weaves it into a mythologizing political rhetoric designed as much to achieve his own political ambition as to realize his less specifically personal political vision. Lucrece's corpse thereafter becomes the public centrepiece of his, and his supporters', political progress.

. . . . .

Brutus' theft and manipulation of Lucrece's subjectivity, which equate with manipulation of her suicide, emphasize how male and political is the world in which Lucrece lives and tries to assert power. It is not a world which overtly demands that she finally maintain power over her selfhood and assert power over others by means of suicide; nonetheless, one could argue that she has so thoroughly internalized Roman cultural norms about ideal femaleness that she has no choice but to use suicide as the way simultaneously to lose, defend and avenge her life – to make it immutable – in the aggressively male, Roman world. And even killing herself, as the speech and actions of Brutus indicate, can provide no guarantees – except for a guarantee of her absence, which makes her past life vulnerable not immutable.

But the story of Lucrece's fashioning by and struggle within her world is of course more elaborate than that, and a glance at *Lucrece* in relation to *Venus and Adonis* may help concisely to suggest what are the main concerns and achievements in Shakespeare's refiguring of the Lucretia story.

Perhaps the way to focus that glance most sharply is to consider something of characterization and Ovidianism in the narrative poems. Characterization in Shakespeare's first narrative poem is rich yet more limited than that in *Lucrece*. The interaction between Venus and Adonis, for all its iconographical and other subtleties, does not have the discursive range of the interactions among Collatine, Tarquin and Lucrece, which offer a Romanized, Petrarchized re-visioning of the Fall. Thus the connections among sexuality, self-knowledge and death in *Lucrece*, although able to be described as straightforwardly as those in *Venus and Adonis*, are implicated in a more intricate network of discourses. Yet at this point in discussion, consideration of the poems' Ovidianism rather than of their characterization may be more revealing of the differences between them, more revealing of the main concerns and achievements in *Lucrece*.

The flamboyant, cunning narrator of *Venus and Adonis* derives mainly from the narrator of the *Metamorphoses*. Like his Ovidian predecessor he treats myth serio-comically, he playfully recreates it, and in treating it ludically he also treats it sceptically, his aetiological mythmaking (when Venus prophesies) maybe suggesting as well a playfully sceptical perspective on historical explanation. What might be called his ludic scepticism is by no means confined to his treatment of myth. By way of broad contrast between the narrative poems' Ovidianism, one could say that the Ovidianism of *Lucrece* is not only more serious in manner but also more intellectually ambitious. The narrator of Shakespeare's second narrative poem is no less a virtuoso rhetorician than his counterpart in *Venus and Adonis*; nonetheless, being closer in manner to the narrator of the *Fasti* than to that of the *Metamorphoses*, there is in him little of his predecessor's sly playfulness. It was suggested a moment ago that the scepticism pervading *Venus and Adonis* is closely linked to the narrator's habit of play: for example, he plays with contrary notions of love by means of the iconography of Venus. Once, at least, that ludic scepticism can be more than incidentally philosophic, as when competing views of what constitutes 'nature' are set in opposition, something one sees again in *Lucrece* and dramatized throughout *As You Like It* and *King Lear*. The narrator of *Lucrece* almost entirely lacks the habit of play to be seen in the narrator of *Venus and Adonis*; as might thus be expected, the former poem's scepticism appears always more seriously philosophic than does that of the latter. The sceptical focus on exemplarity, to take one instance, seems Pyrrhonian rather than Ovidian, carefully balancing 'appearances' against 'judgements' and marking their irreconcilable opposition. So one could describe the poem's treatment of neoplatonism as a means of interpreting human subjectivity. So likewise could one describe the poem's focus on history. In *Venus and Adonis* the aetiological mythmaking centred on Venus' prophecy perhaps plays, as was suggested above, with the notion of historical explanation.[117] Whatever the case, *Lucrece* clearly has a concern with issues of foundationalism, of providence, and of undecidability in connection with both that are beyond the scope and alien to the lighter Ovidian manner of *Venus and Adonis*. The concern and achievement of *Lucrece* that distinguish it, however, most strikingly from its forerunner can be summarized as this: its sympathetic treatment of female subjectivity. The complicated but frequently caricatured Venus with her devalued sexuality is far removed from the complex, tragic Lucrece whose sexuality becomes a dominant political issue in her world. Venus is depreciated in order for Adonis to be enhanced; Lucrece could be numbered among the speakers of the *Heroides*, and very arguably the men who surround her when she dies are more flawed than she.

NOTES

1. Reference to *Lucrece* is from William Shakespeare, *The Poems*, ed. F. T. Prince (1969; rpt. London: Methuen, 1976).
2. See Schoenbaum's *William Shakespeare: A Compact Documentary Life* (1977; rpt. New York: New American Library, 1986), pp. 177–9.
3. Lines 1 and 4–6 respectively.
4. See especially Schoenbaum, *William Shakespeare*, p. 179.
5. On the nature of tragedy in *Lucrece*, see M. C. Bradbrook, *Shakespeare and Elizabethan Poetry* (New York: Oxford University Press, 1952), pp. 110–16.
6. Reference is to Ovid, *Fasti*, trans. Sir J. G. Frazer, *Loeb Classical Library* (Cambridge, Mass. and London: Harvard University Press and Heinemann, 1976).
7. With Petrarchan additions, however.
8. The quotation is from l. 717; see ll. 713–20.
9. That argument will be pursued in the final section of this chapter.
10. Hence the wide agreement that Ovid's *Fasti* is the major pre-text used by Shakespeare.
11. See ll. 721–37 of Ovid's narrative, especially ll. 729–32.
12. An evocation of the criterion of decorum.

13. Cf. the image in l. 694 comparing Tarquin, after his committing the rape, to a 'gorged hawk' – that image in particular evokes the images of predatoriness used to describe Venus in *Venus and Adonis.*

14. See ll. 568–644, especially l. 644; cf. ll. 561–7. The speeches against night, opportunity and time will be considered later in this chapter.

15. Ovid's narrator says of Tarquin: '[T]ransported by blind love he raved' (l. 762). As regards the effect of Lucretia's/Lucrece's chastity on Tarquin, see ll. 765–6 of Ovid's text and especially l. 8 of Shakespeare's, with its qualifying 'Haply'.

16. Reference to Livy is from *Livy*, vol. 1, trans. B. O. Foster, *Loeb Classical Library* (Cambridge, Mass. and London: Harvard University Press and Heinemann, 1976).

17. Shakespeare's qualification to the notion of her chastity's arousing Tarquin should perhaps be mentioned again.

18. The immediately relevant words being in the original: '*[N]ec ulla deinde inpudica Lucretiae exemplo vivet.*'

19. On the Renaissance discourse of exemplarity, see T. Hampton, *Writing from History: The Rhetoric of Exemplarity in Renaissance Literature* (Ithaca and London: Cornell University Press, 1990). See also A. Gelley (ed.), *Unruly Examples: On the Rhetoric of Exemplarity* (Stanford: Stanford University Press, 1995).

20. Giovanni Boccaccio, *Concerning Famous Women*, trans. G. A. Guarino (New Brunswick, N.J.: Rutgers University Press, 1963), pp. 101–3 – here, at p. 101.

21. See ll. 1049–50, 1184–90, and so on.

22. Reference is respectively to Geoffrey Chaucer, *The Complete Poetry and Prose*, ed. J. H. Fisher (New York: Holt, Rinehart & Winston, 1977) and John Gower, *Confessio Amantis*, ed. R. A. Peck (Toronto: University of Toronto Press, 1980).

23. '[G]race', used by the narrator/[?]Lucresse in l. 1804, is retrospectively given an ironically theological connotation, so amplifying its parody of her directly theological use of the word in l. 1731.

24. See Augustine's *City of God*, ed. and trans. D. Knowles (Harmondsworth: Penguin, 1972), 1, 19. Early in Chaucer's tale, in l. 1690, the narrator mentions St Augustine and his 'grete compassyoun' for Lucresse, but does not refer to the dispraise which accompanies the saint's sympathy for and praise of her.

25. And when she ponders suicide, but that will be considered later in this chapter.

26. She alludes to the biblical notion of 'the occasion of sin' in l. 879 and in ll. 881–2 she figures sin in a guise familiar from Christian allegory.

27. See, for example, ll. 1–42 and 596–644.

28. See R. Hillman, 'Gower's Lucrece: A New Old Source for *The Rape of Lucrece*', *Chaucer Review*, 24 (1990), 263–7. The congruence between Shakespeare's Tarquin and Plato's account of the tyrant is discussed in section three, below.

29. The two most acute commentators on the poem's affinities with the complaint are Hallett Smith and Heather Dubrow, whose views are discussed below.

30. On *de casibus* tragedy, see especially Willard Farnham, *The Medieval Heritage of Elizabethan Tragedy* (Berkeley: University of California Press, 1936).

31. Reference is to John Lydgate, *Fall of Princes*, ed. H. Bergen, *Early English Text Society, Extra Series*, 121–4 (Oxford: Oxford University Press, 1918–19).

32. On the tyrant play, see especially R. W. Bushnell, *Tragedies of Tyrants: Political Thought and Theater in the English Renaissance* (Ithaca and London: Cornell University Press, 1990).

33. Cf. ll. 596–602.

34. See Farnham, *The Medieval Heritage*, pp. 271–339.

35. Hallett Smith, *Elizabethan Poetry: A Study in Conventions, Meaning and Expression* (Cambridge, Mass.: Harvard University Press, 1952), p. 103.

36. The essay appears in B. K. Lewalski (ed.), *Renaissance Genres: Essays on Theory, History, and Interpretation* (Cambridge, Mass.: Harvard University Press, 1986), pp. 399–417.

37. Cf. pp. 405–17.

38. As Dubrow's more extended study of the poem in her *Captive Victors*, pp. 80–168, also suggests (H. Dubrow, *Captive Victors: Shakespeare's Narrative Poems and Sonnets* (Ithaca and London: Cornell University Press, 1987)). Reference to Daniel's poem is from *Poems and A Defence of Ryme*, ed. A. C. Sprague (1930; rpt. Chicago and London: University of Chicago Press, 1965).

39. See ll. 1–63; the allusions to Delia are of course new.

40. For examples of the critical approaches and concerns mentioned above, see: M. Platt, *Rome and Romans According to Shakespeare* (Salzburg: English Institute, 1976), pp. 1–40; C. Kahn, 'The Rape in Shakespeare's *Lucrece*', *Shakespeare Studies*, 9 (1977), 45–72; R. S. Miola, *Shakespeare's Rome* (Cambridge: Cambridge University Press, 1983), pp. 18–41; T. French, 'A "badge of fame": Shakespeare's Rhetorical Lucrece', *Explorations in Renaissance Culture*, 10 (1984), 97–106; N. J. Vickers, ' "This Heraldry in Lucrece' Face" ', *Poetics Today*, 6 (1985), 171–84; K. E. Maus, 'Taking Tropes Seriously: Language and Violence in Shakespeare's *Rape of Lucrece*', *Shakespeare Quarterly*, 37 (1986), 66–82; J. Fineman, 'Shakespeare's *Will*: The Temporality of Rape', *Representations*, 20 (1987), 25–76; G. Ziegler, 'My Lady's Chamber: Female Space, Female Chastity in Shakespeare', *Textual Practice*, 4 (1990), 73–100; D. Willbern, 'Hyberbolic Desire: Shakespeare's *Lucrece*', in *Contending Kingdoms*, eds M.-R. Logan and P. L. Rudnytsky (Detroit: Wayne State University Press, 1991), pp. 202–24; P. Berry, 'Woman, Language and History in *The Rape of Lucrece*', *Shakespeare Survey*, 44 (1991), 33–9; L. Woodbridge, 'Palisading the Elizabethan Body Politic', *Texas Studies in Literature and Language*, 33 (1991), 327–54;

H. James, 'Milton's Eve, the Romance Genre, and Ovid', *Contemporary Literature*, 45 (1993), 121–45; J. Bate, *Shakespeare and Ovid* (1993; rpt. Oxford: Clarendon Press, 1994), pp. 65–82; J. O. Newman, ' "And Let Mild Women to Him Lose Their Mildness": Female Violence, and Shakespeare's *The Rape of Lucrece'*, *Shakespeare Quarterly*, 45 (1994), 304–26.

41. In fact, none as far as I am aware.

42. That is likewise implicit in Ovid's narrative.

43. See ll. 1–8, 30–4 of the 'Argument', ll. 20–1 and 36–42, of the poem itself, and ll. 3–7 of the poem on desire as informing his expressions of his tyrannic role in relation to Lucrece.

44. Reference is to Plato, *The Republic*, trans. D. Lee, 2nd edn (rev.) (1974; rpt. Harmondsworth: Penguin, 1979). R. Bushnell discusses Plato's characterization of the tyrant in her *Tragedies of Tyrants*, pp. 9–18.

45. See also ll. 652–65 of Shakespeare's poem, spoken by Lucrece.

46. Cf. ll. 120–89.

47. Reference to Petrarch will be to the edition and translation by R. M. Durling: *Petrarch's Lyric Poems*, trans. and ed. R. M. Durling (Cambridge, Mass. and London: Harvard University Press, 1976).

48. Cf. ll. 519–39, 806–40, 1184–211, and so on.

49. Her doing so is, as well, one of the elements of her characterization that connect her with the personae of the *Heroides*.

50. See l. 17.

51. The 'field' trope is of course derived from heraldry.

52. In general connection with the argument being pursued here, the reader might care to consult two other volumes in this series: R. Kirkpatrick, *English and Italian Literature from Dante to Shakespeare* (1995); R. Sowerby, *The Classical Legacy in Renaissance Poetry* (1994).

53. Compare ll. 397–9, especially 399, with ll. 13–14.

54. Cf. ll. 36–8.

55. In connection with Collatine's hubris, see especially l. 19.

56. Functioning and expressed safely, as he is apparently to be taken as thinking, if he is to be taken as thinking at all.

57. See especially ll. 1751–1806.

58. The phrase is Bakhtin's, from his *Problems of Dostoevsky's Poetics*, trans. C. Emerson (Manchester: Manchester University Press, 1984), p. 293.

59. In conjnction with ll. 87–8, see ll. 386–99.

60. See ll. 90–4, 190–301, 491–504. In ll. 362–4 he is compared to a 'serpent'.

61. See ll. 127–301, especially 181–2, 190–245, 253–80.

62. See ll. 9–14 of the former poem, ll. 13–14 of the latter.

63. See '*Passa la nave* . . .' l. 13, with its reference to passion's defeat of reason.

64. Compare ll. 248–52 with ll. 271–3 and 279–80.

65. Compare ll. 197–201 with 271–3.

66. See l. 348. See also ll. 197–224.

67. Cf. l. 73.

68. See, again, D. Summers's *Michelangelo and the Language of Art* (Princeton, N.J.: Princeton University Press, 1981), here at pp. 171–6.

69. Reference to Milton is from *The Poems*, ed. J. Carey and A. Fowler (London: Longmans, 1968).

70. See ll. 412–13; cf. ll. 386–99.

71. Cf. the discussion of Elegy 19 in the preceding chapter.

72. Cf. ll. 419–20.

73. One aspect of exemplarity subverted in the poem is that of its unquestionable interpretative authority, as asserted by some sixteenth-century writers.

74. For an illuminating account of Montaigne and exemplarity, see T. Hampton's *Writing From History*, pp. 134–97.

75. Castiglione, *The Book of the Courtier*, trans. C. S. Singleton (New York: Doubleday, 1959), pp. 342–5.

76. Approximately ll. 442–742.

77. With reference to parody of the 'warrior of love' trope, cf. ll. 428–41.

78. A trope to be seen throughout the *Rime* and especially in the *Triumph of Chastity*.

79. See ll. 428 and 463–4, for example. The quotation is from l. 469. In objectifying Lucrece the narrator resembles Tarquin but, as well, Lucrece's husband and her father. The narrator's further link with Tarquin, mentioned below, is his complicity with Tarquin's desire.

80. See *Rime* 14, l. 14; cf. Donne's 'The Funeral', ll. 18–19.

81. See Innes's translation (Ovid, *Metamorphoses*, trans. M. Innes (1955; rpt. Harmondsworth: Penguin, 1968)), p. 155.

82. For related portrayals of self-division by Shakespeare's contemporaries, one could turn to Sidney's *Apology* and to Donne's 'Oh, to vex me, contraries meet in one'. Milton uses the notion of self-division to characterize his Satan in *Paradise Lost*.

83. Ll. 719–28, reference being here to l. 721.

84. See ll. 498–9; cf. l. 569.

85. See I. Maclean, *The Renaissance Notion of Woman* (1980; rpt. Cambridge: Cambridge University Press, 1992), pp. 47–67.

86. L. 543; cf. *Rime* 190, ll. 1–11.

87. Reference is to Cicero, *De Inventione, De Optimo Genere Oratorum, Topica*, ed. and trans. H. M. Hubbell, *Loeb Classical Library* (1949; rpt. London and Cambridge, Mass.: Heinemann and Harvard University Press, 1960), here at 1, 2, 2–1, 4, 5.

88. Tarquin's 'passion' is, at the last, wilfully 'blind and unreasoning' – see, again, ll. 267–80, 498–504, 645–68.

89. L. 351. Here, I read 'love' as 'desire' rather than as 'Eros' and 'fortune' as 'chance' rather than as 'Fortuna'. But if Tarquin does allude to Eros and Fortuna, then he is of course choosing those divinities in illegitimate isolation from the rest of the Olympian hierarchy: he is wilfully taking them out of their (for him, inconvenient) context.

90. See Fulke Greville, *Certaine Learned and Elegant Workes (1633)*, introd. A. D. Cousins (New York: Scholars' Facsimiles and Reprints, 1990), Introduction, pp. 9–10.

91. See especially ll. 218–45.

92. Cf. ll. 543–6.

93. Cf. 'The Argument', ll. 11–17.

94. Cicero, *De Officiis*, ed. and trans. W. Miller, *Loeb Classical Library* (1913; rpt. Cambridge, Mass. and London: Harvard University Press and Heinemann, 1975), 1, 43, 153.

95. See her *Rhetoric, Prudence, and Skepticism in the Renaissance* (Ithaca and London: Cornell University Press, 1985), p. 35.

96. That lawful spouse also being Tarquin's friend.

97. Cf. ll. 624–30.

98. See 'The Argument', ll. 1–6; cf. Ovid's account of the taking of Gabii, discussed in this chapter's first section.

99. See, among many others, ll. 746–56, 759–61, 772, 802, 806–26, 1048–50, 1700–8.

100. She possibly and distantly alludes to Diana in ll. 786–7; she does not, of course, call upon the Christian God.

101. See ll. 554 and 673–6, then ll. 117–19.

102. See respectively ll. 774, 778, 779–84.

103. See ll. 809, 819–26, 829, and so on.

104. Cf. ll. 881–3, 908–15, 923–4.

105. See, first, ll. 694–745, especially ll. 722–35; then see ll. 348–52, discussed earlier.

106. As distinct from what was formerly her unwitting complicity with and seeming blindness to the illegitimate rule of the Tarquins.

107. See ll. 1177–80; cf. ll. 1322–3.

108. See ll. 1734–50.

109. Ll. 1189–90; cf. ll. 1186–8.

110. See ll. 1361–5 and ll. 1367–568.

111. Ll. 1534–61; cf. ll. 1564–6.

112. Hers is not, then, a *felix culpa* because there is neither fall nor *culpa*.

113. 'Identity' in the sense that it now has a new 'sameness' of political institutions: not in the sense that it is now homogeneous, essentially one.

114. See ll. 1751–806, especially ll. 1772–85.

115. On Brutus' prudence, see ll. 1807–17.

116. In implicit contrast to Tarquin as a parodically Petrarchan martyr to desire.

117. One must concede that, in *Lucrece*, the aetiological myth focused on the flow of blood from Lucrece's wound may do so too, although it seems more likely to be just an incongruous following of Ovidian convention.

Chapter 3

Shakespeare's Sonnets 1–19: The Young Man, the Poet and Father Time

(I) INTRODUCTION. PETRARCH, SIDNEY AND THE ELIZABETHAN SONNET

Shakespeare's Sonnets were published in 1609; beyond that, however, we know little of their transmission from manuscript to print.[1] They may have been written between 1592 and 1599, that is, from about the time when *Venus and Adonis* was being written until that when *The Passionate Pilgrim* was published. On the other hand, there is no shortage of alternative suggestions. It has been proposed, for example, that most of the Sonnets were written by 1589, that they were probably all written between 1591 and 1595 or 1593 and 1597, or that they were begun in the 1590s but completed thereafter.[2] Because of a remark by Francis Meres it seems likely that a number of the Sonnets were circulating 'among [Shakespeare's] private friends' before and (or) during 1598; yet exactly which sonnets, and did their being circulated (if it happened) affect either their composition or that of any which Shakespeare wrote subsequently?[3] Moreover, to what extent is the order of the poems Shakespeare's? Who was Mr W. H., to whom the publisher of the Sonnets dedicated them, and who was the youth (or, perhaps, who were the youths) to whom and about whom sonnets 1–126 were written? Were those two people one and the same – if, of course, the youth actually existed? Who was the Dark Lady of sonnets 127–52, assuming that she too really lived? The answer to each question is simply that no one knows; at present, to seek an answer is to enter a Sargasso Sea of ink and speculation.[4]

Leaving aside those as yet unresolved questions, one can at least begin to discuss Shakespeare's poems by considering some ways in which they belong to the fashion for sonnets, especially for so-called sequences of them, in England during the 1590s.[5] To do that means, given the centuries-long domination by Petrarch of the European literary language of love, first considering some ways in which the sonnets and other lyrics of Petrarch's *Rime* provided a model for the Elizabethan sonneteers – especially for Sir Philip Sidney, whose post-humously published *Astrophil and Stella* (1591) created the fashion for sonnet sequences in the last decade of the sixteenth century, and of course for Shakespeare, whose Sonnets suggest his awareness of both Petrarch's and Sidney's love poems. As Mario Praz demonstrated in his essay on the Petrarchism of the English Renaissance, when English poets encountered Petrarch's *Rime* (which was approximately from the late 1520s onward) they did so both centuries after its composition and revision and after many changes in continental literary as well as critical responses to it.[6] They thus encountered at much the same time Petrarch's love verse and that by various of his continental successors and commentators.[7] Petrarch himself, nonetheless, apparently remained pre-eminent in their eyes as the great reformulator of the language of love: as the old yet immediate, the intimidatingly authoritative yet sometimes tiresome, original with whose verse they had to come to terms, whether by following, repudiating or rivalling it.

Petrarch

It is certainly true that English poets were interested in Petrarch's paradoxical language and rhetoric of love. But his way of represent-ing the experience of passion was not wholly new to them, for they had seen something very like it in the love verse of their predeces-sors, English or French, who had written in the language and rhet-oric of courtly love verse; moreover, Petrarch's *Rime* almost constantly acknowledges its origins in the Provençal and Tuscan literary tradi-tions of *fine amour*. What was new to them, and what many of them tried to recreate other than Petrarch's language and rhetoric, was the persona whose consciousness that language and rhetoric at once fashion and manifest. To set that priority of the English sonneteers in perspective, something of the concerns, nature and situation of Petrarch's persona in his *Rime* must now be described, albeit briefly.[8] Framing that persona's reflections on his love for an unattainable lady – Laura, whom in *Rime* 211 he says he initially saw and desired on Good Friday 1327 – are two poems of contrition.[9] In the first (1), he looks back on his love as 'youthful error' and delight in an illusory good; in the second (366), he abandons thought of Laura for prayer to the Virgin Mary.[10] He turns, that is to say, from the lady who was once the 'sun' of his life to the lady who is 'clothed with the sun', the favoured servant of that 'Sun' who is God.[11] Between those framing poems, however, the persona relates his experience of love for Laura without suggesting that his passion has now been merely redirected: that sacred eros has simply displaced its profane counterpart.

Telling of and reflecting on moments in his long experience of love, the persona reveals again and again his uncertainty about the status of his passion. Insofar as his love for Laura is sexual he delights in it (22) but also repents of it (290).[12] Insofar as he envisions Laura as a type of the Virgin (30), a Beatrice figure (346) who has led him to pursue virtue (204) and seek heaven (72), he can view his love for her as ennobling and chaste.[13] Yet he acknowledges, too, that even his spiritual love for her is flawed, because in his passion for her he has loved a creature at the expense of the Creator (264), which implies his spiritual like his physical love to be a form of what St Augustine called *cupiditas*: a selfish, God-excluding desire for something made by God.[14] And the poems in which he idolizes Laura, or even blasphemously elides her with Christ, attest to that.[15] The paradoxical language and rhetoric of the *Rime* can be seen, therefore, as fashioning and manifesting a radically divided, self-contradictory persona, one who is all too aware of his confusion but who seems, until the end of the *Rime*, trapped in irreconcilable, paralysing contraries.[16]

A main reason for the persona's being trapped in paradoxes such as those described above lies in himself. In one poem, he reveals himself as responding to a Laura who is, in a number of ways, the projection of his own imaginings and desire, not to a Laura who is independent of them: a revelation that tends to suggest he can have no stable notion of his love for her (70, ll. 31–50).[17] It also tends to undermine his hyperbolic rhetoric of praise throughout the *Rime*.[18] Moreover, his implicit admission that he shapes, at least to some extent, the subjectivity of the Laura he worships can be seen as having significance for two important motifs in the *Rime*, namely, Laura as muse and Laura as a type of Narcissus.

Petrarch's persona identifies Laura as his muse (as in 9, for example) and says, of course, that she inspires him to write (151); he also concedes that she impedes his writing (20).[19] He cannot, he claims, accurately or adequately communicate what she is: his words cannot encompass her (247).[20] In *Rime* 308, to consider one instance, he asserts that although he can partly describe Laura's physical beauty he is unable to describe the beauty of her soul (ll. 9–14). Yet he seems marginally less overwhelmed by her physical than by her spiritual attractiveness. He acknowledges that he can only hint at a couple of its remarkable and myriad aspects. As he laments:

I have often tried in vain to depict in song for the age to come her high beauties, that it may love and prize them, nor with my style can I incarnate her lovely face.

Still now and again I dare to adumbrate one or two of the praises that were always hers, never any other's, that were as many as the stars spread across the sky. . . .

(ll. 5–11; cf. 70, l. 49)

However, if the muse at once baffling and inspiring the persona's art is, by his own admission, partly created by him, then not merely her inexpressibility but also her very capacity to inspire become questionable, for both are contaminated by their partial origins in him: to what extent does her inexpressibility result from his seeing and (or) inferring what he wants to (consciously or otherwise)?; to what degree is her inspiration a matter of him talking to himself? (Moreover, to what degree does her projected subjectivity reflect the instability and diversity of his own?) Precisely those queries link the the motif of Laura as muse to the motif of Laura as a type of Narcissus.

Among the classical myths through which the persona depicts his relationship with Laura – the tale of Daphne being predominant, with its suggestions of sexual desire's sublimation into art – the myth of Narcissus is one of the more telling.[21] In *Rime* 45 the persona explicitly accuses Laura of narcissism (see especially ll. 12–14). Like many of her successors in English sonnets, she is warned against a self-loving preoccupation with gazing into her mirror (see ll. 1–11); but the persona seems so much more obviously to be the Narcissus figure throughout the *Rime* than does his lady. Aware that his understanding of her is flawed, that his words cannot encompass her, and that the nature of his love itself is uncertain (see especially 290 and 360), the persona nonetheless obsessively contemplates Laura as a way of interpreting his experience of desire. That is to say, while he focuses on her because he is drawn irresistibly to her, he simultaneously focuses on her as a way of seeing himself: she is both the object of his passion and, through no fault of her own, his imperfect mirror.[22]

To have examined those contradictions within Petrarch's persona is barely to have outlined his characterization; even so, to have done that much indicates the intricacy of his fashioning and some aspects of it that English sonneteers would recreate. Before English sonneteers can be discussed, however, a few further aspects of Petrarch's persona in the *Rime* need to be mentioned. For a start, although love and, mostly, its discontents dominate him, political concerns also form part of his consciousness. The reader soon learns that the 'scattered rhymes', the 'varied style' (1, ll. 1 and 4) express a desire-riven persona who is troubled, too, by the political fragmentation of his native country (128).[23] Less troubling to the persona than either love or politics are two concerns that reveal further aspects of his characterization: patronage and friendship. At first, patronage and love are distinct in the *Rime*.[24] But subsequently they are represented as the twin rulers of the persona's life (114) and become almost identical (266, 269). Love and friendship occasionally merge, on the other hand, sharing a common language.[25] Thus the love which dominates the persona and his verse does not solely do so; and the interweaving of love, patronage, and friendship in Petrarch's *Rime* has counterparts in the poems of his English heirs.

Sidney's *Astrophil and Stella*

What seems to be the first appearance of the *Rime* in English verse is, as everyone observes, Chaucer's recreation of poem 132 in his *Troilus and Criseyde*: '*S'amor non e . . .*' appears in 1, 400–20 as the beginning of the *Canticus Troili*.[26] If indeed Chaucer's *Song of Troilus* does first and partly bring the *Rime* into English verse, then that might be thought important for more than one reason. That the *Rime* first appears there in English is important as a matter of innovation, to be sure, yet arguably more important is the fact that the innovator was Chaucer, who could be seen thereafter as having lent, in effect, a patriarch's authority to the arrival in England of Petrarchan love verse. It is also arguably more important that Chaucer's poem recreates a Petrarchan sonnet expressing the narcissus motif: the Petrarchan persona, when initially translated into England, appears in his guise as Narcissus refigured. Whether in his guise as another Narcissus or otherwise, however, he seems not to have appeared again in English verse until Wyatt and Surrey began to imitate poems from the *Rime*. Their doing so and its implications are nonetheless not the main concern here, for it was Sir Philip Sidney who directly initiated the fashion in the 1590s for writing sonnet sequences which look warily back to Petrarch. Discussion must therefore focus on how he, then Shakespeare, came to terms with and departed from what might be called the Petrarchan discourse of love.

In the opening sonnet of *Astrophil and Stella* one discovers a speaker, Astrophil, who tells of that moment when he decided to write of his love for his lady, Stella.[27] At that moment, he says, he imagined her as his only reader, and therefore began to seek how to express his desire most truly and persuasively (ll. 1–5). Recounting his attempt to choose a language through which to represent himself as a lover, he in effect relates his attempt to find that language of love through which he could establish his existence as a lover. According to his story, initially he associated literary convention with natural expression, for he describes himself as '[o]ft turning others' leaves to see if thence would flow / Some fresh and fruitful showers upon my sun-burned brain' (ll. 7–8). His narrative insists there on merging the artificial with the natural; art is man's nature, he seemingly determined in anticipation of Burke. Yet immediately he decries his association of artifice with nature. He indicates that, in his preceding words, the catachrestic images of research as potential regeneration imply not his having accurately discerned sameness beneath apparent difference but rather his mistake in having yoked opposites together. 'But words came halting forth, wanting invention's stay; / Invention, nature's child, fled step-dame Study's blows, / And others' feet still seemed but strangers in my way,' he says (ll. 9–11). His elaborate allegory of poetic inspiration then ends: 'Thus, great with child to speak, and helpless in my throes, / Biting my truant pen, beating myself for spite, / Fool, said my Muse to me, look in thy heart and write' (ll. 12–14). What Astrophil would have found when supposedly looking in his heart might be anyone's guess, except that in subsequent poems he mentions very clearly what was there. In his heart lay, notionally then as throughout all his experience of love, an image of his lady.[28] Petrarch's persona had of course claimed that in his heart lay an image of Laura.[29] So Astrophil's muse simultaneously implies his mode of expressing himself as a lover and his very existence as a lover to be grounded in Petrarchan precedent, to be situated in Petrarchan convention. Astrophil's muse thus naturalizes the Petrarchan language and rhetoric of love; she reaffirms its authority and thereby specifically reaffirms the association between artifice and (human) nature, literary convention and natural expression.

The subtly arguing images that unfold the sonnet's elaborate allegory of poetic inspiration are, of course, also comically hyperbolic. They both develop a complicated argument and characterize Astrophil as a melodramatic lover who naively blunders into verse. There is a contradiction, then, between the sophistication of Astrophil's account of his quest for poetic inspiration and his self-characterization as love's fool and stumbling versifier. Yet the sonnet does not confront the reader with a simple juxtaposition of opposites; rather, Astrophil's complicated, allusive argument and the intricate rhetoric with which he puts it forward ostentatiously belie his representation of himself as a mere caricature of the noble lover fashioning noble verse. One recognizes, as one is meant to, the astuteness with which Astrophil stages his amused, good-natured, disingenuous confession of supposed clumsiness and naivety. And thus recognizing the calculatedness of Astrophil's supposedly amazed, climactic discovery that Petrarchan discourse is the natural voice of a true lover's feelings, one recognizes too that Astrophil's own discourse of love will be meta-Petrarchan, not merely that of someone content to be Petrarch's remote and imperfect echo. One perceives that Astrophil is a deliberately and self-revealingly unreliable narrator.

He is an unpredictably and sometimes delightedly unreliable narrator, it could be added. But perhaps the meta-Petrarchism of Sidney's sonnets can be briefly described as follows. In *Astrophil and Stella* there are many motifs derived from the *Rime*; to put it another way, in Sidney's sonnets there are many allusions to Petrarch's. For example, there is an allusion to the idea of the lady's image being carried within her lover's heart (*Rime* 32, 64, 96, 100, and so on). Other examples abound: Astrophil, like Petrarch's speaker, constructs his role as lover in terms of his image of his lady (cf. *Rime* 168, 290, 360 and 361 / *Astrophil and Stella* 1, 9, 39 and so on); love is represented as causing a civil war within Astrophil, as it is within the Petrarchan persona (68–9, 101, 240 / 4, 5, 39, 40); Petrarch's persona celebrates Laura's eyes, Astrophil praises Stella's (3, 9, 11, among a great many instances / 7, 9, 11, likewise). Further examples need not be given; more important is consideration of how such Petrarchan motifs in *Astrophil and Stella* become elements of a meta-Petrarchan text. Sidney achieves that primarily by weaving them into the characterization of a persona who, while therefore recalling the persona of the *Rime*, differs significantly from his predecessor. One difference is of course obvious and powerful. Although Petrarch's persona and Sidney's are both dominated by desire, the former renounces his desire for Laura, whether or not one thinks his doing so to be ambivalent, whereas the latter does not repudiate his desire for Stella. He persists in it, viewing it as radically flawed yet often rejoicing in its transgressiveness.[30] Nor does he turn from his desire although he knows it to be hopeless.[31]

There are further and more specific differences as well. As was mentioned above, Petrarch's persona, for all his tendency to identify Laura with Beatrice, nonetheless finally turns from her service to that of God and of the Virgin, whereas Astrophil does not turn from Stella's service to that of God. But Astrophil is also unlike Petrarch's persona inasmuch as he is a courtier, and a supposed servant of a queen among whose roles is the guise of Petrarchan lady.[32] In having become and in remaining Stella's servant, Astrophil has implicitly placed and continues to place devotion to her before devotion to his politically Petrarchan mistress.[33] He takes great pains, in fact, to emphasize that he has failed as a courtier because he has become love's fool. Through a parody of the judgement of Paris myth he reveals that he has rejected a courtly life focused on political power or on military achievement for a courtly life focused on love of Stella.[34] Astrophil's version of the myth has Phoebus make the choice, not Astrophil himself; moreover, the divinities and hence their genders have of course been altered in order to suit the gender of Astrophil and the chief ways of life supposedly open to him as a courtier. When, however, Phoebus makes the choice in favour of Love/Cupid (the Alexandrian Cupid), he does that not merely in accord with his function as a judge in the affairs of humankind but also in his capacity as god of poetry, who can confer fame.[35] Astrophil the lover and poet celebrates (creates) in verse the choice made by the god of poetry. And Phoebus' choice seems apt, given that the shields of both Jove and Mars attest to the Alexandrian Cupid's power over the two gods.[36] Nonetheless, in approving Phoebus' choice Astrophil signals that as a courtier he has turned from political and military pursuits to the pursuit of his beloved. Choosing with Phoebus in favour of Love, he has diminished the meaning of 'courtiership' in his life: it signifies not 'courtiership' in an inclusive sense but solely his 'courting' of Stella. It may be that in the *Rime* Petrarch's persona intimates his love for Laura to be, for him, a second Fall; in *Astrophil and Stella*, however, Astrophil at once fables that his love for his lady enhances his dignity and intimates that his love means, in addition to his entrapment in *concupiscentia*, his failure if not exactly his fall as a courtier.

The interaction between courtiership and courting forms one of Astrophil's main preoccupations.[37] The reader soon learns, though, that just as in the initial sonnet of *Astrophil and Stella* Astrophil manages both to assert and to disprove his clumsiness as a poet, so throughout the sequence he both asserts and disproves his failure as a courtier. That is not to suggest either Astrophil's constant success as a poet or – insofar as one might draw inferences – his predominant success as a courtier. But it is to suggest for example, with reference to the former, that in sonnet 20 Astrophil's melodrama seems calculated and ludic: he appears to be rewriting, with an elaborate rhetoric of comic insistence and exaggeration (and with the black beauty topos) the Petrarchan motif of the lady's irresistible eye and its conquest of the lover. And it is to suggest that Astrophil, whatever his wry, often elegant gestures of self-deprecation, repeatedly reveals his connoisseurship in courtly aesthetic values and techniques. Surveying some contemporary modes of courtly writing (sonnet 3), he indicates at once his knowledge, control, and transcendence of those modes (ll. 1–8), for all his then gracefully confessing to his narrow limitations as a poet (ll. 9–11), and thus indicates that he will not simply reproduce the Petrarchan mode whose authority he finally reasserts (ll. 12–14). In sonnets 7 and 70 he plays with the *ut pictura poesis* motif. In 42 he works variations on the motifs of *Venus Victrix* and of *Venus Verticordia*. In 48 he rewrites the motif of Virtue reconciled with Pleasure, ending the poem with elaborately melodramatic, sexually punning speech.

Moreover, as regards Astrophil's self-confessed failure as a courtier, one might suggest that although he does virtually proclaim himself a failure he also chooses to reveal something of what his political and military talents as a courtier, if now obscured by passion, nonetheless are. In sonnet 30, for example, Astrophil shows himself turning his back on political matters, yet in doing so he concisely displays his knowledge of European politics and his status as a person whose political views are sought by those more ostensibly involved with politics than he is (ll. 1–11 and 12, respectively). Further, he carefully points to his family connection with major political events (ll. 9–10) – one of the many broad hints, to be qualified by the emphasis on metafictionality in *Astrophil and Stella*, that Astrophil is a mask for Sidney.[38] Therefore his self-deprecatory last words, in which he says he 'know[s] not how' he answers political questions (l. 14), imply not his incompetence as a courtier but the talent that his passion for Stella has suppressed ('for still I think of you,' he goes on to tell her in l. 14). Astrophil indicates his skills as a political analyst in other poems, too, though insofar as he uses them he does so in the service of love: he subordinates politics to desire, making political analysis a means for examining his experience as a lover (see, for example, 29 and 85). In sonnet 107, however, he uses political analysis in order to ask that Stella temporarily release him from his duty to her, presumably so that he may engage in politics other than those of love.

Astrophil's representation of his political skills and potential accords with the way in which he represents himself as a martial figure. The two are not, however, entirely in agreement. In sonnet 41 Astrophil images himself as a triumphant knightly hero, a truly chivalric hero because he attributes his military success to the 'heavenly' influence of his lady (ll. 12–14, specific reference being to l. 13). In sonnet 53, by way of contrast, Astrophil presents himself as a knight who once could not even advance against his opponent. Yet there Astrophil also relates that he failed because Cupid, his lord, would not allow him to act in the service of Mars – which he had been doing successfully (ll. 1–8). As Astrophil tells it, Cupid asserted his lordship by ordering him to look at Stella. Love's true servant that he was, and is, he did look at her, becoming overwhelmed by her beauty and thereupon unable to move. So the beauty which supposedly empowered him on one occasion supposedly disabled him on another. Astrophil thus suggests that he does not lack military talent but that his military, much like his political, skills and potential are constrained by passion: although passion is claimed, in 41, to have benefited him militarily at least once, 53 seems to imply that his service of the Alexandrian Cupid precludes him from service of Mars, a notion congruent with the fable of choice in 13. Astrophil images himself as a courtier who has failed in chief concerns of male courtly life solely because desire rules him.

According to Castiglione's *The Courtier* and other such studies of the courtier's life, of course, love is itself an important concern of the male courtier. So while one might reasonably propose that Astrophil's (*de facto*) choosing Love over Jove and Mars (sonnet 13) has diminished the meaning or actuality of 'courtiership' in his life, another way of putting the idea might be this: Astrophil's life, inasmuch as he sets it before his readers, reveals different, important aspects of the male courtier's life in conflict. Moreover, in the love-engendered conflict which characterizes Astrophil one witnesses conflict among authorities and discourses important to, if not only to, the Elizabethan courtly world. Much of that conflict concerns the nature of human love. Astrophil reveals his experience of love as being divided between spiritual love (of the neoplatonic kind advocated in *The Courtier*) and physical love (of the voracious kind denigrated in *The Courtier*). Yet he obliquely and directly reveals that the two loves are not separable or often distinguishable.[39] Further, just as the speaker's desire in the *Rime*, whether spiritual or physical, is variously and finally indicated to be a manifestation of *cupiditas*, so Astrophil's desire seems inescapably, whether spiritual or physical, but more obviously in the case of the latter, to be a manifestation of *concupiscentia*: concupiscence, probably in Calvin's meaning of the term.[40] There is in *Astrophil and Stella*, then, conflict within the boundaries of Castiglione's neoplatonic discourse of love (spiritual versus physical desire) and conflict between neoplatonic and Protestant discourses of love (Castiglione's and Calvin's). The contradiction, a qualified one as has just been suggested, between neoplatonic and Protestant discourses implies a number of things. The most important of those would seem to be that neoplatonic, spiritual *eros* is *concupiscentia* under another name. If such an elision is being argued, as seems to be so, then in acknowledging his inability to distinguish carnal from spiritual love Astrophil is also indirectly acknowledging that the Petrarchan discourse of love – the authority of which he has reaffirmed from the start of *Astrophil and Stella* – is natural to humanity in its experience of fallen desire and therefore the 'natural man's' discourse of love. He would be reaffirming both the Petrarchan persona's condemnation of carnal love and, in relation to *concupiscentia* rather than to *cupiditas,* that persona's condemnation of creature-centred spiritual love (the persona's condemnation, that is, of his own profane discourse) without taking them as examples to be followed, for he does not turn from Stella whereas the *Rime* ends with rejection of Laura. Astrophil's experience of love as self-conflicting and (hence) conflict-generating thus expresses conflicts between neoplatonic and Protestant discourses and appears to deconstruct, through a curious mingling of reaffirmation and denial, the authority of Petrarchism as a courtly discourse of love.

Yet the neoplatonic discourse of love as represented in *Astrophil and Stella* is not, one hardly need say, associated with Castiglione and nobody else. In other words, the discourse of love implicated in what seems to be Astrophil's intricate reaffirmation and negation of Petrarchism does not have Castiglione as its sole authority. There may be allusion to his *The Courtier* (see, for example, 5, 1–4 and 9–11) but there are allusions as well to Ficino (songs 3 and 5) and to Plato himself (25). So the opposition staged between the neoplatonic and the Protestant involves, at least in the case of the former, a varied cast of authorities. Plato, Ficino and Castiglione are set against Calvin, yet this warring of authorities and of discourses is not as straight-forward as it might be thought. Castiglione and Calvin implicitly contradict each other in sonnet 5 (ll. 1–11; cf. *The Courtier* 4, 62 and *Institutes* 1, 11, 8–9).[41] However, Astrophil sometimes analyses his confused experience of love in terms that suggest the (immediate) irrelevance of Calvinist categories, since he can of course evaluate the uneasy physicality of his love – as he can its spirituality – with reference to neoplatonic categories alone.[42] But perhaps the most important point about the conflict of discourses is implicit in the ending of *Astrophil and Stella*. The sequence ends without narrative closure or resolution of its warring discourses: at its end remain desire without fulfilment and discursive conflict without conclusion.

(II) NARCISSUS CALLED TO ACCOUNT

The relations between Shakespeare's Sonnets and the Petrarchan discourse of love are intricately initiated in the early poems, the Petrarchan elements of which mingle sometimes harmoniously, sometimes discordantly, with the non-Petrarchan. It has long been recognized that the first seventeen of Shakespeare's Sonnets, which urge a young man to marry and have children, draw on images and ideas used by Erasmus in one of the model letters he wrote for his *On the Writing of Letters*.[43] That letter illustrates how to write persuasively and by way of example it exhorts an imaginary young man to marry and have children, thereby perpetuating both himself and his ancestry. Thomas Wilson translated and printed the letter in his *The Art of Rhetoric* (1553); it is specifically to Wilson's translation that Shakespeare was indebted in the early sonnets.[44] It has also been long recognized, however, that in those early sonnets Shakespeare drew possibly on images and ideas from a couple more Erasmian texts and definitely from those in yet other texts written neither by Petrarch nor by his successors. Erasmus' colloquy *The Wooer and the Maiden* and his *The Education of a Christian Prince* may have provided him with material. Writings by Ovid (in Golding's translation) and by Marlowe contributed as well to the early sonnets. But how did they and other such texts contribute, and to what? How did they, and those Petrarchan or Petrarch-derived (or significantly Petrarch-affiliated) texts on which Shakespeare drew, interact? Within that broadly inclusive category of the Petrarchan one would have to list, for example, the *Rime*, Sidney's *Arcadia* as well as his *Astrophil and Stella*, and Samuel Daniel's *Delia* (1592). What relations with the Petrarchan discourse of love are initiated, then, in the early poems? In trying to answer those questions I shall focus on the first nineteen sonnets, for the eighteenth and nineteenth poems directly continue the concerns of their predecessors whereas the twentieth poem appears to introduce changes of emphasis and of theme.

The way to begin is probably by considering the use of the Narcissus myth in the first four sonnets. It was suggested above that in his *Rime* Petrarch's speaker accuses Laura of narcissism but in fact constantly displays his own, destabilizing preoccupation with himself. It was also suggested that, in English sonnet sequences modelled more or less on the *Rime*, the Narcissus myth often functions in a similar way. The male speaker of the poems often tells his beloved to stop gazing narcissistically into her mirror yet in effect uses her as a mirror in which to ponder his own experience of desire. The male speaker tends to do that, in fact, whether or not he warns his lady against preoccupation with her mirrored image. Petrarch's speaker is aware of his ironic self-absorption; how many of his descendants in English sonnet sequences understand themselves so well is debatable.

Sidney's Astrophil is a useful case in point, given the popularity and influence of *Astrophil and Stella*. He appears to acknowledge, in the eighteenth and ninety-fourth sonnets, for instance, the narcissism implicated in his courtship of Stella. Elsewhere he makes that disclosure without even appearing to be aware that he does so. For example, in sonnet 27 he denies allegations of narcissism and asserts that he is, rather, an opposite to Narcissus: 'Yet pride I think doth not my soul possess,/ Which looks too oft in his unflatt'ring glass' (ll. 9–10). But his denial nonetheless emphasizes his preoccupation with himself; a similar ambiguity can be seen in sonnet 90. In sonnet 34, Astrophil implies distinctly that his art is narcissistic but there, likewise, his revelation seems unselfconscious. Questioning himself, he asks: 'How can words ease, which are/ The glasses of thy daily vexing care' (ll. 2–3). His answer, in part a Petrarchan one, suggests obliviousness of or indifference to the narcissism hinted at in the question: 'Oft cruel fights well pictured forth do please' (l. 4). There he unwittingly acknowledges that, even if he did begin – as he claimed in the opening poem – with the notion of writing for Stella alone, he now also writes for himself about himself. There he intimates that, obsessed with Stella, he is obsessed too with the images of his frustration and loss mirrored in his words.[45] In the first four of Shakespeare's Sonnets, however, the reader sees a different if not wholly dissimilar evocation of the Narcissus myth, one that will dominate the initial nineteen poems and thereby form a prelude to use of the myth in sonnets 20–126.

The opening poem unmistakably associates the young man, to whom it is addressed, with Narcissus:

> But thou, contracted to thine own bright eyes,
> Feed'st thy light's flame with self-substantial fuel,
> Making a famine where abundance lies –
> Thyself thy foe, to thy sweet self too cruel.
>
> (ll. 5–8)

Although Shakespeare's persona uses the myth to suggest the self-absorption of the young man whose beauty he celebrates so elaborately in this and in the other early sonnets, he does not use it to imply that between himself and the young man there exists a relationship akin to that between a Petrarchan lover and the idealized object of his desire. In this poem, as in the next eight, his tone resembles that of a benign counsellor, being at times sharp, at times playful, but always respectful whether he speaks in praise of the young man or in reproach of him, in persuasion or encouragement. Such a tone of address is decorous,

of course, as Shakespeare's persona reveals that the young man belongs
to some great family, that he has, in conjunction with his respons-
ibility to marry and so perpetuate his beauty in the world through his
offspring, a responsibility to father legitimate children and so per-
petuate the aristocratic dynasty of which he is apparently the latest
member (for example, see 10, ll. 7–8). And therein, in the persona's
constant dwelling on the young man's obligation to marry and breed,
lies the obvious yet not simple difference between the use of the
Narcissus myth in the early sonnets and its use in the *Rime, Astrophil
and Stella*, or even in sonnets 20–126.

It is the words 'contracted to thine own bright eyes', in the lines
quoted above, that help to clarify the matter. Through those words
the persona implies both the young man's narcissism and its intensity.
The youth is not like the speaker of Donne's 'The Extasy', who tells
of his gaze, and that of his mistress, as entwined (ll. 7–8). The young
man's gaze is self-reflexive, like his archetype's, his narcissism being
so intense that it is as if he were betrothed ('contracted') to himself,
to his own self-regarding eyes. Moreover, his supposed betrothal to
himself is also, and therefore, self-diminution: a 'contraction' into
himself of his existence as distinct from an expansion of his existence
through marriage and breeding (contrast 'The Sun Rising', ll. 21–
30).[46] The youth's being represented as 'contracted to [his] own bright
eyes' has other functions, too. In addition to suggesting his narcissism
and its intensity, the trope introduces all the Erasmian and related allu-
sions which imply the unnaturalness, and hence self-destructiveness,
attendant upon the youth's self-love and refusal thus far to marry
another. Allusions to Erasmus in the early poems can be seen in
sonnet 2, perhaps more distinctly in and after sonnet 3; it is clear, in
any event, that some images in the initial sonnet accord, at least, with
the images which Shakespeare derived from Erasmus' model letter
and, perhaps, other writings. Those allusions will not be itemized
here, nor will those to the related non-Petrarchan texts with which
the early poems have links; that has been already and usefully done.
More functional at this point might be an account of some important
ideas that the allusions to the Erasmian text(s) evoke and contribute
to the portrayal of the young man as another Narcissus, the allusions
to other non-Petrarchan texts being considered thereafter.

An immediately relevant as well as important idea, evoked by
allusions to the Erasmian model letter, is simply that through one's
children one achieves something like immortality, renewing and
perpetuating one's finite, declining existence. In his letter, as trans-
lated by Wilson, Erasmus writes:

Now again, what a joy shall this be unto you, when your most fair wife shall make you a father in bringing forth a fair child unto you, where you shall have a pretty little boy running up and down your house . . . by whom you shall seem to be newborn. . . .
For what man can be grieved that he is old, when he seeth his own countenance which he had being a child to appear lively in his son? Death is ordained for all mankind, and yet by this means only nature by her providence mindeth unto us a certain immortality, while she increaseth one thing upon another, even as a young graff buddeth out when the old tree is cut down. Neither can he seem to die that, when God calleth him, leaveth a young child behind him.

(Wilson, pp. 94–5)

There are allusions to the model letter, and specifically to the quoted passages, from the second sonnet onward. But the idea of approximating immortality through one's children is, in that Erasmian text to which the early sonnets certainly allude, part of a group of ideas centred on marriage and procreation. Directly or indirectly, allusions in the early sonnets evoke the main components of that ideational group or cluster, which are frequently expressed through images of ploughing, crops and the like. Marriage, according to Erasmus' model letter, was instituted by divine law and is one of the principles of natural law. The Erasmian persona observes that God, 'after the general flood, being reconciled to mankind, is said [to have] proclaim[ed] this law first of all, not that men should live single, but that they should increase, be multiplied, and fill the earth. But how, I pray you, could this thing be, saving by marriage . . . ?' (Wilson, p. 81). Later, he remarks: '[I]f a man following the law of nature do labor to get children, he is ever to be preferred before him that liveth unmarried for none other end but because he would be out of trouble and live more free' (Wilson, p. 83). Soon after, he refers to the condemnation of 'the single life of bachelors' by the law of Moses (ibid.). To avoid marriage and children is, then, to defy divine law and to act unnaturally. It is also, according to Erasmus' letter, to deny one's civic responsibility, one's duty to the maintenance of civil society:

Therefore, as he is counted no good gardener that being content with things present doth diligently prune his old trees, and hath no regard either to imp or graff young sets because the selfsame orchard (though it be never so well trimmed) must needs decay in time, and all the trees die within few years, so he is not to be counted half a diligent citizen that being content with the present multitude hath no regard to increase the number.

(Wilson, pp. 87–8)

Again:

> If that man be punished who little heedeth the maintenance of his tillage (the which although it be never so well manured, yet it yieldeth nothing else but wheat, barley beans, and peasen), what punishment is he worthy to suffer that refuseth to plough that land which being tilled yieldeth children?
>
> (Wilson, p. 92)

After all, the elements of the world itself, Erasmus' persona suggests, maintain life by something like marital union:

> What say you of the sky or firmament that is ever stirring with continual moving? Doth it not play the part of a husband while it puffeth up the earth, the mother of all things, and maketh it fruitful with casting seed (as a man would say) upon it [?]
>
> (Wilson, p. 86)

That is the group of ideas, or field of argument, evoked by the Erasmian allusions in the early sonnets; even though its more otherworldly elements are at best marginal to depiction of the youth as another Narcissus, its main components are crucial to that depiction.

They imply, of course, that the youth's narcissism exiles him from the world, no matter how resplendent and how prominent he may seem to be within it. Primarily they suggest that his self-love denies him personal renewal, immortality insofar as that can be conferred by one's child (or children), and thus that his self-love denies the world the continuance of his beauty. Yet in doing so they indicate as well that his narcissism sets him in defiance of natural law, makes him evade his responsibility to civil society and, ultimately, detaches him from the pattern of marital union which pervades not merely the human world but even the physical world. In his guise as Narcissus, then, the youth both resembles and differs from the ladies praised and complained of, or to, in the verse of Petrarch and of his English successors. Like them he is accused of narcissism; unlike them, he is accused of a narcissism which hurts not a lover but himself, his family and the world because he will not marry and breed. Furthermore, he is male; but that difference, striking though it may be, cannot be seen as merely straightforward. Although throughout the first nineteen sonnets Shakespeare's persona does not celebrate a female object of desire in Petrarchan terms, he does represent the youth as a counterpart to the ideal lady of Petrarchan tradition. The young man is identified in sonnet 1 as 'beauty's rose' (l. 2) and the persona mentions his 'bright eyes' (l. 5); the persona warns the young man, in sonnet 2, that age will mar his perfect beauty with wrinkles (ll. 1–2); in sonnet 3, the young man is associated with the beauty of spring (at the same time he is associated with the implicitly ideal beauty of his mother in her youth, the relevant phrase being 'the lovely April of her prime', l. 10).[47] As the phrase just quoted makes clear, the third sonnet's intimation that the young man has an androgynous beauty elaborates on the persona's declaration in sonnet 1: 'Thou . . . art now the world's fresh ornament/ And only herald to the gaudy spring' (ll. 9–10). There the youth, initially figured as another Narcissus, becomes also another Adonis, whom Shakespeare feminizes in *Venus and Adonis* chiefly by means of Petrarchan imagery. It is interesting, moreover, that in *Venus and Adonis* the goddess of love compares Adonis to Narcissus but her anachronistically Petrarchan comparison seems wrong in several important respects, whereas in sonnet 1 the young man becomes an Adonis who is indeed narcissistic (see ll. 11–12). Thus do the non-Petrarchan and Petrarchan elements in the Sonnets begin to interact; thus, in part at least, Shakespeare initiates his poems' relations with Petrarchan discourse.

How Shakespeare developed his representation of the youth as Narcissus, and what that means for his poems' interactions with Petrarchan discourse, come into focus if one returns to the opening sonnet. It was suggested above that the Erasmian allusions in the early sonnets imply the narcissistic youth's various estrangement from the world. The first sonnet indicates some specific and important aspects of that. For a start, the persona's remark to the youth, 'Thyself thy foe, to thy sweet self too cruel' (l. 8), in effect depicts the young man as a counterpart to a narcissistic Petrarchan lady, but a counterpart whose 'cruel' self-love injures himself rather than a lover, so that it is as if he were involved in a Petrarchan relationship with himself. Moreover, when the persona later ends the oblique, momentary picturing of the youth as another Adonis with the words, 'Within thine own bud buriest thy content,/ And tender churl mak'st waste in niggarding' (ll. 11–12), he intimates that the youth, as Adonis/ Narcissus, turns away from *Venus Genetrix* – which Adonis likewise does in *Venus and Adonis* – and also that he turns away from the reconciliation of chastity with pleasure in marriage (cf. ll. 5–6), a denial of the proper accord between *Virtus* and *Amor*.[48] Erasmus' speaker in the model letter uses that 'reconciliation' motif when praising marriage and so does the young man in *The Wooer and the Maiden*.[49]

The representation of the youth as Narcissus is then deftly developed, in the second sonnet, by the speaker's saying to the young man:

Then being asked where all thy beauty lies –
Where all the treasure of thy lusty days –
To say within thine own deep-sunken eyes
Were an all-eating shame and thriftless praise.

(ll. 5–8)

That the quatrain alludes to the parable of the talents (Matthew 25: 14–30; cf. the subsequent quatrain) seems clear and has been variously noted. But how does the allusion work? It initiates, I think, a calling to account of Narcissus, that is, a process in which the young man in his role as Narcissus is told to what and to whom he must answer for his narcissism. The speaker's evocation of the parable of the talents implies, for a start, that the youth will have to answer to human judgement rather than to divine law and the God who framed it. The imagined punishment of the young man is set firmly in the present world ('all-eating shame and thriftless praise', l. 8) and its being so agrees with what occurs in the next poem, where Narcissus is made accountable to himself. Sonnet 3 distinctly suggests that, for all the otherworldly implications residual in the secularized biblical allusion and penumbral to the Erasmian ones, the emphasis in these poems falls on what is and what will be in the realm of mortality. 'Look in thy glass and tell the face thou viewest,/ Now is the time that face should form another,' the speaker begins. *Carpe diem*, he counsels, yet he does not simply urge that point. The wit of his opening words lies in his telling Narcissus to look in the mirror and to give wise advice to himself: stop being merely narcissistic and give your renewed, living image to the world.[50] Perhaps the finest touch in this gracefully and ingeniously persuasive sonnet is, however, the speaker's remark to the youth that he lives as a mirror to his mother's past, extraordinary beauty: 'Thou art thy mother's glass, and she in thee/ Calls back the lovely April of her prime' (ll. 9–10). If the young man is to look in the mirror and speak wisdom to his image, a wisdom that will not end his self-love but productively deflect it (for unless he loves someone else and breeds, the prime object of his love will not survive), he is also to recognize that he himself is a mirror because he reflects the beauty of his mother. In him her past beauty lives, for her as for others, and so he manifests the pattern of renewal, a prudent and generous self-love, at the same time as his improvident self-love, his contentment with just the image to be viewed in his 'glass', repudiates both. He must transform his narcissism or allow it to transform him into its tomb: 'Or who is he so fond will be the tomb/ Of his self-love to stop posterity?' (ll. 7–8).

Finally, in the fourth sonnet, Narcissus is shown that he will be answerable to nature: 'Then how when nature calls thee to be gone,/ What acceptable audit canst thou leave?' (ll. 11–12). The parable of the talents is again secularized. Nature has lent beauty to the youth; to clear the debt he must propagate that beauty. Yet it is not solely the fact of God's replacement by nature that desanctifies the parable. Shakespeare's persona insistently images the bounty of nature and the youth's responsibility to nature in economic terms: '[u]nthrifty loveliness' and 'spend' in the opening verse, then 'thy beauty's legacy' in the next; '[n]ature's bequest' as well as 'lend' in verse three, and 'lends . . . free' in verse four; then on to 'beauteous niggard' (l. 5), 'bounteous largess' (l. 6), '[p]rofitless usurer' (l. 7) and so on. The speaker's secularizing of the parable cannot be doubted, but how his economic imagery is to be interpreted, in this poem and in the poems that follow, seems less clear. Earlier images, for example those of 'niggarding' (1, 12), of 'worth' (2, 4) and of 'sum[ming an] account' (2, 13), are amplified by the iteratively economic images in the fourth sonnet; that strand of images accords, moreover, with the Erasmian images of 'increase' (1, 1), of ploughing, crops and the like.[51] Thus, if one pursues the argument unfolded largely through the economic and the Erasmian imagery, the speaker has indicated to the narcissistic young man why, to whom and to what he will be called to account. Nevertheless, is the speaker imposing on the aristocratic youth a merely bourgeois world view? And, if he is, does that not merely reflect Shakespeare's milieu as a professional playwright and suggest the limits of his speaker's perspective on experience? To seek answers to those questions one must turn to the rest of the early sonnets.

(III) THE ECONOMY OF NATURE, FATHER TIME AND
THE WISDOM OF NARCISSUS

Sonnets 5–19 do not suggest, I think, that Shakespeare's speaker imposes a bourgeois world view of profit and loss on the aristocratic young man but, rather, that he pictures the youth as being necessarily caught up in the economy of nature. In other words, the Erasmian images of 'increase' and the economic images of profit and loss in the first four sonnets combine to establish as a point of reference for the rest of the early poems – and in fact for all the subsequent ones – the classical notion that the world as a whole functions in diverse patterns of birth, growth, decline and renewal, of need and fulfilment, of forfeit and compensation.[52] The language of everyday economics helps to provide metaphors for the more intricate economy of the world. Shakespeare's speaker remarks in sonnet 64, for example:

> . . . I have seen the hungry ocean gain
> Advantage on the kingdom of the shore,
> And the firm soil win of the watery main,
> Increasing store with loss, and loss with store.
>
> (ll. 5–8)

His phrase in the next line, 'interchange of state', epitomizes the process imaged by simple economic imagery and chiasmus in line 8. It could be argued, of course, that Shakespeare's speaker is thus naturalizing capitalism; one might reply, however, that his speaker is using capitalism – or something like it – as a way of making immediate to the youth the great forces acting upon and surrounding him. In effect, Shakespeare's speaker makes Narcissus look beyond the mirror and see a representation of his place in the scheme of things.

What that representation is, and what it implies about the youth and about Shakespeare's speaker, can be discovered in part from the fifth sonnet. That poem, like a number of the remaining early sonnets (7, 15, 19, for example), images the working of the world, the economy of nature in process, as if it were an ever-unfolding, courtly pageant:

> Those hours that with gentle work did frame
> The lovely gaze where every eye doth dwell
> Will play the tyrants to the very same
> And that unfair which fairly doth excel:
> For never-resting time leads summer on
> To hideous winter and confounds him there,
> Sap checked with frost and lusty leaves quite gone,
> Beauty o'ersnowed and bareness everywhere.
> Then were not summer's distillation left
> A liquid pris'ner pent in walls of glass,
> Beauty's effect with beauty were bereft,
> Nor it nor no remembrance what it was.
>   But flow'rs distilled, though they with winter meet,
>   Leese but their show, their substance still lives sweet.

In the ceremonial drama of the sonnet's opening quatrains, Shakespeare's speaker presents the 'hours' as 'gentle[women]' who have favoured the young man but who will also tyrannize over him. They resemble, then, the ladies of courtly love poems – but so does the youth. He is presented in Petrarchan terms, being at once the beautiful creature gazed upon by all and the desired creature possessing alluringly beautiful eyes ('The lovely gaze where every eye doth dwell'). Time, as personified by the 'hours', has made him pre-eminent in the world yet, nonetheless, as vulnerable as anything else in it. The ritual of Father Time's leading summer to 'hideous winter' argues the common fate of beauty in the economy of nature. But as the epilogue of the last six lines suggests, especially through allusion to Sidney's *New Arcadia* (in ll. 9–12), the economy of nature preserves beauty for time to bring forth again.[53] The miniature pageant and its epilogue seem, therefore, to offer the aristocratic young man an elegant, ambiguous representation of his place in the scheme of things.

The representation of the young man's place in the economy of nature is, of course, ambiguous insofar as it implies him to be an androgyne; it is also ambiguous because it suggests that, for all his being uniquely beautiful and hence prominent in the world, the natural forces which have produced and favoured him will treat him as they do everyone and everything else. That notion is implicit in the preceding sonnets and is suggested again in sonnets 6 and 7. From sonnet 10 onward, however, it gains a social dimension. In the tenth sonnet one learns, although there are hints before then (as in 3, ll. 9–10, for example), that the young man belongs to some great family. From sonnet 10, therefore, one perceives that the fifth sonnet and its successors emphasize the vulnerability of a person who is socially prominent as well as prominent because of his unique beauty.[54] The aristocratic young man is emphasized in the fifth and subsequent poems to be, so to speak, caught up in power relations of another class altogether: he is outclassed when choosing to deal dismissively with – in choosing narcissistically to ignore – the economy of nature.

His dealings, or non-dealings, with the economy of nature are characterized in sonnet 5, as in the subsequent early poems, by his relations with time, which are really time's relations with him. The miniature pageant that the speaker stages in the sonnet has manifestations of time as its supporting cast – given that the young man is its central figure. Those forms of time (the hours, Father Time, the seasons) represent time as the chief agent in the economy of nature and as both benign and maleficent. The hours benignly made the youth but will certainly undo him; Father Time ('never-resting time', l. 5) brings the beautiful and abundant summer to 'hideous winter' (l. 6) and to destruction. Throughout the rest of the early sonnets Shakespeare's speaker continues to image time as the dominant force in the economy of nature and to allude to time's beneficence. But the allusions are negative. 'As fast as thou shalt wane so fast thou grow'st – / In one of thine, from that which thou departest' (11, ll. 1–2) and

'[S]weets and beauties do themselves forsake,/ And die as fast as they see others grow' (12, ll. 11–12), for example, suggest time's nurturing of new life yet stress time's ruining of pre-existent life. Moreover, Shakespeare's speaker most often and most dramatically presents time as Father Time, the spoiler and devourer, and it is appropriate that he should do so. To the narcissistic youth who has turned away from *Venus Genetrix*, who has not transformed his narcissism, time can ultimately and solely mean decline and desolation. The figure of Father Time thus becomes one of the more disquieting images that the young man, already compelled to view himself as Narcissus, has set before him.

The characterization of Father Time in the early sonnets has many aspects and has received much comment.[55] Nevertheless, to glance again at how Shakespeare's speaker fashions him seems necessary for at least two reasons: evoking his image is one of the speaker's main tactics of persuasion; to consider how the speaker fashions, and uses, his image is to understand more distinctly both the wisdom of Narcissus – what is identified as wisdom in the case of this Narcissus – and how the speaker represents himself in relation to the young man. It has been frequently pointed out that the Father Time of the Sonnets derives in particular from Ovid's depiction of time in *Metamorphoses* 15, especially as rendered by Golding. It is also true that the Father Time imaged for the young man by Shakespeare's speaker has a life of his own: a universal malice, a precise vindictiveness, reminiscent of Saturn's yet not of his alone. In sonnet 16 the speaker calls Father Time a 'bloody tyrant' (l. 2), which connects him with Saturn but, for that matter, with Tarquin, Richard III and other Shakespearean tyrants. Some of the more powerful moments in the characterization of Father Time throughout the early sonnets are those when one sees his malice and vindictiveness expressed through exercise of his tyrannic power, or by the results of its having been exercised. Sonnet 5 shows Time's irresistible, tyrannic authority being inflicted upon summer, and suggests not merely his destructive power but his vigorous malice.[56] The speaker warns, in sonnet 6, that the same malice will be exercised specifically upon the summer of the youth's beauty, for he too will be led on to hideous winter and confounded. '[W]inter's ragged hand' will, literally, ꞏdeface' him (l. 1): a graceful, violent, brutal image of disfigurement. Since the young man is Adonis as well as Narcissus, it is not surprising that Shakespeare's speaker often associates him with the summer and the sun. In sonnet 12, when recounting his meditations on Time's universal malice, the speaker associates the young man with both. The decline of 'the brave day' (l. 2) and the death of summer bring him, he says, to reflect that the youth 'among the wastes of time must go' (l. 10).[57] Yet perhaps the most powerfully individuated image of Father Time in the early sonnets occurs in sonnet 19.

Behind the characterization of Time in the poem stands the figure of Saturn the tyrant and child-devourer as recreated in Ovid's *'tempus edax rerum'*; Shakespeare's speaker alludes to his Ovidian original in the sonnet's opening words, 'Devouring time. . . .' Then, however, he works variations on that archetype. He represents Time as a predatory tyrant, concerned to demean and to defile rather than to ingest. Father Time is not pictured, for example, devouring the beasts which themselves are great predators; instead, the speaker describes him humiliating them, making the lion's paw harmless and drawing the tiger's teeth (ll. 1 and 3). In fact, the speaker does not picture Father Time consuming anything or anyone. Time is variously shown throughout the poem to be a tyrant who, as was remarked above, exercises his power with universal malice and precise vindictiveness. He 'makes the earth devour her own sweet brood' (l. 2): he compels her to be, like him, a cannibal; he remakes her in his own likeness. Moreover, not only does Time cruelly kill the 'long-lived phoenix' (l. 4). He also makes incineration the price of its renewal. One recalls that the narcissistic youth, by contrast, blazes splendidly toward total extinction; he '[f]eed[s his] light's flame with self-substantial fuel,/ Making a famine where abundance lies' (sonnet 1, ll. 6–7). The speaker's characterization of Father Time as the tyrant who demeans and defiles is then curiously developed in relation to the young man. 'O carve not with thy hours my love's fair brow,/ Nor draw no lines there with thine antique pen./ Him in thy course untainted do allow . . .' the speaker says (ll. 9–11). Demeaning the young man by defiling his beauty will be the tyrant's sport, according to the speaker, who would not have it so but who acknowledges that it cannot be otherwise.[58] In the lines just quoted, nevertheless, Father Time resembles stage tyrants in plays by Shakespeare, and by some other early modern writers, not solely because of his ludic vindictiveness but, as well, because of his being an artist. Early modern stage tyrants – Richard III, for example – tend to theatricality, to acting and toying with the differences between illusion and actuality; they are malign artists, in their own ways.[59] Father Time, as the speaker reluctantly acknowledges, will be both sculptor and limner of the young man, disfiguring him into a parody of what he was, transforming him with grotesque artistry ('antique pen', l. 10). But the motif of transformation through the power of art has a further dimension in the last part of the sonnet, for there, of course, Father Time has himself been transformed by the speaker. At the end of sonnet 15 the speaker announces that in his verse he 'engraft[s the young man] new', making good the damage done by time (l. 14), the implication being that otherwise (except through procreation) Narcissus will disappear from the world. At the end of sonnet 19 he says, in effect elaborating on the assertion with which sonnet 15 concludes: 'Yet do thy worst, old time; despite thy wrong,/ My love shall in my verse ever live young.' The imaging of Time as tyrant-artist emblematizes paradoxically the defiance in that final couplet. The speaker admits that Time's tyrannic power is unstoppable (l. 13); his picturing of Time's malign artistry has suggested how Time's power will be exercised upon the youth. Nonetheless, in so picturing Father Time the speaker also exercises power over him: first, Time the transformer is thus subjected to transformation; in addition, by representing Time as an artist – a defacer, a caricaturist – the speaker transforms Time into a rival whom he can defy, with whom he claims he can deal because of his own artistry's power to eternize. In sonnet 19 Time becomes a rival, and surpassable, artist before the appearance in the Sonnets of the so-called 'rival poet'.

As that poem and others suggest, then, recreating Ovid's *'tempus edax rerum'* enables Shakespeare's speaker to argue dramatically, to put before the young man a series of scenes representing his involvement in a conflict at once personal and universal. To ignore the economy of nature, the speaker thereby proposes, is to become a helpless victim of the dominant, tyrannic, hostile force within it. However consideration of Father Time in the early sonnets, in addition to clarifying the speaker's attempted persuasion of the young man, also illuminates both what wisdom is for the narcissistic youth and how the speaker relates to him. The poems insist repeatedly that, for the young man and not for him alone, wisdom in the domain of Father Time means continuance through marriage and breeding. In fact, the speaker says of the young man's having offspring: 'Herein lives wisdom, beauty, and increase;/ Without this, folly, age, and cold decay' (11, ll. 5–6). But what form of wisdom would Shakespeare's contemporaries have taken that to be, given their debates about the term and its meanings? The beginning of Sonnet 10 indicates an answer to the question. There the speaker says: 'For shame deny that thou bear'st love to any,/ Who for thyself art so unprovident.' The last word of the couplet, 'unprovident', again shows human economics being used as a metaphoric field for the economy of nature. The word evokes, too, the notion of prudence (*prudentia*).[60] Sonnet 11 subsequently uses the word 'wisdom', as the verses quoted from it a moment ago make plain, in the context of effective personal action in the world, that is, to label an instance of the 'practical knowledge of things to be sought for and of things to be avoided' – Cicero's description of prudence.[61] The speaker implies that the wisdom of Narcissus, the wisdom needed by the narcissistic young man, is ultimately *prudentia*; pre-eminent in the world, he nonetheless cannot afford to disdain the economy of nature, for to do so is improvidence, mere 'folly' (11, l. 6), imprudence. The wisdom he lacks is that which Lucrece lacks, but she seems to have been denied the acquisition of it whereas no such claim seems able to be made for him.

If, in the early sonnets, the speaker tries most forcibly through the characterization of Father Time to persuade the youth to prudence, then examining the representation of Father Time of course illuminates the relations between the speaker and the youth. But doing so reveals that the relations between them are more subtly nuanced than might at first be thought. Although the speaker does seek to move the young man to 'wisdom', and does at last present himself as defying Time on the youth's behalf – having referred to his 'love' for the young man and announced thereafter that he is 'all in war with time for love of' him – there is more to the portrayal of their relationship than that.[62] One way of concisely identifying other elements of it might be to look again at how the speaker associates the young man with the sun as well as with Father Time. Insofar as the youth is both Adonis and Narcissus, the speaker's linking him with the sun and summer is not in itself unusual, as has been remarked above. The elaborate pageant unfolded throughout the first dozen lines of sonnet 7, for example, suggests the youth is a sun on earth. Yet that pageant offers no mere celebration of him; rather, it astutely makes celebration inseparable from devaluation, and how it does so indicates the intricacies in the speaker's portrayal of his relating to the young man.

Early in the pageant Shakespeare's speaker celebrates the sun, and by implication the youth, in terms of pre-eminence: the sun's 'sacred majesty' is honoured by people and, too, they 'adore his beauty' (ll. 4 and 7 respectively). The speaker subsequently pictures, however, the sun's inevitable decline, emphasizing that even it is trappped in time, becomes enfeebled and ceases to be honoured (ll. 9–12) – which must, by constraint of the analogy, logically if not necessarily be acknowledged as the fate of the now-resplendent youth. And the speaker accordingly explicates the end of the pageant for him, saying: 'So thou, thyself outgoing in thy noon,/ Unlooked on diest unless thou get a son' (ll. 13–14). What does the poem indicate, then, about portrayal of the relationship between the speaker and the young man throughout sonnets 1–19? For a start, the speaker's choosing to celebrate the youth in terms of analogy with the sun, while appropriate because the young man is Adonis as well as Narcissus, also harmonizes with the Petrarchan imaging of him elsewhere in the early sonnets. Thus, like Laura, the anonymous young man is praised and characterized syncretically; but if the speaker honours and identifies him by using Petrarchan motifs among others, and declares his 'love' for him, moreover, it does not seem that the relationship between the two is represented in the early sonnets as Petrarchan and erotic. Further, the speaker's choice of an analogy between the sun and the youth allows for the linking of celebration to devaluation. Picturing the sun's inevitable decline and forewarning the youth of his, an option spectacularly repudiated in sonnet 18, the speaker acts as counsellor to Adonis-Narcissus in addition to being the singer of his praises.

The role of counsellor has a couple of aspects in the poem which typify the speaker's self-presentation in that guise throughout the first nineteen sonnets. One aspect is courtly wit, appropriate to a counsellor no less than to a eulogizer of the highborn, or more highly placed, as Castiglione and Puttenham well knew. In this poem the speaker's wit appears especially in the tropes with which he variously fashions the figure of the sun, tracing its progress from triumph to decay: 'Lifts up his burning head' (l. 2), 'golden pilgrimage' (l. 8), 'Like feeble age he reeleth' (l. 10), for example. Elsewhere his wit can be seen not only in other sonnets that resemble courtly pageants but also in those that play elaborately with paradoxes and conceits (such as sonnet 8) or, doing so, allude as well to the wit of courtly predecessors (such as sonnet 14, with its allusion to and reworking of *Astrophil and Stella*, 26). The second aspect to the speaker's role of counsellor is mediation. Through his wit he seeks to mediate wisdom, *prudentia*, to the young man. When the narcissistic youth apparently remains unpersuaded, in effect refusing to be counselled into wisdom, the speaker proceeds to offer less and less counsel, more and more praise, asserting that through his artistry he will generate in his verse a double of the vulnerable young man, a living icon of beauty beyond the power of Father Time (the turning point seems to be sonnets 15–17). Yet neither in the early sonnets nor in their successors does he create that icon. His declarations of his art's time-transcending power are everywhere but the likeness of the youth is nowhere, a curious absence, despite the speaker's appeals to the inexpressibility topos.[63]

The failure of the speaker's role as counsellor, and his abandoning it for that as eternizer of the young man's beauty, seem however to be less a problem notionally resolved than a problem which leads to another in the portrayed relations between him and the youth. Announcing that he will become the young man's champion against Time (as in 15, ll. 13–14, also 18, ll. 9–14, and 19, ll. 13–14), the speaker runs the risk of seeming to put himself forward at the young man's expense – and he appears to be aware of that danger. In sonnet 16, almost straight after he has declared himself to be 'all in war with time for love of' the youth (15, l. 13), the speaker asks:

> But wherefore do not you [the young man] a mightier way
> Make war upon this bloody tyrant time?
> And fortify yourself in your decay
> With means more blessed than my barren rhyme?
>
> (16, ll. 1–4)

Fathering a child, the speaker proceeds to elaborate, will mean that the young man generates a living likeness '[m]uch liker than [his] painted counterfeit' (l. 8), an accomplishment beyond the capacity of 'this time's pencil or [the speaker's] pupil pen' (l. 10). The speaker ends with: 'To give away yourself keeps yourself still,/ And you must live, drawn by your own sweet skill' (ll. 13–14). The suggestion is, I think, not merely that the youth's penis is mightier than the 'pencil[s]' of contemporary artists or the 'pen' of the speaker: that his sexual art can triumph over the art of painter and of (this) poet, engendering life as theirs cannot. The suggestion appears to be as well that the young man has the capability to be his own champion, if he will choose to be so; he has the ultimate artistry, the truly heroic virtue as it were, needed to overcome the malign artistry of Father Time and, therefore, to make championship by the speaker unnecessary. The close of sonnet 11 in part anticipates, deliberately or otherwise, such a suggestion: 'She [nature] carved thee for her seal, and meant thereby/ Thou shouldst print more, not let that copy die.' The speaker implies that the young man's nature-given role as the one exemplar of beauty lends singular importance to the fact that his ability to reproduce himself is unique. On the other hand, the reader soon learns in subsequent poems that the young man will not transform his narcissism, and that he will live – as the speaker indirectly reveals – as *copia* in the speaker's verse.[64]

. . . . .

The speaker of the early sonnets, unlike Sidney's Astrophil or the persona of the *Rime*, never queries the nature and status of his 'love';

nor does he indicate what either may be. Nonetheless, in the *Rime* love, patronage, and friendship intermingle, as has been discussed above, and it seems that in Shakespeare's early sonnets they do so as well. The implied social pre-eminence of the young man addressed by the speaker, and the respectful, celebratory, often intimate manner of his address, as well as his counsel that the youth marry for dynastic – but not solely dynastic – reasons, at least suggest as much.[65] Thus one can see the variously Petrarchan discourse of the poems as interactive with other discourses and, at the same time, as linked ultimately to the Petrarchism of clientage: as reflecting the contemporary adaptation of Petrarchan discourse to the pursuit of favour from socio-political superiors. Sonnets 20–126 imply, however, problems within that and related discourses, problems which appear to defy resolution.

NOTES

1. All reference to the Sonnets is from *Shakespeare's Sonnets*, ed. S. Booth (New Haven and London: Yale University Press, 1977).

2. See, for some examples: Hallett Smith, *Elizabethan Poetry: A Study in Conventions, Meaning and Expression* (Cambridge, Mass.: Harvard University Press, 1952), p. 171; M. R. G. Spiller, *The Development of the Sonnet* (London: Routledge, 1992), p. 152; A. Ferry, *The 'Inward' Language* (Chicago and London: University of Chicago Press, 1983), p. 174. For a useful summary of views on the date of the Sonnets, see K. Muir, *Shakespeare's Sonnets* (1979; rpt. London: Allen & Unwin, 1982), pp. 1–4.

3. Meres's reference to the Sonnets, from his *Palladis Tamia*, is quoted by Booth on p. 545.

4. I am not suggesting that such speculation is useless but merely that, at present, speculation is all we have – however informed and judicious it may be.

5. On the Elizabethan sonnet and on Shakespeare's Sonnets, see: H. Smith, *Elizabethan Poetry*, pp. 131–93; C. S. Lewis, *English Literature in the Sixteenth Century Excluding Drama* (Oxford: Clarendon Press, 1954), pp. 327–8, 490–8; J. W. Lever, *The Elizabethan Love Sonnet* (London: Methuen, 1956); N. Frye, *Fables of Identity* (New York: Harcourt, 1963), pp. 88–106; A. Ferry, *All in War with Time: Love Poetry of Shakespeare, Donne, Jonson, Marvell* (Cambridge, Mass. and London: Harvard University Press, 1975), pp. 3–63; P. Jones (ed.), *Shakespeare: The Sonnets* (London: MacMillan, 1977); A. B. Kernan, *The Playwright as Magician: Shakespeare's Image of the Poet in the English Public Theatre* (New Haven: Yale University Press, 1979), pp. 1–48; K. Muir, *Shakespeare's Sonnets*; A. Ferry, *The 'Inward' Language*; H. Dubrow, *Captive Victors: Shakespeare's Narrative Poems and Sonnets* (Ithaca and London: Cornell University Press, 1987), pp. 169–257; H. Bloom (ed.), *Shakespeare's Sonnets* (New

York: Chelsea House, 1987); P. Fumerton, *Cultural Aesthetics: Renaissance Literature and the Practice of Social Ornament* (Chicago and London: University of Chicago Press, 1991), pp. 67–110; M. R. G. Spiller, *The Development of the Sonnet*; W. Wall, *The Imprint of Gender: Authorship and Publication in the English Renaissance* (Ithaca and London: Cornell University Press, 1993), pp. 23–109; J. Bate, *The Genius of Shakespeare* (London: Picador, 1997), pp. 34–64. Among recent articles, other than those collected in the volumes edited respectively by Jones and by Bloom, see especially: J. Hedley, 'Since First Your Eye I Eyed: Shakespeare's *Sonnets* and the Poetics of Narcissism', *Style*, 28 (1994), 1–30; L. Engle, 'Afloat in Thick Deeps: Shakespeare's Sonnets on Uncertainty', *PMLA*, 104 (1989), 832–43.

6. Petrarch's *Rime* dates from the late 1320s or early 1330s and was revised until his death in 1374. Reference to Mario Praz is from his *The Flaming Heart* (1958; rpt. New York: Norton, 1973), pp. 264–86, especially pp. 268–72.

7. Those successors and commentators were chiefly Italian or French.

8. Reference to Petrarch's *Rime* is again from Durling's edition and translation, as it will be in subsequent chapters: *Petrarch's Lyric Poems*, trans. and ed. R. M. Durling (Cambridge, Mass. and London: Harvard University Press, 1976).

9. In conjunction with *Rime* 211 see 3.

10. Cf. 361–5.

11. On Laura as the sun of the speaker's life see, for example, 4.

12. See also: 62; 235; 280.

13. In conjunction with 72, see also 290, 351, 357.

14. In conjunction with 264, see 355, 363–6.

15. See respectively 9, 30, 198, 218, 311 and 4 (cf. 3).

16. See 1, 2, 17, 68, 69, and so on.

17. Cf. 264.

18. With 70 compare 156, 168, 186, 247.

19. See, with 20, 307–9; cf. 5.

20. See, again, 307–9.

21. On the myth of Narcissus in medieval (and by implication subsequent) verse, see F. Goldin, *The Mirror of Narcissus in the Courtly Love Lyric* (Ithaca, New York: Cornell University Press, 1967).

22. Cf. 168 and 361.

23. Cf. 53.

24. See 10 in relation to 9 and 11; cf. 40.

25. See 48, ll. 5–6, 244 and 120.

26. Reference to Chaucer is again from Fisher's edition: Geoffrey Chaucer, *The Complete Poetry and Prose*, ed. J. H. Fisher (New York: Holt, Rinehart & Winston, 1977).

27. Reference to Sidney's verse is from the modernized version of W. A. Ringler's text in R. M. Bender (ed.), *Five Courtier Poets of the English Renaissance* (New York: Washington Square Press, 1967).

28. See sonnets 32, 88 and 105 – cf. 39.
29. As far as I know, W. A. Ringler was the first to comment on this, in his edition of Sidney's poems (Oxford: Clarendon Press, 1962), p. 459. Cf. *Rime* 64, 96, 100, 125.
30. See 68, ll. 12–14, 71, 72, 73, 77–83.
31. See 107 and 108.
32. Along with several other things, such as his equivocating hints that he is a seriocomic disguise for Sidney, his emphatic 'Rich' allusions suggest that he is notionally at Elizabeth's court.
33. See especially 75; cf. 107.
34. See 13, ll. 1–4, 5–8, 9–14 respectively.
35. See the pun on 'blaze' in l. 13.
36. Of course, Astrophil's oblique assertion is the superiority of Stella's beautiful likeness – here, as a heraldic device, that is, as a sign of gentlemanly status – over all other images.
37. For a recent account of the topic of courtship, see C. Bates, *The Rhetoric of Courtship in Elizabethan Language and Literature* (Cambridge: Cambridge University Press, 1994).
38. For emphases on metafictionality in *Astrophil and Stella*, see 45, 58, 66–7, 69, 80–1, 93.
39. See especially 72, ll. 1–4 and 13–14; cf. 14 and 18.
40. Compare, for example, 5, ll. 5–8 with Calvin's *Institutes* 1, 11, 8–9; see also 72, ll. 1–4 and 13–14; compare 71–2 with *Institutes* 2, 8, 41 and 44. Reference to the *Institutes* is from the Bevington translation, 2 vols (1845; rpt. Grand Rapids: Eerdmans, 1983).
41. Reference to *The Courtier* is from C. S. Singleton's translation (New York: Doubleday, 1959).
42. In 71, l. 14, the voice of Desire is what Ficino would identify as 'bestial love', and what precedes it could be identified with reference to Plato, Ficino or Castiglione.
43. See the translation by C. Fantazzi in the *Collected Works of Erasmus*, vol. 23, ed. J. K. Sowards (Toronto: University Press, 1985). The most recent long discussion of Erasmian influence on sonnets 1–17 is by K. M. Wilson, *Shakespeare's Sugared Sonnets* (London: Allen & Unwin, 1974), pp. 146–76.
44. Reference to Wilson is from P. E. Medine's edition of *The Art of Rhetoric* (University Park: Pennsylvania State University Press, 1994).
45. See, as well, 45, especially l. 14.
46. Reference to Donne's verse is again from Smith's edition: John Donne, *The Complete English Poems*, ed. A. J. Smith (1971; rpt. London: Allen Lane, 1974).
47. In connection with the 'beauty's rose' image, see Daniel's *Delia* 31, *passim* and 42, ll. 5–8. In connection with the 'bright eyes' image, see sonnet 5, l. 2. Likewise, in connection with the monitory reference to ageing see *Delia* 42, ll. 9–10; cf. 33, ll. 1–4. There are of course parallels in the verse of Ronsard. Reference to Daniel's verse is from

A. C. Sprague, (ed.), *Poems and A Defence of Ryme* (1930; rpt. Chicago and London: University of Chicago Press, 1965).

48. See E. Wind, *Pagan Mysteries in the Renaissance* rev. edn (1958; rpt. Harmondsworth: Penguin, 1967), pp. 81–96.

49. See C. R. Thompson, trans., *The Colloquies of Erasmus* (Chicago and London: University of Chicago Press, 1965), p. 95.

50. Cf. ll. 3–4 and l. 14; the wise advice is Erasmian, as the echoes in ll. 5–6 reveal.

51. See *Hero and Leander* 1, 229–80. Reference to Marlowe's verse is again from Orgel's edition: S. Orgel (ed.), *Christopher Marlowe: The Complete Poems and Translations* (Harmondsworth: Penguin, 1971).

52. Cf. Aristotle, *Parts of Animals*, trans. A. L. Peck, Loeb Classical Library (Cambridge, Mass. and London: Harvard University Press, 1961), 2, 14; *idem.*, *Politics*, trans. H. Rackham (*ibid.*, 1959), 1, 1, 4–12; [Aristotle] *Oeconomica*, trans. G. C. Armstrong (*ibid.*, 1969), 1, 3 *passim*; Cicero, *On the Nature of the Gods*, trans. H. Rackham (*ibid.*, 1933), 2 *passim*; Thomas Aquinas, *De Principiis Naturae*, ed. J. Pauson (Fribourg: Société Philosophique, 1950); Richard Hooker, *The Works*, ed. J. Keble, 7th edn rev. R. W. Church and F. Paget (1887; rpt. New York: Burt Franklin, 1970), *Lawes* 1, 3 *passim*.

53. See Sidney's *New Arcadia*, ed. V. Skretkowicz (Oxford: Clarendon Press, 1987), p. 333.

54. Cf. 13, ll. 9–14.

55. The classic study of Father Time is E. Panofsky's in his *Studies in Iconology* (1939; rpt. New York: Harper & Row, 1962), pp. 69–93. On Father Time in relation to the Sonnets and other writings of Shakespeare, see especially: J. B. Leishman, *Themes and Variations in Shakespeare's Sonnets*, 2nd edn (1961; rpt. London: Hutchinson, 1968), pp. 95–148; L. Woodbridge, *The Scythe of Saturn: Shakespeare and Magical Thinking* (Urbana and Chicago: University of Illinois Press, 1994), in particular at pp. 210–16. I have also consulted the writings of Claudian, Comes, Cartari and Fraunce on the iconography of Time.

56. See 'confounds' in l. 6; see also ll. 3–8.

57. In l. 2, 'hideous' is transferred to 'night'. On the death of summer, see ll. 7–8: 'Summer's green all girded up in sheaves/ Borne on the bier with white and bristly beard'.

58. Ll 8 and 13: 'But I forbid . . .', 'Yet do thy worst . . .'.

59. I am indebted for this point about the theatricality of stage tyrants to R. W. Bushnell's *Tragedies of Tyrants: Political Thought and Theater in the English Renaissance* (Ithaca and London: Cornell University Press, 1990), pp. 56–63.

60. In his 'Shakespeare's Sonnet 15 and the Art of Memory', R. B. Waddington associates that poem, and some others outside numbers 1–19, with *prudentia* – primarily in connection with the art of memory, as his essay's title indicates. I argue here that *prudentia* is a concern throughout all the early sonnets, as well as in later ones; moreover, I

link 'prudence' chiefly to the notion of the economy of nature. Waddington's essay – a fine study – is in *The Rhetoric of Renaissance Poetry From Wyatt to Milton*, eds T. O. Sloan and R. B. Waddington (Berkeley, Los Angeles, London: University of California Press, 1974), pp. 96–122.

61. See ll. 1–6 of the sonnet. The reference to Cicero duplicates that in Chapter Two.

62. The parenthetic quotations are from 10, l. 13 and from 15, l. 13.

63. For example, directly in sonnet 17 and indirectly in sonnet 18; cf. 20 and 53.

64. See: 'copy' in 11, l. 14; 17 *passim*; and 18, ll. 9–14.

65. In the early sonnets, 'love' seems therefore to be represented as friendship with/attachment to an idealized, socio-political superior.

Chapter 4

Shakespeare's Sonnets 20–126: The Poet, the Young Man, Androgyny and Friendship

(I) INTRODUCTION. NARCISSUS AND ADONIS

Although sonnets 20–126 echo much of the praise, anxiety and ironic insight as expressed in their immediate predecessors, the differences between the two groups of poems are more striking than are the similarities.[1] Certainly, for example, in the later sonnets the aristocratic youth is imaged again as a figure of sun-like resplendence and pre-eminence; but one has merely to juxtapose sonnets 7 and 33 in order to illustrate the important dissimilarities between earlier and later comparisons of the youth to the sun. Sonnet 7 represents the young man as virtually another sun to the world: supposedly above all in status and beauty, yet nonetheless subject to time and therefore destined to decline and to suffer disregard. Sonnet 33, on the other hand, pictures the youth as the sun of the speaker's life, suggesting that, in his role as the sun of the speaker's existence ('my sun', l. 9), the young man is not merely brilliant, and not merely trapped in time, but necessarily flawed. He is subject to contamination because he is a sun in and of the world, being indeed a son of the world, and not even the sun in the heavens is free from imperfections. Moreover, he is one of a class (social and otherwise), not singular. As Shakespeare's speaker says in reconciling himself to the young man's imperfection: 'Suns of the world may stain when heav'n's sun staineth' (l. 14).[2]

Important differences can be seen also in later imaging of the youth as another Narcissus and allusion to the economy of nature. While it is true that sonnet 84 implicitly condemns the young man's narcissism (ll. 13–14), sonnet 103 explicitly justifies it (see especially ll. 1–8 and 13–14). Furthermore the Narcissus motif becomes variously linked to, not just used by, Shakespeare's speaker. In sonnet 62 he asserts, then denies, his own narcissism; elsewhere, however, he indicates that his love for the youth is in fact narcissistic. The later sonnets suggest a closeness between Shakespeare's speaker and the youth which is not stated or implied − if at times it is foreshadowed − by the earlier poems, and they depict him focusing, self-absorbed, on his relations with the young man.[3] In particular, they imply both his tendency to use the young man as a mirror in which to ponder his experience of love and his tendency to impose his own ideals and needs on the young man.[4] They depict, too, his preoccupation with the power and ingenuity of his own art, something foreshadowed distinctly in sonnets 18 and 19.[5] No less marked are the differences in allusion to the economy of nature; nonetheless, for present purposes they can be more briefly identified. Sonnets 64 and 126 may evoke, with others, the notion as signified in sonnets 1−19, yet a number of poems do not, dwelling on economic value and exchange as merely social phenomena. The forty-ninth sonnet, for example, begins with the speaker considering the young man's love for him in terms of limited expenditure (ll. 1−4). Sonnet 87 opens with the relationship between the speaker and the youth being imaged as a one-sided financial arrangement which favours the aristocratic, younger man (ll. 1−4). That such differences are important to the characterization of the youth is clear enough; the changes to the Narcissus motif are, however, arguably more so.

It was suggested a moment ago that, in sonnets 20−126, changes to the Narcissus motif are in part concerned with representation of the young man and in part with representation of Shakespeare's speaker: the young man appears to be both condemned for and justified in his narcissism; the speaker tends to focus narcissistically on his experience of love and on his art, to project his ideals and needs on the young man. Those changes emphasize important, underlying continuities between Shakespeare's Sonnets and Petrarch's *Rime*, despite the evident and major discontinuities between the two. Of course it is no slight difference between the Sonnets and the *Rime* that the former mostly contains poems expressing love for an androgynous young man. And the young man, for all his being imaged in ways which evoke the images of Laura, cannot be seen as her direct counterpart. She is the sun, for example, whereas he is a stained sun. Nor is he the sole object of the speaker's attachment; but the other, the so-called Dark Lady, is apparently less perfect than he and certainly nothing like the sun. Nonetheless, in sonnets 20−126 one can see evident and major continuities with the *Rime*, continuities that are variously adumbrated in sonnets 1−19.

The most revealing of those is not that in 1−19, and likewise in 20−126, the depiction of the young man evokes at times the portrayal of Laura – nor that there he is accused of narcissism, an accusation directed too at Laura in the *Rime*. More revealing are the affinities in sonnets 20–126 between Shakespeare's speaker and Petrarch's insofar as each appears – in ways previously mentioned – rather to be another Narcissus than does his beloved.[6] Recognizing those affinities, one perceives that although the youth may to some extent resemble Laura in being sun-like, in being beauty itself and so on, he resembles her beyond their sharing such attributes. Just as the subjectivity of Laura in the *Rime* cannot be separated from that of the Petrarchan persona, so the subjectivity of the young man cannot be disentangled from that of Shakespeare's speaker. In each case the subjectivity of the beloved expresses at least in part the desires of the speaker and becomes the focus of the speaker's reflections on the process of loving. In each case, as a result, the beloved cannot be seen as having a selfhood independent from the speaker's manipulative desire, appearing instead to be caught in the fictions of loving that the speaker weaves, sometimes knowingly, around at once the beloved and himself.[7]

Perhaps the most useful way to begin considering some implications of the speaker's being a Narcissus in the manner of Petrarch's persona, and thus of Sidney's Astrophil, is to examine for a moment sonnets 22 and 31, which were mentioned earlier as manifesting different aspects of his narcissism. Sonnet 22 begins:

> My glass shall not persuade me I am old
> So long as youth and thou are of one date,
> But when in thee time's furrows I behold,
> Then look I death my days should expiate.
> For all that beauty that doth cover thee
> Is but the seemly raiment of my heart,
> Which in thy breast doth live, as thine in me.
> How can I then be elder than thou art?

> (ll. 1–8)

The speaker declares that not his mirror, but rather the face of the young man, will convince him that the last phase of his life has come. In the face of the young man, then, and not in a mirror, can be seen the true image of his life's physical progress: in that sense, a truer image of himself than his mirror can reflect. Moreover, the speaker suggests that the self-knowledge that he gains, and will gain, from finding his truer likeness in the face of the young man both derives from love and expresses the speaker's experience of loving. That becomes clear when Shakespeare's speaker proceeds to justify his declaration by affirming a concept expounded in Ficino's *Commentary on the Symposium of Plato* – and further declares that his emotions and the core of his physical existence lie within the youth, for within the youth lives his heart (ll. 5–7). In the *Commentary* Antonio the theologian says, '[T]he lover removes himself from himself and gives himself to the beloved,' adding, 'Therefore the beloved takes care of him as his own possession' – which is relevant at once to the last six lines of sonnet 22 and to almost all the rest of the poems, including the Dark Lady sonnets.[8] Because the beautiful youth encloses the heart of the speaker, the speaker's life manifests itself through the young man. Hence the question, 'How can I then be elder than thou art?' (l. 8).[9] Hence, too, the implication that self-knowledge gained from gazing on the youth derives from love of him and is part of the experience of loving him, that gazing on the youth helps the speaker to understand his experience of love, here, his miraculous experience of union and renewal through love. What is the octave of sonnet 22 but the speaker's meditative gazing on the youth in order both to celebrate him and to ponder loving him?

Sonnet 22 begins, therefore, by unfolding a narcissistic fiction generated from a fable of identity. A similar strategy can be seen in sonnet 31, except that there can also be seen distinctly the speaker's imposing on the young man his own needs and ideals. Once again Shakespeare's speaker evokes the notion that a lover's heart dwells within his beloved. He says to the youth:

> Thy bosom is endeared with all hearts,
> Which I by lacking have supposed dead;
> And there reigns love and all love's loving parts,
> And all those friends which I thought buried.
> How many a holy and obsequious tear
> Hath dear religious love stol'n from mine eye,
> As interest of the dead, which now appear
> But things removed that hidden in thee lie.
>
> (ll. 1–8)

There the speaker fashions the graceful and intricate fiction that within the young man still survive those friends of whom the speaker had thought himself deprived by death. On the youth, that is to say, the speaker imposes an idealizing and self-consolatory fiction which functions at the same time as a fable of identity, a fable of spiritual union in love, and so allows the speaker to meditate on his experience of loving. In fact the poem proceeds to deny both the Petrarchan turn in the *Rime* from *cupiditas* and Ficino's idea that (male) friendship draws its participants to God, the speaker's fictions leading him to assert that the young man is the *telos* of his life. He says at the sonnet's close, referring to the friends he had once thought lost: 'Their images I loved I view in thee,/ And thou, all they, hast all the all of me' (ll. 13–14). It is as if he were imaging anew and personally the relations of the Many and the One.[10]

Sonnets 22 and 31 do not merely express, however, the speaker's narcissism; they also indicate that narcissism's implications for sonnets 20–126 as a whole. What seems particularly important is the depiction, in sonnet 31, of the young man as a transcendent, inclusive being and of the speaker as spiritually united to him. Just such a representation of the young man opens the second group of sonnets, initiating a distinct change of emphasis both in how he is portrayed and in portrayal of the speaker's relations to him. That is to say, sonnet 31 indicates those fictions which, from sonnet 20 onward, the speaker will especially impose on the young man and on his relations to him, sometimes self-consciously but at others not. Through those fictions, as one learns, the speaker can neither possess nor define the young man, yet in them he does ensnare himself.

(II) SONNET 20. FICTIONS AND DISCOURSES

To focus on sonnet 20 is to see the fictions and discourses that will dominate the rest of the poems, as far as sonnet 126, at once asserted and brought problematically together:

> A woman's face, with nature's own hand painted,
> Hast thou, the master mistress of my passion –
> A woman's gentle heart, but not acquainted
> With shifting change, as is false women's fashion;
> An eye more bright than theirs, less false in rolling,
> Gilding the object whereupon it gazeth;
> A man in hue all hues in his controlling,
> Which steals men's eyes and women's souls amazeth.
> And for a woman wert thou first created,
> Till nature as she wrought thee fell a-doting,
> And by addition me of thee defeated,
> By adding one thing to my purpose nothing.
>> But since she pricked thee out for women's pleasure,
>> Mine be thy love, and thy love's use their treasure.

As might be expected, because of its sexual playfulness and its having been written by Shakespeare, sonnet 20 has evoked vigorous scholarly disagreements. The most lively are among those scholars who believe, or fear, that the Sonnets are autobiographical. Some argue that the poem suggests – and, in conjunction with other of the initial 126 poems, reveals – that the person who has been apotheosized as the Greatest English Dramatist was a same-sex lover, which therefore queers the icon at the centre of the canon.[11] In contradiction, some argue that sonnet 20 shows this same Greatest English Dramatist to have had no personal interest whatsoever in homoerotic attachments, whatever a number of his other sonnets might be taken to imply. Thus the canon's centrepiece remains reassuringly heterosexual. While the nature of sexuality as represented in the Sonnets is an important issue, there seems no need, nonetheless, for interpretation of sonnet 20 to be limited by debates over ownership of Shakespeare or over sexuality and the canon. In any event, to consider the fictions and discourses that Shakespeare's speaker attempts to merge in the poem – and which interact in so many of the other sonnets focused on the young man – makes it hard for one to support either extreme in the debate about Shakespeare's sexuality, assuming in the first place that one could believe, in the absence of proof, that the Sonnets are simply autobiographical.[12]

Sonnet 20 begins with Shakespeare's speaker portraying the young man as an androgyne and so imposing on him a fiction of transcendence and inclusion. In developing that fiction, moreover, the speaker unfolds another (which itself expresses the notion of transcendence and inclusion), the second implying his spiritual rather than his physical unity with the youth. Those fictions thus bring together discourses of gender and of friendship. To be more exact, they interplay discourses of androgyny and of misogyny, of Petrarchism and of friendship, in what seems an attempt to merge not so much the last two – for the discourse of friendship is woven into the discourse of divided desire (*caritas/cupiditas*) in the *Rime* – but the first with them. The second and the fourth are already linked, misogyny being recurrent in the ancient and Renaissance discourses of friendship.[13] It could be suggested that the sonnet's famous 'master mistress' trope (l. 2) crystallizes the attempt, the self-contradictoriness of the image indicating not a harmonizing of disparate things but their precarious, unstable fusion. In order to clarify the play of discourse in the sonnet, however, and therefore the implications of the 'master mistress' trope, one must focus for a while on the discourses themselves which the speaker's fictions evoke.

In portraying the young man as an androgyne Shakespeare's speaker does not, of course, suggest that he is literally a hermaphrodite. The youth has a 'woman's face' but nature has also 'pricked [him] out for women's pleasure' (ll. 1 and 13 respectively). He is androgynous but male. Nonetheless, being imaged as androgynous (ll. 1–9) and, in an Ovidian moment of ludic explanation for his androgyny, being reported as originally made female till nature reconsidered and altered his sex (ll. 9–13), the youth is clearly linked with an old, powerful and various discourse. In *Asclepius* Trismegistus describes God as androgynous.[14] One strand of mythographic tradition identifies Venus as an androgyne.[15] So Spenser images Nature in his *Cantos* – which Shakespeare does not in sonnet 20.[16] Leone Ebreo, reflecting on Genesis and on Plato's *Symposium*, wrote that Adam was an androgyne – prior to the creation of Eve.[17] Androgyny could be seen in Shakespeare's time, then, as a principle expressed in different notions of the divine and informing the generation of life. We could be seen to inhabit a universe shaped and renewed by androgyny. Thus, as a trope, it could be readily used to signify transcendent inclusiveness and perfect union.

How the discourse of androgyny relates to the speaker's strategy in sonnet 20 starts to become clear when one looks at the discourse of friendship also current at the time of Shakespeare. To examine the literature of friendship from ancient times to Shakespeare's is to recognize at once its homosocial and at times homoerotic emphases.[18] Those emphases appear, to cite an early instance, in Plato's *Lysis*, although the notion of male friendship with women is not excluded.[19] In the *Nichomachean Ethics* Aristotle affirms the reported view that 'friends . . . are . . . the greatest of all external advantages' but offers a picture of friendship which has no female presence.[20] A no less distinctly homosocial emphasis marks Cicero's dialogue *De Amicitia*. There Laelius asserts that friendship surpasses family ties in value; a friend, he says, is 'another self'. Both his account of friendship's origins and his examples of friendship are male. By way of conclusion he says: 'This is all that I had to say about friendship; but I exhort you both [his fellow participants in the dialogue] so to esteem virtue (without which friendship cannot exist), that, excepting virtue, you will think nothing more excellent than friendship.'[21] To turn from Plato, Aristotle and Cicero, whose influences on Renaissance friendship literature were so pervasive, to Plutarch, Ficino and Montaigne is to see an intensification of the emphases that have just now been discussed.

In the case of Plutarch's dialogue, 'Love', there is certainly an intensification but also a counter-emphasis. Protogenes, speaking in praise of adult male friendship, and sexual involvement, with boys says: 'For love, when it seizes a noble and young soul, ends in virtue through friendship; but these violent passions for women, at the best, aim only at carnal enjoyment, and reaping the harvest of a beauteous prime.' He adds: 'For the end of passion is pleasure and fruition: but love, when it has once lost the promise of friendship, will not remain and continue to cherish merely for beauty that which gives it pain, where it gives no return of friendship and virtue.'[22] Protogenes is of course arguing that men experience friendship, and ideally should have sex (for him, an aspect of friendship with boys), only with other males. However Daphnaeus responds: '[T]his boy-love denies that pleasure is its aim: for it is ashamed and afraid to confess the truth: . . . the pretext is friendship and virtue.'[23] The father of Flavianus and Autobulus, who open the dialogue, subsequently asserts that marriage too participates 'in divine friendship'.[24] The dialogue ends by implicitly favouring heterosexuality and marriage; it does not, nonetheless, conclusively condemn male same-sex relations. What would seem to be immediately relevant is that the homosocial and misogynic emphases already noted in the ancient discourse of friendship are intensified in Plutarch's dialogue, in part by its linking the homosocial with the homoerotic. That having been granted, there is as well in the dialogue a clear counter-emphasis on the actuality and attractions of friendship with women in marriage. The discussion of such male–female friendship came to be a motif in Christian accounts of marriage, an example occurring in Tilney's *The Flower of Friendship* (1568). There Master Pedro asks: 'What is then more necessary than Matrimony, which containeth the felicity of man's life, the *Flower of Friendship*, the preservation of Realms, the glory of Princes, and that which is most of all, it causeth immortality[?]'[25] His question is pertinent to the calling of Narcissus to account in sonnets 1–19.

But to read Ficino and Montaigne on friendship is to discover sentiments closer to those of Protogenes than to those of Master Pedro. Since, however, Ficino expresses his views primarily in the *Commentary on Plato's Symposium*, drawing heavily on *De Amicitia* in order to elaborate on Plato's text, while Montaigne in his essay 'On Friendship' aligns his views with those expounded in *The Ethics* and in *De Amicitia*, that could hardly prove a surprise.[26] In Ficino's dialogue one reads this description of how male friendships may begin:

[A]t the same time that the soul is perceiving a certain man in sensation, and conceiving him in the imagination, it can contemplate, by means of the intellect, the reason and definition common to all men through its innate Idea of humanity; and what it has contemplated, it preserves. Therefore, since the soul can preserve in the memory the image of a handsome man once it has conceived and reformed that image within itself, the soul would be satisfied to have seen the beloved only once. But the eye and the spirit, which, like mirrors, can receive images of a body only in its presence, and lose them when it is absent, need the continuous presence of a beautiful body in order to shine continuously with its illumination, and be comforted and pleased.

(p. 115)

Of the friendship between an older and a younger man one reads:

A man enjoys the beauty of a beloved youth with his eyes. The youth enjoys the beauty of the man with his Intellect. And he who is beautiful in body only, by this association becomes beautiful also in soul. He who is only beautiful in soul fills the eyes of the body with the beauty of the body. Truly this is a wonderful exchange. Virtuous, useful, and pleasant to both. The virtue certainly is equal to both. For it is equally virtuous to learn and to teach. The pleasure is greater in the older man, who is pleased in both sight and intellect. But in the younger man the usefulness is greater.

(p. 58)

The homosocial and homoerotic emphases in the quotations are clear but one should add that, in Ficino's *Commentary* as a whole, homoerotic desire is naturalized and sanctified, while sexual enactment of homoerotic desire is carefully denounced.[27]

Montaigne, in his essay 'On Friendship', also condemns the sexual expression of homoerotic desire. Prior to doing so he remarks:

As for marriage, not only is it a bargain to which only the entrance is free, continuance in it being constrained and compulsory, and depending upon other things than our will, but it is a bargain commonly made for other ends. There occur in it innumerable extraneous complications which have to be unravelled, and are enough to break the thread and disturb the course of a lively affection, whereas in friendship there is no business or traffic with anything but itself. Moreover, the normal capacity of women is, in fact, unequal to the demands of that communion and intercourse on which the sacred bond is fed; their souls do not seem firm enough to bear the strain of so hard and lasting a tie. And truly, if that were not so, if such a free and voluntary relationship could be established in which not only the soul had its perfect enjoyment, but the body took its share in the alliance also, and the whole man was engaged, then certainly it would be a fuller and more complete friendship. But there has never yet been an example of a woman's attaining to this, and the ancient schools are at one in their belief that it is denied to the female sex.

(p. 95)

Then he writes: 'As for that alternative, permitted by the Greeks, our morality rightly abhors it' (*ibid.*). But of course he later asserts that '[i]n ["a proper kind of"] friendship [the participants] mix and blend one into the other in so perfect a union that the seam which has joined them is effaced and disappears' (p. 97 – the 'another self' motif). And: '[P]erfect friendship . . . is indivisible. Each gives himself so absolutely to his friend that he has nothing to dispose of elsewhere' (p. 100). In light of those and the preceding remarks one has no trouble understanding why Montaigne identifies friendship as a bond more important than family ties (see pp. 92–4).

Some knowledge of the early modern discourses of androgyny and of friendship seems essential if one is to appreciate the ambitiousness and precariousness of the speaker's fictions in sonnet 20. Shakespeare's speaker begins, after all, by portraying the young man as an androgyne. Portrayal of the youth as in that way at once transcendent and inclusive enables the speaker to picture him as the object of desire by both sexes and ultimately to celebrate him, via the mock-etiology of ll. 9–12, as desired at his inception by Nature herself (cf. l. 1): in effect, as the object of universal desire. The fiction of androgyny confers on the young man a quasi-divine status and, at the same time, links him with the mystical and the mythic (and not only the playfully mythic). Further, it generates the hyperbole of universal desire and subsequently a fiction of spiritual union, of friendship. But although the speaker's picturing the youth as an androgyne can be seen, given what has been described above, to suggest the ambitiousness of his fiction-making in the sonnet, in fact the ambitiousness – and precariousness – of his fiction-making has greater complexity than that. His fabling androgyny is part of a more intricate and unstable process.

At the poem's start, Shakespeare's speaker indicates that the young man both subsumes and supplants femaleness. The speaker merges the discourses of androgyny and of misogyny, drawing on the cliches of women's fickleness and falsehood to suggest that the youth does not merely incorporate femaleness with maleness but, rather, that he incarnates a femaleness which leaves to those who are solely female the flaws innate to women. Moreover, the femaleness embodied by the young man recalls some of the qualities attributed to Laura in the *Rime* and thence to her literary descendants: true gentleness of heart and unsurpassed brilliance of eye. The young man therefore seems at once to subsume ideal femaleness and to supplant all remaining femaleness. By implication, in being an androgyne and subsuming perfect femaleness he transcends Laura.[28] The verse addressed to him can be inferred, then, to subsume and to transcend, perhaps supplant, its Petrarchan ancestry – and the paradigmatic myth of Salmacis and Hermaphroditis.[29]

If the fiction of androgyny implies that the young man surpasses Laura as an object of desire and veneration, it implies too that he embodies the virtues of true friendship. When, at the end of sonnet 20, Shakespeare's speaker identifies his connection to the young man in terms of friendship, in terms of spiritual rather than sexual union, his doing so develops from the praise given to the young man, earlier in the poem, at the expense of women. There the youth is celebrated for his capacity to feel affection, for his constancy, honesty and freedom from uncontrolled desire, all of which Cicero lists as virtues essential to true friendship and thereby bequeathes to the early modern discourse of friendship.[30] Thus the virtues which contribute to the youth's surpassing Laura also make him capable of being a true – indeed, perfect – friend. Those virtues as well as his beauty draw the speaker to him, leading the speaker to say, 'Mine be thy love. . .'. As a fiction of transcendence and inclusion, the androgyny attributed to the young man brings together not only both genders but the image of Laura and the ideal of the true (male) friend. One sees, that is to say, a fiction of androgyny engendering a fiction of spiritual union and so bringing together discourses of androgyny and of misogyny, of Petrarchism and of friendship.

Yet ambitiousness seems inseparable from precariousness in the speaker's imposing those fictions on the young man. Shakespeare's speaker seeks to portray the youth as someone whose capacity for affection co-exists with constancy, honesty and freedom from un-controlled desire. However, when the speaker contrasts the youth to women in general, telling him that he has '[a]n eye more bright than theirs, less false in rolling' (l. 5), 'less' appears to deny inconstancy and deception in the young man's behaviour but nonetheless concedes their presence, or the possibility of their presence. His implicit tran-scendence of Laura becomes doubtful – and so, as a result, does the status of the verse addressed to him. The description of the youth wavers between the ideal of a static, harmonious androgyny and its opposite, an androgyny contaminated by the 'shifting change' and 'false[hood]' notionally typical of women. Subsequent representations of the young man as androgynous also waver between those contraries or alternate between them.[31] That is to say, in the case of the latter, if one poem asserts the ideal then another denies it. The ideal is eventu-ally revealed to be an unsustainable fiction; but there is, nonetheless, finally in sonnets 20–126 a sceptical counterbalance of opposites, such as can be seen in the narrative poems. The fiction's unsustainability is demonstrated and its sustainability is also unqueried. So it is with the other fictions of transcendence and inclusion that Shakespeare's speaker imposes on the youth from sonnet 20 onward. In them too occurs a wavering or alternation between contraries ending in a counterbalance of opposites.[32] It might be remarked here as well that whereas the narrative poems link death, sexual experience and self-knowledge, albeit differently, in the characterizations of Adonis and of Lucrece, sonnets 20–126 link the consciousness of mortality, desire and self-knowledge in the characterization of Shakespeare's speaker.

The fiction of spiritual union generated from that of androgyny is therefore also rendered precarious, for if the young man does not necessarily have the virtues which elevate him above women then he does not necessarily have those virtues which make him capable of true friendship. Moreover the nature of the speaker's attachment to him is of course by no means transparent. One could read the last two lines of sonnet 20, which declare or anticipate the spiritual union of the younger and the older man, in terms, say, of Ficino or of Montaigne. Both writers focus on spirituality in male friendship and Ficino discusses the relationship between an older man and a younger; but Ficino mentions the intellectual benefits gained by the younger man in such a friendship and Montaigne writes of friendship as excluding matters of business. Shakespeare's speaker asserts through-out sonnets 20–126 that the young man gains fame from their asso-ciation, not wisdom or virtue; in addition, the speaker uses the language of friendship in addressing a patron, which jars with the opinion expressed in Montaigne's essay that friendship and business are separate concerns.[33] However, Shakespeare's speaker implies that he is his patron's true friend, a notion which would seem to accord partly with this statement in 'On Friendship': 'In this noble relation-ship [true friendship] services and kindnesses, which keep other friend-ships alive, do not deserve even to be taken into account, by reason of the complete fusion of the wills' (p. 99). Be that as it may, there is finally another problem evoked by the assertion, in the sonnet's last lines, of emotional rather than physical involvement between the speaker and the youth. A sexual pun on 'nothing' (l. 12) leads to another on 'pricked' (l. 13) and that, in turn, to one on 'treasure' (l. 14). The syntax of the last line, too, remains ambiguous.[34] Thus the speaker's denial of sexual interest in the youth is insistently sexual and unclear. Reference to Ficino might clarify the speaker's playfully erotic denial of homoeroticism; for all that, its playfulness and con-trariety make it elusive.

By the end of sonnet 20, then, the 'master mistress' trope of line two comes to signify a more intricate, problematic relationship between the speaker and the young man than it does even at first. Its initial suggestion that the youth is the speaker's chief object of desire, a desire erotic in intensity and perhaps in kind, brings together notions of androgyny and of misogyny, of Petrarchism and of friendship. The discursive interplay subsequent to and inseparable from the trope at once widens and directs that confluence of notions; in doing so, it manifests the ambitiousness and precariousness of the fictions that the speaker imposes on the young man and in which he recurrently ensnares himself. Now is the moment at which to begin examining that interplay of discourse, that ambitiousness, precariousness, and ensnarement, as they variously appear in the other poems about or addressed to the young man.

(III) DESIRE AND ITS DISCONTENTS

The sonnet that perhaps most resembles 20 is 53, 'What is your substance, whereof are you made', which offers even more elevated praise to the young man than does its predecessor. In the later poem Shakespeare's speaker again portrays the young man as an androgyne, likening him both to Adonis and to Helen of Troy. According to the speaker, however, to '[d]escribe Adonis' would be 'poorly' to imitate the youth; and the speaker implies as well that Adonis himself was only a poor imitation of the young man, who preceded his mythical counterpart as a type of perfect male beauty (ll. 4–5). Moreover, according to the speaker, if the youth is Helen born anew to the world he is also Helen idealized – and therefore a Helen who supersedes her former self. Helen of Troy is thus supplanted by the young man just as Laura is by him in sonnet 20. 'On Helen's cheek all art of beauty set,/ And you in Grecian tires are painted new', the speaker says (ll. 8–9). He implies that Helen of Troy merely prefigured the young man. Hence the speaker's comparing the youth to Adonis and to Helen of Troy suggests forcibly that the fiction of transcendence and inclusion imposed on him in this later sonnet resembles yet differs from that imposed on him in sonnet 20. Although in the former he appears again in the role of androgyne, he is nonetheless a more transcendent, more inclusive figure than the latter indicates him to be. The reason for that can be seen clearly at the poem's beginning and near its end. There the speaker virtually apotheosizes the young man, identifying him as the incarnation of Beauty itself and so characterizing him once more in terms of the relations between the Many and the One. 'What is your substance, whereof are you made,/ That millions of strange shadows on you tend?' he asks at the beginning of the sonnet. Near the end of the poem he says: 'And you in every blessed shape we know' (l. 12). Given the young man's being Beauty incarnate, a familiar motif in Petrarchan discourse, one understands how he can simultaneously precede Adonis and be prefigured by Helen of Troy. And from that fiction of transcendence and inclusion follows a fiction of spiritual union. The speaker says to the youth: 'In all external grace you have some part,/ But you like none, none you, for constant heart' (ll. 13–14).

Those fictions that the speaker imposes on the young man could hardly be more ambitious; but they are no more ambitious than precarious. One problem lies in the speaker's comparing and contrasting the youth to Adonis. Shakespeare's *Venus and Adonis*, written at about the time his Sonnets seems to have been begun, presents an Adonis who is an androgyne uncertain of his selfhood, a figure to be viewed at once comically and sympathetically. Can the analogy in sonnet 53 between Adonis and the androgynous young man fail to evoke the particular Adonis of Shakespeare's first narrative poem? In addition, the comparison and contrast between the youth and Helen of Troy appears distinctly to make the speaker's praise discordant – and to do so at the centre of the sonnet. Helen of Troy symbolizes female beauty in the poem, albeit female beauty which is perfected in the young man; however, she is often associated in sixteenth- and in seventeenth-century texts not only with surpassing beauty but also with sexual betrayal and with ruin. Shakespeare's Lucrece associates her with both those latter things. Troilus associates Helen with destruction, saying in *Troilus and Cressida*: 'Fools on both sides [of the Trojan War]! Helen must needs be fair/ When with your blood you daily paint her thus.'[35] Another instance of that can be seen in Wither's generic use of Helen's name: 'Where Hellen is, there, will be Warre;/ For, *Death* and *Lust*, Companions are.'[36] In sonnet 53, moreover, Shakespeare's speaker compares the youth to a Helen whose beauty has been heightened by artifice, a different representation of him from that given in the opening line of sonnet 20 ('A woman's face, with nature's own hand painted'). The fiction of transcendence and inclusion imposed on the youth seems again to be unstable. Far from manifesting unity in multiplicity – inasmuch as he is attended upon by 'millions of strange shadows' but incarnates Beauty itself and embodies a unique constancy of heart – the young man manifests indeterminacy and contradiction within multiplicity.

That wavering between opposites which marks portrayal of the youth as an androgyne occurs, too, in the final line of the sonnet, where the speaker implies a spiritual oneness between the youth and himself. When Shakespeare's speaker says to the young man, 'But you like none, none you, for constant heart', for an instant 'like' reads as a verb and so makes the speaker both assert and deny the young man's constancy.[37] Thus the youth appears at the end of the poem both as a true friend and as totally incapable of true friendship. If, then, he is implied to subsume flawless female beauty into his perfect maleness and to have a constancy beyond that of anyone else, he is nonetheless indicated to be at once flawed and inconstant. In sonnet 53 as in sonnet 20, androgyny, misogyny, Petrarchism and friendship curiously intermingle.

Much of what can be seen in those poems can be seen in other of the sonnets where Shakespeare's speaker directly images the young man as an androgyne or implies his androgyny. Sonnets 41 and 54, for example, show the speaker describing the young man in terms that accord with the portrayals of him in 20 and in 53. The youth is called '[g]entle' and '[b]eauteous' in sonnet 41 (ll. 5–6), recalling the description of him in the first eight lines of sonnet 20, his beauty being referred to in each of the quatrains and in the final couplet. Perhaps, too, the proverb rewritten in ll. 5–6 feminizes the youth; it seems to make him resemble the Adonis of *Venus and Adonis*.[38] In sonnet 54, furthermore, Shakespeare's speaker addresses the young man as 'beauteous and lovely youth' (l. 13, cf. ll. 1–4), the words serving to point an analogy between the young man and the beauty of roses. The speaker's praise elaborates not only on his depiction of the young man in sonnets 20, 41 and the like, but also on this claim in sonnet 53:

> Speak of the spring and foison of the year;
> The one doth shadow of your beauty show,
> The other as your bounty doth appear,
> And you in every blessed shape we know.
>
> (ll. 9–12)

That sonnets 41 and 54 image the youth in terms akin to those of 20 and of 53 can be readily evidenced; and there is another important similarity between the two sets of poems. Sonnets 41 and 54 ambiguously celebrate the young man. In each the speaker's praise is qualified, especially in 41. There the speaker refers to the 'pretty wrongs' of the beautiful young man, asserts that his gentleness and beauty make him vulnerable, then represents him as the victim of his 'beauty' and 'youth' as if they were external forces compelling him to err (ll. 1, 5–6, and 10).[39] Blame, praise, and an ingenious, insistent magnanimity come together in portrayal of the young man, the speaker suggesting that stability and constancy dominate him whatever his acts of falsehood and inconstancy. As the speaker says at the poem's beginning:

> Those pretty wrongs that liberty commits,
> When I am sometime absent from thy heart,
> Thy beauty and thy years full well befits
> For still temptation follows where thou art.

In sonnet 54 the speaker's analogy between roses and the young man contains this contrast between 'roses' and 'canker blooms':

> The canker blooms have full as deep a dye
> As the perfumed tincture of the roses,
> Hang on such thorns, and play as wantonly,
> When summer's breath their masked buds discloses. . . .
>
> (ll. 5–8)

While the contrast begun in that quatrain goes on to emphasize what 'canker blooms' lack, namely, the fragrance which emanates from other roses and which is subsequently preserved in perfume, the lines introducing the contrast do so by comparing 'canker blooms' with their counterparts. That comparison is important because, at the poem's end, scent-bearing roses become a similitude through which the youth is invited to understand himself and his relationship with the speaker. The comparison focuses initially on colour, 'tincture', raising notions of both artificial colouring and of essential identity (l. 6). Then, far more problematic, it focuses on luxuriant beauty, the reference to 'thorns' and the sequence 'play', 'wantonly', 'discloses' raising and juxtaposing notions of pain and of unrestrained sexuality. The result would seem to be the generating of a contradiction which is unresolved in the poem and which aligns it with sonnet 41. Although the speaker asserts at the end of the sonnet that he will preserve in (immortal) 'verse' the 'truth', or constancy, of the young man – just as the makers of perfume preserve the fragrance essential to roses – he has already associated pain as well as sexual inconstancy with scent-bearing roses and thereby made them an ambiguous analogue to the young man. The youth is invited to interpret himself and his relationship with the speaker in terms of a similitude where overt praise merges gracefully with oblique disparagement. It seems that in sonnet 54, as in 41, celebration and depreciation of the young man are inseparable.

Yet with such important similarities between the two sets of poems coexist equally important differences. In sonnet 41, for example, the speaker implicitly imposes on the young man that fiction of transcendence and inclusion which he also imposes on him in sonnets 20 and 53; however, he problematically elaborates on it so as almost to excuse the young man's flaws and, as does not occur in the other two poems, confines himself within it, for all his obvious discontent and disillusionment. Another important and related difference is that in 41 the speaker, while narcissistically fictionalizing the youth, uses his representation of the youth as a means to ponder his own experience of loving: as a mirror in which to reflect upon himself. Narcissism in a variant form distinguishes sonnet 54 from 41 as well as from 20 and 53. There the speaker not only imposes his own ideals and needs on the young man but ends in self-celebration.[40] His ambiguous encomium of the youth finally also becomes unambiguous praise of his own creative power – unambiguous, at least, in relation to the genuineness and scope of that power if not its application to the youth.

Having focused on such similarties and differences, one can now consider something of how they, and the play of discourse in which they are implicated, relate to sonnets 20–126 as a whole. Perhaps, by way of beginning, one should start with a point made earlier: that although Shakespeare's speaker recurrently imposes fictions of transcendence and inclusion on the young man in sonnets 20–126, the first and most elaborate of those being the fiction of the youth's androgyny, he fables the young man's perfection in other ways as well. Sonnet 20, the sonnets discussed above and, especially yet not solely, the sonnets environing 94, directly or indirectly portray the youth as an androgyne. However sonnets 31 and 37 represent him as a transcendent, inclusive but not androgynous figure. The first plays with the fiction of spiritual union pervasive in sonnets 20–126, linking it with the notion of the Many and the One; the second uses no specific, subordinate fiction in idealizing the young man. In sonnet 63, to cite a further example of difference, the speaker idealizes the young man partly through the fiction that he is a sun on earth: a fiction of transcendence but of neither inclusion nor androgyny; a fiction deployed both to elevate and to depreciate him in sonnet 33.[41] The contrariety of sonnet 33 is, moreover, of immediate rather than of incidental relevance here. It serves to illustrate the point that, irrespective of the terms through which the speaker fables the perfection of the youth, the celebratory fictions imposed on the young man seem to waver or to alternate between contraries. For example, sonnet 31 belongs to a cluster of poems (29–31) where the speaker asserts that his 'dear friend' compensates for the misfortunes in his life (30, l. 13; see the final couplet of each sonnet). The speaker alters the motif of compensation in sonnet 32 (see ll. 9–14); then, in a subsequent group of sonnets (33–35) he dwells on a rupture between the youth and himself, finding it necessary that he compensate for the young man's disregard and doing so with excuses not easily or simply fashioned. Thereafter, in sonnets 36–39, the speaker returns to fabling the youth's perfection – a short-lived return. A further group of poems (40–42) reveals the speaker reflecting on his loss of a female lover to the young man, a loss which seems primarily to evoke tortuous excuses of the 'dear friend' and focus on that friend's sexuality.[42]

Finally here, in order to clarify the general point made a moment ago about the process of wavering or alternation between contraries in the Sonnets, I should like to glance at how sonnet 67, one of the poems in which Shakespeare's speaker idealizes the youth as transcendent, inclusive and androgynous, is involved in a mode of alternation much like that affecting 31. In 67 the speaker depicts the young man as the quintessence of beauty and as the last trace of the golden age, a representation elaborated upon in the next poem.[43] But in sonnet 69 he continues that portrayal of the youth only to disfigure it. Initially asserting that others who view the young man likewise affirm his beauty, the speaker goes on to say that while they gaze on the young man this also happens:

> They look into the beauty of thy mind,
> And that in guess they measure by thy deeds;
> Then, churls, their thought – although their eyes were kind –
> To thy fair flow'r add the rank smell of weeds;
> > But why thy odor matcheth not thy show,
> > The soil is this, that thou dost common grow.
>
> (ll. 9–14)

Line 12 at once anticipates the final line of 94, with the damning proverb it reformulates, and leads to 'common grow', which certainly refers to conduct inappropriate to the youth's social class but, in doing that, may refer particularly to his sexual behaviour. To read the last six lines of the poem is to see that although the speaker displaces and supposedly disagrees with the suggestion of an incongruity between the youth's beautiful appearance and notional 'beauty of . . . mind', the connection '[t]hey' make between the youth's 'deeds' and 'mind' appears more credible than the mere disassociation of the two protested by the speaker on the basis of allegedly privileged knowledge. Not only the conduct of the young man is scrutinized in the Sonnets, however; nor is he alone made subject to fictions.

If Shakespeare's speaker fictionalizes the young man, so too he fictionalizes himself. In other words, if the speaker imposes idealizing fictions on the young man – fictions that threaten to collapse, or that he denies, or wilfully refuses to deny, and iterates – so too he problematically assumes a number of roles, imposing fictions on himself. They are not separable from those through which he variously fashions the youth and in their own ways they also can be idealizing. They are not separable, it is true, because the speaker's fictionalizing of himself necessarily interacts with his fictionalizing of the young man. Yet what seems more important is this: they are linked with the discourses of androgyny and of friendship, of Petrarchism and of misogyny as are the fictions imposed on the youth. The speaker's self-idealization is likewise less than straightforward, for his fictions tend to represent him in terms of idealized, empowered devotion and extreme, hence idealized, devoted but powerless unworthiness. At the last, moreover, they are profoundly and subtly changed when the idealization of the young man is considered with deepened scepticism. Before such doubt and change can be discussed, of course, one must consider the speaker's antithetic idealizings of himself.

A useful place to begin is with sonnets 35–37. In the first of those poems the speaker memorably describes as 'civil war' his experience of compensating for, of excusing, some 'trespass' committed against him by the youth (ll. 12 and 6 respectively). 'Such civil war is in my love and hate,' he says. Although he sounds like Romeo, his words allude not to civil strife but to that self-division which is essential to the Petrarchan psychology of love. In fact the Petrarchan psychology, and rhetoric, used by the speaker in line 12 pervade the sonnet from line 7 to its end. It is clear that they have been repositioned – the addressee is male and truly flawed – yet they are Petrarchan nonetheless. Furthermore, sonnet 36 indicates that the Petrarchan psychology and rhetoric of 35 have not been entirely relocated, because the speaker immediately addresses the young man through the discourse of friendship: 'Let me confess that we two must be twain,/Although our undivided loves are one' (ll. 1–2). The discourse of friendship, as has been mentioned in Chapter 3, is merged with that of love in Petrarch's *Rime*; here, in sonnets 35–36, they are juxtaposed if not fused.[44] Amid and after the reworking of Petrarch in those poems there emerge two fictions which the speaker recurrently imposes on himself. First, in 36, he represents himself as the utterly unworthy, powerless, devoted friend of the young man. He clearly emphasizes the intensity of his devotion, taking on the Petrarchan role of love's martyr (ll. 13–14).[45] That Petrarchan role having been taken on, it seems that in sonnet 37 the speaker takes on another and thus presents what is the second of his self-imposed fictions: that of the ageing lover whose desire abides although his time slips from him. So the speaker has portrayed himself in sonnets 22 and 32; so, for example, he does again in sonnets 62–63 and 71–74. In 37 the role appears with a variation, for it is presented initially through a comparison between the speaker and 'a decrepit father'. Shakespeare's speaker announces:

> As a decrepit father takes delight
> To see his active child do deeds of youth,
> So I, made lame by fortune's dearest spite,
> Take all my comfort of thy worth and truth.
>
> (ll. 1–4)

But he begins with a statement of likeness, not of identity, and soon he proceeds to address the youth in language that suggests the registers of sonnets 36 and 53 rather than a register of fatherhood.[46] The speaker's momentary comparison of himself to a 'decrepit father' draws attention, however, to aspects of the two fictions that need further discussion, and consideration in light of another Petrarchan fiction, or role, adopted by him.

Authority seems inescapably to be one of those aspects. The speaker cedes authority to the youth, much as Petrarch's persona does in the *Rime* to Laura and to Colonna. The analogy is appropriate not only because Shakespeare's speaker can be seen as adopting a number of Petrarchan roles but also because the young man appears at times in the Sonnets both to transcend Laura (20, 53) and to be the speaker's patron.[47] A hybrid in his androgyny, the youth is likewise a hybrid insofar as he evokes in the speaker at once personal and, as it were, social desire: he is truly the 'master mistress' of the speaker's 'passion'. Quite decorous, then, is the speaker's Petrarch-derived manoeuvre of identifying the young man as his muse. In sonnet 38 he asks: 'For who's so dumb, that cannot write to thee,/When thou thyself dost give invention light?' (ll. 7–8). And he continues: 'Be thou the tenth muse, ten times more in worth/Than those old nine which rhymers invocate' (ll. 9–10). Yet the speaker does not altogether cede authority to his 'master mistress' in sonnets 20–126, as so many of them testify. He did not entirely cede it to the youth in sonnets 1–19; Petrarch's persona does not entirely cede it to Laura, although Colonna remains unchallenged. Shakespeare's speaker proclaims again and again throughout the Sonnets what the older friend can offer to the younger, the client to the patron. As he declares in 55:

> Not marble nor the gilded monuments
> Of princes shall outlive this pow'rful rhyme,
> But you shall shine more bright in these contents
> Than unswept stone, besmeared with sluttish time.

(ll. 1–4)

If as 'dear friend', patron, muse, the young man supposedly authorizes the speaker's verse, the speaker nonetheless emphasizes throughout the Sonnets that his verse expresses too his personal authority as a maker, for it will preserve the young man and, in fact, keep him alive until the end of the world. The lines quoted above predict that the youth's life will survive death resplendently because of the resplendent verse which celebrates him now and which will continue to do so undimmed. In sonnets 18 and 63, the speaker says that his verse will confer life beyond death on the young man, not merely commemorate him: 'His beauty shall in these black lines be seen,/And they shall live, and he in them still green' (63, ll. 13–14; cf. 18, ll. 9–14). The speaker's art lives and cannot die; accordingly, whatever is part of it lives transcending time and death – until the end of all things. Thus the fiction of his being the perfectly devoted, inspired, empowered encomiast of the youth gestures toward the young man as the author of his creativity yet implies distinctly and often the uniqueness of that creativity, which transforms not only the inspiration given by the youth but the youth himself. Moreover while Ovid and Horace do seem to influence the speaker's choice of words when he uses the eternizing motif, as for example in sonnet 55, his deployment of it in relation to the 'master mistress of [his] passion' seems to resemble that by Petrarch's persona when he celebrates Laura. The persona of the *Rime*, as does Shakespeare's speaker, negotiates problems concerning authority, mediation and art's transforming power; in addition, he negotiates those problems with reference to a venerated object of desire, as does Shakespeare's speaker, not merely with reference to himself, as do Ovid and Horace.[48] The speaker's fiction of himself as the idealized celebrant of the young man therefore appears mainly to be Petrarchan rather than Roman.

Further problems are implied to beset Shakespeare's speaker, of course. One problem is that, while he alternates between presenting himself as empowered and as powerless, he at times must also confront others' attempts to gain the favour of the youth. In a group of sonnets, 78–86, he variously considers such rivals and their writings.

At some points within those sonnets he portrays himself as enabled to write only by the youth, only for whom and of whom he writes (for example, 78, ll. 9–14). Elsewhere he represents himself as being intimidated by 'a better spirit', much as Antony claims his genius to be by that of Octavian (80, ll. 1–10, here at l. 2). Elsewhere again, he can assertively indicate the 'virtue' (strength) of his creativity and the life-conferring authority of his 'gentle verse' (81, ll. 13 and 8 respectively). So, in contrast, the speaker can admit to his art's inadequacy to satisfy the expectations of the young man – whose expectations he acknowledges in a manner at once deferential and latently ironic – and the young man's right to turn to work by others (82, ll. 5–8). Accordingly, in sonnets 83 and 84, the speaker praises but likewise reproaches his friend and patron. On the other hand, in sonnet 85 the speaker says that his 'muse' is 'tongue-tied' and that he 'think[s] good thoughts, whilst other write good words' (ll. 1 and 5 respectively). Then in the following poem he asks:

> Was it the proud full sail of his great verse,
> Bound for the prize of all too precious you,
> That did my ripe thoughts in my brain inhearse,
> Making their tomb the womb wherein they grew?
>
> (ll. 1–4)

Back in sonnet 69 the speaker talks of others, not him, imposing a fiction on the youth – a fiction that seems more credible, less fictional, than his claim to have privileged knowledge of the youth's immaculate mind. In sonnet 85 the impinging 'others' to whom he alludes are of course rivals who celebrate the young man. And as the lines quoted above indicate, in 86 he alludes to a particular rival, a powerful and even sinister figure who has translated the likeness of the young man into alien verse.[49] It is interesting to see how the speaker, at the end of 86, manages the recounted situation of rivalry by asserting the defiant authority of his creative power and at once submitting that to the authority of the youth. 'I was not sick of any fear from thence', he says with reference to his mysteriously aided rival (l. 12), continuing: 'But when your countenance filled up his line,/Then lacked I matter, that enfeebled mine' (ll. 13–14; cf. 80, ll. 1–4). The speaker cunningly announces the depletion of his verse in a final couplet which implies that, whatever the achievements of his rivals, his considerable art exists solely for the young man. One could more broadly make the point in this way. After an eerily witty characterization of a rival and defiance of him, the speaker disingenuously admits to a loss of creativity: a loss attributed to the youth and shrewdly acknowledged in terms that stress the speaker's entire devotion to and artistic dependence upon the young man. Now as has been indicated earlier, the impinging of the world upon, or its intrusion into, the relationship between the speaker and the youth is a problem for the speaker repeatedly in the Sonnets.[50] His conflict with rivals is, then, both a specific manifestation of the world's intrusiveness and a direct challenge to his role as the perfectly devoted, empowered celebrant of the friend, patron and muse. How astutely the speaker can deal with rivalry may be gathered from 86. That sonnet, moreover, both illuminates and is illuminated by 112, in which the speaker alludes to his oppression by the world and says to the youth: 'You are my all the world, and I must strive/ To know my shames and praises from your tongue;/None else to me, nor I to none alive' (ll. 5–7). There the speaker envisions anew the commonplace '*multum in parvo*', rendering it in effect as '*non multum sed omnia in parvo*' in order to describe the importance of the youth to him: that of being a world within the malign, mundane world.[51] Yet once more one sees the intricacy with which Shakespeare's speaker can interplay the discourses of friendship, Petrarchism and patronage.

Such intricacy notwithstanding, it is out of the contradictions within, between and among the poems focused on rivalry that those poems concerning the speaker's separation from his 'master mistress' seem to develop. The breaking of their relationship is signalled at the start of sonnet 87:

> Farewell, thou art too dear for my possessing,
> And like enough thou know'st thy estimate.
> The charter of thy worth gives thee releasing;
> My bonds in thee are all determinate.

The last of the sonnets focused on the young man, an elegiac lyric of twelve lines, less directly but no less clearly bids the youth farewell. In sonnet 126 the speaker says:

> O thou, my lovely boy, who in thy pow'r
> Dost hold time's fickle glass, his sickle hour,
> Who hast by waning grown, and therein show'st
> Thy lovers withering, as thy sweet self grow'st —
> If nature, sovereign mistress over wrack,
> As thou goest onwards still will pluck thee back,
> She keeps thee to this purpose, that her skill
> May time disgrace, and wretched minute kill.
> Yet fear her, O thou minion of her pleasure;
> She may detain but not still keep her treasure.

Her audit, though delayed, answered must be,
And her quietus is to render thee.[52]

As juxtaposition of the poems emphasizes, the speaker uses the
rhetorics of different economies in farewelling the young man.
He employs the rhetoric of commerce throughout 87, interweaving with it both relevant legal terms and terms which incongruously
evoke the Senecan theory of giving and receiving gifts – a theory
long before incorporated into the discourse of patronage.[53] Developing his suggestion, in the group of poems concerned with rivalry,
that the youth holds no merely high opinion of his own merits, the
speaker indicates that the young man no doubt has a lofty sense of
his own worldly value and that their relationship can be seen as a
one-sided financial arrangement. The speaker does not imply that
the young man's probable self-appraisal is exaggerated; nor does he
imply that the relationship between them could ever have been
other than adversely one-sided. After all, he often testifies elsewhere
in the Sonnets to the youth's extraordinary qualities, especially in the
rivalry poems.[54] Elsewhere in the Sonnets his self-abasement before
the young man is frequent enough, too; again, that is especially so in
the poems concerned with rivalry. But in 87 the impersonal, delimiting rhetoric of commerce coldly extinguishes the warmth of the
discourse of friendship, the fervour and defiance of limitation that
are part of Petrarchan discourse. Moreover, as has been suggested
above, that rhetoric jars in the sonnet with those words which evoke
the Senecan theory of giving and receiving of gifts. Thus 'dear' in
the opening line soon has its meaning of 'beloved' overshadowed by
its significations of economic cost and of class superiority. The overshadowing or perhaps contaminating of 'beloved' as a signification
begins the speaker's account, paradoxically through the formal language
of finance and financial law, of his broken intimacy with the young
man.[55] In that context, when the speaker asks, 'For how do I hold thee
but by thy granting [?]' (l. 5), 'granting' brings irreconcilably together
the notions of financial dealing and of gift-giving. The young man's
bestowal of himself on the speaker was both the 'granting' of a 'patent'
(l. 5 then 8) and the 'granting' of a 'fair gift', the speaker claims. Except,
the speaker also says, that what was a gift made in self-ignorance by
the young man – or in ignorance about the gift's receiver – turned out
to be soon-expired 'bonds' (l. 4; cf. ll. 9–10). The dissonance between
the rhetoric of commerce and the evocative language of gift-giving
increases when the speaker observes that the youth, having bestowed
himself as a gift, subsequently took himself back increased in value.[56]

Seneca's theory of giving and receiving gifts posits that upon receiving a gift one thanks the giver, praises the gift, and seeks to reciprocate the giver's generosity. The speaker's slyly reproachful wit near the end of the sonnet lies, I think, not in implying that he has enhanced the youth in some way despite having been given such a gift in error, but in indicating that when the young man reconsidered his own value, after he had made a gift of himself, he simply took himself away from the speaker. 'So thy great gift, upon misprision growing,/Comes home again, on better judgement making', the speaker observes (ll. 11–12). The sonnet's closing lines sharply contradict those euphorically ending sonnet 29. At the end of 87 one reads: 'Thus have I had thee as a dream doth flatter:/In sleep a king, but waking no such matter.' At the end of 29: 'For thy sweet love remember'd such wealth brings,/That then I scorn to change my state with kings.'

In sonnet 126 the speaker appears to farewell the young man with the finality but not the dissonance with which he does so in sonnet 87. Through the rhetoric of the economy of nature he portrays the youth as isolated: transcending and remote from those who love him; pre-eminent and privileged in the natural cycle as if the central figure in a vast pageant. It is a portrayal of the youth that has striking counterparts among the first nineteen sonnets. Here furthermore, as in some of those poems, the speaker indicates that while the young man transcends others he is nonetheless subject to natural process – and thus at once the central figure and another victim within the pageant unfolding around him. As the speaker warns in the last lines of the poem: 'Her [nature's] audit, though delayed answered must be,/And her quietus is to render thee' (ll. 11–12). Those are certainly words of farewell; for all that, they are not words which abandon the speaker's idealizing of the youth. That is to say, at the end of the main group of sonnets focused on the young man, after the wavering and alternation to be seen throughout the speaker's imaging of the youth and of his relationship in general with the youth, one sees the speaker finally picturing the young man as the 'lovely boy', as the Adonis-like object of desire described in sonnet 20.[57] In order to suggest what I take to be the larger importance of that ending to sonnets 20–126, however, I should like to turn to the sonnets between the two poems of farewell.

(IV) LOSING AND KEEPING

In between sonnets 87 and 126 one sees representations of the young man and of the speaker which accord with those in the sonnets prior to the first poem of farewell. Again can be seen the speaker's idealizing of the youth along with the wavering and alternation that query it; again, as well, can be seen the the speaker's antithetic self-idealizations. Yet although there are important likenesses between the last of the sonnets focused on the young man and those preceding them, there are also important differences. Chief among the latter seem to be these. The speaker's praise of the young man, although no less elaborate or apparently intense than it was before, both coexists with and has for its prelude disparise more elaborate and apparently more intense than any directed previously at the youth.[58] Furthermore, although the speaker asserts his perfect devotion to the youth and the power of his art much as he has beforehand in the Sonnets, his disparise of himself is now more self-accusatory and hence more self-abasing than that he has deployed earlier. Two other differences are of greater consequence than either of those, however. The doubt that the speaker has generated in celebrating the young man becomes stronger – which does not mean that the speaker stops idealizing the youth, as sonnet 126 attests. In addition, the speaker announces that his love – his capacity to love unalterably – rises above physical changes to the person he loves or imperfections within himself. Love is of eternity, he suggests, so transcending time and the merely finite. Sonnets 20–126 therefore end in celebration of the speaker rather than in praise of the young man. Just so, Shakespeare's speaker has earlier promised immortality to the youth but has instead immortalized himself.

If in sonnets 78–86 the speaker reveals anxiety about competition for the young man's favour, in sonnets 88–93 he reveals anxiety about losing the young man. The unease caused by rivals led the speaker both to remark upon flaws in the young man and to ponder losing him. But in the poems concerned more closely with loss the speaker in effect discredits his idealizing of the youth while nonetheless continuing it. Moreover, his intensified self-disparise is clearly self-celebrating. Through those paradoxes seems to be expressed a twofold denial: on the one hand, that the young man embodies the integrity, the harmonious stability, attributed to him in sonnet 20 and often thereafter; on the other, that the young man can actually be lost to the speaker. I do not mean to suggest, as regards the first aspect of denial, that the speaker ceases to impose idealizing fictions of transcendence and inclusion on the youth. For example, amid his ostentatious self-disparise and his depreciation of the young man he still praises the young man's beauty in terms that recall the fiction of androgyny unfolded in and after sonnet 20. His fiction of the youth as androgyne has now, however, been all but discredited. It is not that the speaker denies the youth's possession of androgynous beauty; rather, he cannot view the youth's notional androgyny as being an harmonious reconciliation of opposites. The wavering and alternation inseparable from the fiction of the youth as androgyne have at last, so to speak, fragmented it. Thus one sees the speaker acknowledge that the young man is quite capable of duplicity (88, ll. 4, 7 and 14; 89, ll. 5–6; 90, l. 8; 92, l. 9; 93, *passim*). One also sees the speaker praise the youth's beauty in ways that evoke the notion of his androgyny, describing him as 'blessed-fair' (92, l. 13), and subsequently adding (after comparing himself to 'a deceived husband', in 93, l. 2):

> But heav'n in thy creation did decree,
> That in thy face sweet love should ever dwell,
> What'er thy thoughts or thy heart's workings be,
> Thy look should nothing thence but sweetness tell.
>
> (ll. 9–12)

In later sonnets the young man is portrayed again as an Adonis figure and as Beauty incarnate. The speaker celebrates him much as in sonnet 53; and it appears that the speaker's praise of the youth is, at least within the frames of sonnets such as 97–99, less problematic than the similar praise offered in the fifty-third sonnet. Certainly in 97–99 the speaker's celebration of the young man is less immediately compromised than that in 88–93.[59]

Elaborate praise and dispraise coexists, then, in sonnets 88–93; nonetheless it is clear that, in diversely and continuously acknowledging the young man's capacity to be duplicitous, the speaker dispraises the youth with a deepened doubt – and so with an apparent intensity – not seen previously in the Sonnets. The final lines of 93 seem decisive in that regard: 'How like Eve's apple doth thy beauty grow,/If thy sweet virtue answer not thy show.' What a various falling-off was there in such a case, the speaker implies. It is also clear in sonnets 88–93, however, that the speaker's self-depreciation and self-abasement are more elaborate and profound than previously in the Sonnets. If the young man proves duplicitous, the speaker repeatedly suggests, then his duplicity will not be opposed. The speaker presents himself as love's powerless martyr, only too well aware of his own failings and limitations – and entirely devoted to the young man, notwithstanding his recognition of the young man's imperfection. For example, the speaker says:

> When thou shalt be disposed to set me light
> And place my merit in the eye of scorn,

Upon thy side against myself I'll fight,
And prove thee virtuous, though thou art forsworn.
With mine own weakness being best acquainted,
Upon thy part I can set down a story
Of faults concealed, wherein I am attainted,
That thou in losing me shall win much glory.

(88, ll. 1–8)

He concludes that same poem with: 'Such is my love – to thee I so belong – /That for thy right myself will bear all wrong.' In the next sonnet he says: 'Speak of my lameness, and I straight will halt,/ Against thy reason making no defence' (89, ll. 3–4). At the end of the poem he adds: 'For thee, against myself I'll vow debate,/For I must ne'er love him whom thou dost hate.' In 90, having told the youth, 'Then hate me when thou wilt, if ever, now,/Now while the world is bent my deeds to cross' (ll. 1–2), he concludes: '[O]ther strains of woe, which now seem woe,/Compared with loss of thee will not seem so.' And in 92 the speaker declares his unalterable love for the young man:

But do thy worst to steal thyself away,
For term of life thou art assured mine,
And life no longer than thy love will stay,
For it depends upon that love of thine.

(ll. 1–4)

The farewell to the young man is not, therefore, an end to friendship with him according to the speaker. He announces the end of friendship only to deny its end and loss of the young man – and thereby to celebrate himself or, more exactly, his capacity for love beyond change. There is power amid powerlessness in the speaker's role as love's martyr.

The speaker's claim of perfect devotion has already been identified as an element of his self-idealization. What can be seen in light of the poems discussed above is that his claim implies him to be in fact empowered whether he appears to be so or not. That is to say, the speaker represents himself as having awakened, amid his losing the young man, to the power and, indeed, dignity of his own transcendent capacity to love. I shall pursue that self-representation presently, as well as the speaker's awareness of the fragility and even wilfulness in his idealizing the youth. For the moment, however, the three poems that directly follow 88–93 must be considered, since in them the speaker compacts the praise and dispraise of the youth recurrent throughout 88–93, re-evaluates the process of praising and dispraising him, and offers a blazon of the young man that is perhaps more revealing of him – and of the speaker himself – than any yet seen in sonnets 20–126.

Interpretations of sonnet 94 disagree about many things, not least about whether the poem implicitly praises or dispraises the young man. In my view, the poem praises the young man in such a way as to turn praise itself into depreciation, doing so appropriately because the youth is presented as someone who depreciates what is praise-worthy in himself – or allows it to be depreciated.[60] Earlier in the Sonnets the speaker obliquely praises the young man by suggesting that he is another sun: the sun of the speaker's life. Yet in sonnet 33, as has been mentioned above, the sun metaphor is used at once to praise and to dispraise the young man. Shakespeare's speaker remarks that '[t]he region cloud' has obscured '[his] sun', coming between himself and the youth, then finally and gnomically observes: 'Suns of the world may stain when heav'n's sun staineth' (ll. 9, 12, and 14 respectively). A similar strategy occurs in sonnet 94. The difference between the speaker's strategy in 33 and that used by him in 94 seems, however, to have at least two major elements. First, in 94 the fiction of transcendence imposed by the speaker on the young man overgoes that deployed in 33. Next, the more hyperbolic fiction is likewise the more problematic. It implies higher celebration and harsher condemnation of the youth. The opening quatrain of sonnet 94, for example, appears to reveal the speaker associating a specified class of people with Aristotle's 'Unmoved Mover', or equivalent to God. There one reads:

> They that have pow'r to hurt, and will do none,
> That do not do the thing they most do show,
> Who moving others are themselves as stone,
> Unmoved, cold, and to temptation slow. . . .

The speaker seems to suggest that those whose 'pow'r' is self-controlled, evident – perhaps duplicitous – but restrained, and who arouse emotion in others while themselves being virtually impervious to or immovable by emotion, are as gods of this world. Accordingly, in the subsequent quatrain, he describes them as 'rightly' receiving heavenly gifts and carefully protecting the 'riches' nature has given them; hence they are self-possessed possessors of whatever 'excellence' has been bestowed upon them, whereas '[o]thers' are mere 'stewards' of such things. He says:

They rightly do inherit heaven's graces,
And husband nature's riches from expense;
They are the lords and owners of their faces,
Others but stewards of their excellence.

(ll. 5–8)

Assuming, for the moment, that one accepts the broad outline just given of the sonnet's initial quatrains, what is one nonetheless encountering?[61]

One encounters in those lines, I think, a blazon that both celebrates the 'unmoved movers' of this world and mocks them. The speaker acknowledges their power over others and themselves; he attributes that power, on the other hand, not to aristocratic virtues – to *virtu* or to *sdegno*, for instance – but to a cold narcissism, an inertia allied with or begetting prudence.[62] In them prudence seems an unlovely wisdom. The blazon could in certain respects fit Angelo from *Measure for Measure* or maybe some of the figures in portraits by Bronzino. It is also a blazon which in certain ways fits the young man as he is portrayed in sonnets 1–19 and thereafter as well.[63] Its aptness to the youth becomes clearer when the speaker continues:

The summer's flow'r is to the summer sweet,
Though to itself it only live and die;
But if that flow'r with base infection meet,
The basest weed outbraves his dignity:
    For sweetest things turn sourest by their deeds;
    Lilies that fester smell far worse than weeds.

The final line of the sonnet distinctly echoes the twelfth line of 69, in which the speaker refers to 'the world's' (l. 1) disparaging opinion of the difference between the physical appearance and mental condition the youth.[64] Furthermore, as a whole the last six lines of sonnet 94 recall the oblique or direct accusations of vice coexistent with beauty that are made against the youth in sonnets such as 33–35, 40–42, 67 and 84.[65] Thus in sonnet 94 the speaker seems to celebrate the young man not as another sun of this world but rather as one of its gods, its 'unmoved movers', and not to suggest that aristocratic virtue has so elevated him but rather that his apotheosis results from his narcissism, on which the speaker has elsewhere recurrently focused. The poem draws toward its end, moreover, with the speaker apparently recounting to the youth, relating to him, an unflattering commonplace: that while self-contained beauty – something attributed to the young man again and again in the Sonnets – need generate nothing and yet be valuable, its moral contamination makes it odious by comparison with even the ordinary and less attractive.[66] The final couplet of the sonnet might therefore be read as suggesting that the youth is a fallen god of this world.[67]

What makes him so spectacularly paradoxical a being is pursued further in sonnets 95 and 96. The contradiction between outer beauty and inner ugliness in the young man, implied rather than openly announced in sonnet 94, is now directly identified by the speaker. Reflecting upon it, he compacts the praise and dispraise of the youth proffered in sonnets 88–93 – as well as elsewhere – and re-evaluates the process of praising and dispraising him. Tracing the paradoxicality of the young man, the speaker acknowledges his perfect (androgynous) beauty and the ugliness, the corruption, which mar it from within; he acknowledges the doubleness which not only makes the youth's existence a contradiction, rather than a harmony of opposites, but fragments it. In 95 the speaker begins by elaborately comparing the young man's developing reputation to a budding though cankered rose: 'How sweet and lovely dost thou make the shame/ Which, like a canker in the fragrant rose,/ Doth spot the beauty of thy budding name!' (ll. 1–3). Usually the speaker compares the young man's physical beauty to that of a rose, thereby contributing to the portrayal of him throughout the Sonnets as at once androgynously and perfectly beautiful. Here, as a result, picturing his reputation through rose imagery inevitably evokes those uses of it which suggest his personal beauty. Moreover the next line of the sonnet appears to allude, at least in part, to the physical beauty which the comparisons to roses usually celebrate. 'O in what sweets dost thou thy sins enclose!' the speaker says, as if in parodic anticipation of Herbert's lines, 'Sweet spring, full of sweet dayes and roses,/ A box where sweets compacted lie' ('Vertue', ll. 9–10).[68] In sonnet 96 the speaker says to the young man:

> As on the finger of a throned queen
> The basest jewel will be well esteemed,
> So are those errors that in thee are seen,
> To truths translated, and for true things deemed.
>
> (ll. 5–8)

The simile at once feminizes and idealizes the young man, evoking the notion of his androgynous, perfect beauty with more directness if perhaps less resonance than does the rose imagery in the previous sonnet. Matters of directness and resonance aside, however, there is an emphatic contrast in each case between outer, perfect beauty and interior ugliness. Furthermore, in each case the speaker focuses on that contrast in terms which indicate at once the confusingly graceful coexistence of opposites in the young man and their manifesting his self-division, the radical fragmentation of his existence. The latter are forcibly suggested, for example, by 'canker' and 'spot' being played against 'rose' and 'beauty', or by 'errors' being set against 'truths'. One is shown the young man's doubleness; and his potential for duplicity is likewise put before the reader.[69] If the fiction of the youth's androgyny is evoked, it does not have harmony and integrity among its elements.

That fiction's discrediting has important consequences for praise of the young man. Its discrediting of course lays bare its fictionality, a consequence that the speaker does not consider at this point; when, earlier, he discredited his fable of the young man as another sun, and laid bare its fictionality, he did not then pursue the implications of his having done so. He continued to impose vulnerable, precarious fictions on the youth, which is what happens now.[70] On the other hand, a simpler and even more obvious consequence certainly is considered by the speaker, namely, that the contrariety which discredits the fiction makes praise of the young man curiously problematic. The mingling of beauty and vice, aesthetic grace and moral ugliness in the youth virtually transforms condemnation of him into celebration:

> That tongue that tells the story of thy days,
> Making lascivious comments on thy sport,
> Cannot dispraise but in a kind of praise;
> Naming thy name blesses an ill report.
>
> (95, ll. 5–8)

His very imperfections are perceived as enhancements (96, ll. 5–8). Praise of the youth should have limits but dispraise itself becomes 'a kind of praise'. Thus it is ultimately not praise of the young man that his contrariety makes problematic but interpretation of him:

> Some say thy fault is youth, some wantonness,
> Some say thy grace is youth and gentle sport;
> Both grace and faults are loved of more and less;
> Thou mak'st faults graces that to thee resort.
>
> (96, ll. 1–4)

As has been suggested earlier, in these later sonnets one sees intensified dispraise of the young man and intensified doubt about representing him as an icon of the ideal. Such dispraise and doubt are often linked in the later poems, as they are here in 94–96 and as might in any event be expected. Yet, it could be asked, if at least some of the idealizing fictions imposed on the youth are discredited in various of the later as in a number of the earlier sonnets, how can mere doubt be said to exist: surely, at different times, the speaker's doubt has become disbelief? Surely, in other words, one discovers not scepticism in sonnets 20–126 but doubt that is superseded by disillusionment?

Were there only doubt and disillusionment in those sonnets then indeed they could not be associated with scepticism, except insofar as scepticism might be seen as a prelude to disbelief. But in sonnets 20–126, as has been shown above, doubt and disillusionment are not simply sequential nor are they alone dominant. In sonnet 96 the speaker implies that interpretation of the youth is problematic because of his contrariety; yet what makes interpretation of the speaker's portrayal of him problematic in sonnets 20–126 is likewise its contrariety – that recurrent wavering and oscillation which implicate or juxtapose contrary views of the young man. For example, sonnet 96 is followed by three poems where the speaker suggests that the young man is at once Adonis and Beauty incarnate. It may be that sonnets 95–99, and some or all of their fellows, are not in the order designed by Shakespeare; whatever the case, at present we have solely the order of the 1609 edition in which to read the Sonnets. It may be, should the 1609 edition evince the authorial order of the Sonnets, that in 97–99 the speaker is unwittingly revealing himself to be another of those whose judgements are confounded by the youth's appearance. Whether or not that in turn is so, however, the point remains that a brace of poems critical of the young man is succeeded by three which celebrate him as though no criticism of him – much less such searching criticism – had been expressed immediately before or at all. Doubt and certainty, disbelief and faith coexist in sonnets 20–126; their speaker's general view of the young man, inasmuch as it can be discerned, is hard to describe otherwise than as sceptical.

Two elements of that view need to be discussed further before the account of sonnets 20–126 in this chapter can conclude: intensified doubt about representing the young man as an icon of the ideal; the speaker's assertion of his transcendent capacity to love. Since the speaker's intensified doubt about portraying the youth as an icon of the ideal has been already considered above, in relation to his intensified dispraise of the young man, only a few additional remarks will now be made. They concern sonnet 83, for in that poem one sees the speaker's conscious acknowledgement and confrontation of doubt; one sees, too, the unresolved contradictions evoked by it. Here is the sonnet:

I never saw that you did painting need,
And therefore to your fair no painting set;
I found, or thought I found, you did exceed
The barren tender of a poet's debt;
And therefore have I slept in your report,
That you yourself, being extant, well might show
How far a modern quill doth come too short,
Speaking of worth, what worth in you doth grow.
This silence for my sin you did impute,
Which shall be most my glory, being dumb;
For I impair not beauty, being mute,
When others would give life, and bring a tomb.
    There lives more life in one of your fair eyes
    Than both your poets can in praise devise.

As elsewhere in the Sonnets, Shakespeare's speaker does not query the perfection of the young man's beauty but rather the personality behind it and his understanding of that personality. He suggests clearly in the opening and closing lines of the poem that the youth's beauty was and is beyond any need of heightening by art. Within the frame of those lines, however, he also suggests clearly that his understanding of the young man has erred, for in the young man he formerly discerned no flaw. He thought the youth beyond not only the want of enhancement by art but the desire for it, yet the desire was there. What the speaker in fact communicates to the young man, and so to the reader, is doubt more problematic than the obvious contrasts that he draws might be taken to imply. Certainly the speaker contrasts past ignorance or self-delusion to present, disillusioning knowledge, the perfect beauty of the youth to the youth's vanity, his insight and silence to the obtuseness and misused words of a rival. More important, he contrasts wise doubt to naive belief.

In the sonnet's initial quatrains the speaker says that, once believing the young man to be above both the want and the desire of enhancement by art, he thought the youth's transcendence of others would be sufficiently displayed by its mere existence. He thought that the youth's presence in the world required no enhancement – that, as it were, epiphany would suffice the young man and the witnessing world. In saying those things to the young man, the speaker acknowledges past error and current uncertainty. He implies that he was wrong about the youth: that the personal beauty of the young man is informed by personal vanity; that the young man's existence is a discord not, as the speaker indicates he believed, a harmony. In addition, the speaker ambiguously raises the notion of the young man's 'worth', suggesting his uncertainty about what that 'worth' might be.[71] His uncertainty is suggested by his choice of words ('what worth in you doth grow . . .', l. 8) and, too, by his having identified, in the previous lines, the excellence of the youth as a matter of physical appearance. The consequences of his uncertainty are no less interesting than the nature of the doubt itself. While the speaker's disillusionment necessarily involves his having recognized the youth's self-division, and although he is uncertain about what the 'worth' of the young man might be, he still retains his belief that the young man is a transcendent being, a mystery, to which he is uniquely responsive because into which he has privileged if not perfect insight. So the speaker implies in the sonnet's third quatrain.[72] As a result, in his address to the young man he casts himself in the role of devotee – one familiar to him – with that role having a number of contradictions. The speaker represents himself as devoted to the young man and as at once powerless yet powerful in his devotion. He is powerless because, according to his self-portrayal, his art cannot do justice to the beauty of the youth.[73] The youth's beauty renders art superfluous – except, of course, insofar as the youth desires celebration of his beauty.

On the other hand, the speaker also portrays himself as powerful in his former voicelessness: powerful because his silence expressed wisdom, the insight which will make silence his 'glory' when rightly understood. There are more important contradictions in the speaker's role as devotee, however, and they centre on his uncertainty, his doubt of the young man's 'worth'. The speaker represents himself in the sonnet as having been and as still being uniquely responsive to that mystery which is the young man; as was mentioned above, by way of explanation he indicates that he has a privileged if not perfect insight into the mysterious object of his devotion. But he reveals that contradiction informed his responsiveness, his insight, in the past and does so now; further, he reveals that contradiction separates his present devotion from the devotion he used to pay the youth. In the past, the speaker suggests, he rightly perceived the young man's mysterious physical perfection while wrongly inferring a correspondent perfection of mind. Now, he also suggests, aware of his error he retains his perception of the youth as mysteriously, transcendently beautiful but recognizes that the 'worth' of the young man is uncertain. In his disillusion he can appreciate both past error and accuracy in his judgement; moreover, his disillusion having generated doubt, he is paradoxically now a devotee who better understands at once his former self and the object of his devotion – and who now gives the object of devotion better self-understanding as well as better understanding of the devotee who seems to have failed in duty yet has signally fulfilled it. The speaker's intensified, albeit partial doubt about representing the youth as an icon of the ideal evokes contradictions that are unresolved, in this sonnet as in those which follow.

Transcendence of a kind is not solely the youth's possession, of course, for the speaker asserts his own transcendent capacity to love, beyond change in the beloved or change in circumstances. The best-known example of such an assertion in the Sonnets as a whole is sonnet 116, although there Shakespeare's speaker indirectly puts the assertion forward. Other remarkable and more direct instances are sonnets 123–125, just before the speaker farewells the young man. In the first place, nonetheless, here is sonnet 116, for it is indeed 'the most universally admired of Shakespeare's sonnets'.[74]

> Let me not to the marriage of true minds
> Admit impediments. Love is not love
> Which alters when it alteration finds,
> Or bends with the remover to remove.
> O no, it is an ever-fixed mark
> That looks on tempests and is never shaken;
> It is the star to every wand'ring bark,
> Whose worth's unknown, although his height be taken.
> Love's not time's fool, though rosy lips and cheeks
> Within his bending sickle's compass come.
> Love alters not with his brief hours and weeks,
> But bears it out ev'n to the edge of doom.
>   If this be error and upon me proved,
>   I never writ, nor no man ever loved.

Recent commentary on the poem has drawn attention to its frequent negatives and insistent idealism.[75] The point is rightly made that the speaker often says what love is not in order to suggest what love is; moreover, his view of what love is seems unrelentingly, uncompromisingly idealistic. Perhaps, though, the speaker's negatives and idealism are better seen as parts of a strategy than as parts of an argument; that is to say, perhaps they are better seen as parts of an argument which is first about the speaker himself and then about love.[76] The frame to the speaker's various blazon of love is self-reference: 'Let me not . . .' and 'upon me proved,/ I never writ . . .'. He begins and ends the sonnet with assertion of his belief in and commitment to the notion that human love — perfect human love, which alone may be called love between people – exists and can be achieved. What he says about such love is, then, simultaneously a statement about himself. The negatives that recur throughout what he says do not necessarily mar it, however, and turn his attempted self-representation into unwitting self-parody; on the contrary, they indicate his belief that human love, as he conceives of it, is a rare phenomenon most readily understood by contrasts with its widespread counterfeit. His passionate celebration of perfect and so, for him, real love's immutability – focusing in particular on that love's transcendence of change in the beloved, in circumstances, and even of time – implies his impassioned belief in and commitment to a notion of human love beyond common human experience. And it is worth mentioning that the 'marriage of true minds' image, the 'star to every wand'ring bark' image with its evocation of Petrarch, and the grotesque picturing of time's power over physical beauty, are appropriate in Shakespeare's day to consideration of love within male friendship no less than to consideration of love between men and women. The speaker is indicating that the elevated notion of human love to which he declares his allegiance informs his attachment to the young man – the friend whose loss the later sonnets show him confronting. The young man, and hence the reader, are to infer that loss and separation cannot change the speaker's devotion, for his is a transcendent capacity to love: the youth may be lost to the speaker yet never can be lost to him.

What sonnet 116 implies sonnets 123–125 declare. At the beginning of 123, for example, the speaker announces: 'No! Time, thou shalt not boast that I do change'. He proclaims at the poem's end: 'I will be true [to the friend] despite thy scythe and thee.'[77] Those statements are the more compelling because, in between them, the speaker reflects on time's play with the world and with human knowledge of it, knowledge contaminated in any event by human self-centredness.[78] Thus the speaker's certainty frames a meditation on the mutability of our world and of our understandings of it. 'Love alters not', the speaker says in 116, implying that therefore neither does he. Here his assertion of unalterable devotion is explicit. He acknowledges that time changes the material world, that it deceives us and we deceive ourselves; but, he suggests, in loving he knows himself at least to the extent that he can assert his love to be immutable.[79] Moreover, in sonnet 124 the speaker likewise explicitly asserts that his capacity to love transcends time and so change or circumstance. Since, he indicates, his 'dear love' is not merely 'the child of state' (l. 1), then

... it was builded far from accident;
It suffers not in smiling pomp, nor falls
Under the blow of thralled discontent,
Whereto th'inviting time our fashion calls.

(ll. 5–8)

And in 125 he announces himself to be in his love '[a] true soul', not
a suitor of material gain whose devotion is tied to change and
circumstance. Thus it is that in 126 the speaker can call the youth
'my lovely boy' (l. 1), even though the 'lovely boy' has ceased to be
his. Sonnets 20–126 end elegiacally yet with the speaker celebrating
his transcendent capacity to love.

NOTES

1. It should be mentioned again that, when I refer to 'early' or 'late'
    poems among Shakespeare's Sonnets, to 'predecessors' and 'subsequent'
    poems and the like among them, identification is being made in terms
    of numerical order alone.
2. There is a no less striking contrast between sonnet 18 and sonnets 33–
    34. It should be mentioned, however, in relation to sonnet 33, that
    the speaker's equivocation in the last line involves not merely a play
    on sun/son but a calculatedly false logic. In that line, the analogy
    between the staining of 'heaven's sun' and the staining of that sun 'of
    the world' which is the youth deliberately blurs the issue of agency, a
    process initiated in l. 5.
3. Sonnets 21–26 introduce portrayal of that.
4. See, by way of examples, sonnets 22 and 31 respectively.
5. Sonnets 21, 23, 24 likewise introduce portrayal of that preoccupation,
    but see also 38, 47 and, with their uses of the eternizing motif, 54–55.
6. Sonnets 1–19 may depict the speaker as preoccupied with his own art,
    and they may foreshadow, for instance in 10, 13–14, the subsequently
    announced closeness between him and the young man, but they barely
    hint at the other dimensions to his narcissism. Sonnets 1–19 do show
    the speaker idealizing the youth, that is, fashioning a diversely idealized
    image of him; on the other hand, the dynastic imperative that apparently
    informs his doing so makes it significantly unlike the subsequent, more
    seemingly personal and more precarious imposition of ideals on the
    young man.
7. The subjectivity of the beloved could not, of course, in any case be
    completely distinguished from that of the speaker/lover; my point is,
    however, that in Petrarch's love verse, as in Shakespeare's Sonnets,
    one cannot know the degree to which subjectivity is imposed on the
    object of desire by the speaker, especially since the speaker does at
    times indicate his awareness that he refashions his beloved. Petrarch's

speaker seems not himself to know the extent to which Laura is the independent object of his desire and refashioned by him. A similar uncertainty, although less directly expressed than in *Rime* 70, can be seen in the Sonnets. For a general account of diversity in English Petrarchism see Heather Dubrow, *Echoes of Desire: English Petrarchism and Its Counterdiscourses* (Ithaca and London: Cornell University Press, 1995).

8. Reference to Ficino's *Commentary* is again to the translation by Sears Jayne (*Commentary on Plato's Symposium on Love* (1985; rpt. Woodstock: Spring, 1994)), here at 2, 8 *passim*. Antonio is speaking, of course, about the lover's soul, not his heart. Charita's song in the *Old Arcadia*, 'My true love hath my heart and I have his', accords with what Antonio says in 2, 8 and of course has a more immediate likeness to Shakespeare's sonnet. It may be, among other relevant possibilities, that Shakespeare directly drew on Sidney's poem. Whatever the case, Shakespeare's poem affirms the notion that the lover's essential self − soul or heart − leaves him or her to dwell within the beloved.

9. What the young man might discover upon finding his reflection in the speaker is not mentioned.

10. Blasphemy is, of course, a familiar motif in *fine amour* verse including Petrarch's − but here, the transgression is also against the precedent of Petrarch's *Rime* and the imperatives of Ficino's *Commentary*. For another example of ingeniously blasphemous love verse transgressing the Petrarchan repudiation of *cupiditas*, see Constable's sonnet 'My God, my God, how much I love my goddess', a poem playing with Psalm 22 and some of Christ's words on the cross. See also 'To his Mistress upon occasion of a Petrarch he gave her . . .'. Reference to Constable's verse is from the edition by Joan Grundy (Liverpool: Liverpool University Press, 1960). On sacred parody of neoplatonic love lore in Constable's religious sonnets, see my *The Catholic Religious Poets from Southwell to Crashaw: A Critical History* (London: Sheed & Ward, 1991), pp. 73−85. On the relations of the Many to the One as a preoccupation in early seventeenth-century verse, see J. Smith, 'On Metaphysical Poetry', *Scrutiny*, 2 (1933), 222−39.

11. Reference to the 'canon' does not have to imply, of course, the notion that there is now and always has been a fixed number of hierarchically ordered texts identified for study by secondary and tertiary students and for appreciation by the 'common reader'. The canon has always varied, texts having been inserted into or removed from the 'great tradition'. But it seems reasonable to suggest that, since the earlier nineteenth century, Shakespeare has been central to many competing versions of what the canon might be. For example, see H. Bloom, *The Western Canon: The Books and School of the Ages* (New York: Harcourt Brace, 1994), pp. 45−75.

12. By 'simply autobiographical' I mean 'telling the "true story" of Shakespeare's involvement' with whomever; I do not mean 'uncomplicatedly

autobiographical'. There is at present no proof that the sonnets are or are not autobiographical. A host of other issues arises, of course, concerning what would constitute the autobiographical itself; those issues, however, seem to me neither able to be resolved in relation to the Sonnets nor within the ambit of this discussion.

13. The Renaissance discourse of friendship is built on and so includes the discourse of friendship from the ancient world.

14. See *Hermetica*, ed. and trans. Walter Scott (1924; rpt. Boston: Shambhala, 1993), *Asclepius* 3, 20b–21. I refer to Trismegistus as a speaker in the dialogue, not as the author of the text.

15. For an example of Venus' being represented as an androgyne, see Alexander Ross, *Mystagogus Poeticus*, ed. S. Orgel (New York: Garland, 1976), p. 409.

16. See *The Faerie Queene*, ed. A. C. Hamilton (London and New York: Longman, 1977), 7, 7, stanza 5.

17. Reference is to *The Philosophy of Love*, trans. F. Friedeberg-Seeley and J. H. Barnes (London: Soncino, 1937), 3, pp. 343–65.

18. Habington, in his character 'A Friend' (1635), wrote subsequently to the title: 'Is a man'. See *Poems*, ed. K. Allott (Liverpool: Liverpool University Press, 1969), pp. 99–100, here at p. 99. Thus the emphases can still be seen well after Shakespeare's death, the homosocial emphasis in that particular case. I owe this reference to Dr Liam Semler.

19. See *Lysis*, trans. B. Jowett, in *The Dialogues of Plato*, 2 vols (1892; rpt. New York; Random House, 1937), 1, 206–11, pp. 33–9.

20. See *The Ethics of Aristotle*, trans. J. A. K. Thomson (1953; rpt. Harmondsworth: Penguin, 1974), 9, 9, p. 277 and 9, 12, p. 284. On the latter page one reads: 'So we find friends who drink together for physical training, hunting or philosophy.' The passage cited initially accords with Socrates' remark in *Lysis*: 'I should greatly prefer a real friend to all the gold of Darius, or even to Darius himself: I am such a lover of friends as that' (Jowett, 212, p. 40). Aristotle's discussion of friendship does not exclude but does not emphasize the homerotic.

21. *De Amicitia*, trans. W. A. Falconer, in *De Senectute, De Amicitia, De Divinatione, Loeb Classical Library*, (1923; rpt. Heinemann, 1971), 5, 19–20 (see 14, 49–50), 8, 36–12, 42 and 21, 80. The extended quotation is from 27, 104. In 23, *passim*, Laelius agrees with Plato and with Aristotle on the importance of friendship to human happiness.

22. Reference is to *The Complete Works*, various transs, introd. R. C. Trench, 6 vols (New York: Crowell, 1909), *Essays*, vol. 2, p. 31.

23. *Ibid.*, p. 33.

24. *Ibid.*, p. 34.

25. See *The Flower of Friendship: A Renaissance Dialogue Contesting Marriage*, ed. and introd. V. Wayne (Ithaca and London: Cornell University Press, 1992), p. 105. Spelling and punctuation have been modernized by me in the quoted lines. Calvin, of course, describes tolerance and friendship (*tolerantia* and *amicitia*) as two of the elements of marriage.

On the origins of Christian discussions of friendship between men and women, in or outside marriage, see C. White, *Christian Friendship in the Fourth Century* (Cambridge: Cambridge University Press, 1992), initially at pp. 10–12.

26. Reference to Ficino is from the Jayne translation of 1985. Reference to Montaigne's 'On Friendship' is from *Essays*, trans. J. M. Cohen (Harmondsworth: Penguin, 1958). I have also used *The Complete Essays*, trans. M. A. Screech (London: Allen Lane, 1991).

27. See respectively and especially pp. 130–45 of the *Commentary* and pp. 158–68.

28. The object of devotion in the poem is not simply another child of Laura represented as transcending her mother: a perfect female supplanting her not notionally perfect archetype.

29. On the paradigmatic status of that myth, see Hallett Smith, *Elizabethan Poetry: A Study in Convention, Meaning and Expression* (Cambridge, Mass.: Harvard University Press, 1952), p. 74 and W. Keach, *Elizabethan Erotic Narratives: Irony and Pathos in the Ovidian Poetry of Shakespeare, Marlowe, and their Contemporaries* (New Brunswick, N.J.: Rutgers University Press, 1977), p. 191. The fiction of the young man as androgyne transcends the myth of Salmacis and Hermaphroditus in the sense that the union of male and female in the youth is indicated to be neither discordant nor flawed, even though it is obviously the case that the young man is not a hermaphrodite.

30. See ll. 1–5 and *De Amicitia* 4, 17–24. Some further virtues are mentioned as well. Cicero's insistence on virtue as the basis of true friendship, and the list of virtues ascribed to the young man, can of course be variously seen in Ficino's *Commentary* and in other of the texts discussed above in relation to the discourse of friendship.

31. Representations, that is to say for present purposes, until sonnet 126.

32. Again, I am not suggesting that the Sonnets unfold a narrative.

33. Those remarks about business and friendship may echo Aristotle's negative comments on friendships that involve mere 'usefulness'.

34. See Booth's edition (*Shakespeare's Sonnets*, ed. S. Booth (New Haven and London: Yale University Press, 1977)), pp. 164–5.

35. 1, 1, 86–7.

36. George Wither, *A Collection of Emblems, Ancient and Moderne* (London, 1635), 1, 27.

37. As Booth also notes, while reading the line differently. See p. 225 of his edition.

38. Compare the more usual form of the proverb as given in *Titus Andronicus*: 'She is a woman, therefore may be wooed;/ She is a woman, therefore may be won' (2, 1, 82–3). Booth, at p. 201, and many other editors discuss the rewriting of the proverb in sonnet 41. How one interprets that rewriting will to some extent depend on – or help determine – whether one believes 'he' or 'she' should appear in l. 8 as the subject of 'prevailed'. In any event, the immediate point here is that the

role-reversal indicated in ll. 5–6 apparently feminizes the youth, aligning him with Shakespeare's Adonis; then that reversal of roles is itself reversed in the following lines (assuming, as seems most likely, that 'he' should precede 'prevailed' in the eighth line).

39. Compare sonnet 5, which also pictures the youth as caught up in a drama enacted by personified forces. In 5, the drama does not displace responsibility for the youth's behaviour.

40. The eternizing topos here iterates at once the narcissism of its use by the speaker, and his apparent duplicity in using it, in sonnets 1–19.

41. Again, see sonnet 7 – where the motif is problematic if not as disparaging of the youth as it appears to be in 33.

42. See, for example, the opening quatrain of sonnet 40 and its closing lines: 'Lascivious grace, in whom all ill well shows,/ Kill me with spites, yet we must not be foes.' Whether the latter verses are homoerotic in appearance only, because formed from the (at times) homoerotic language of clientage, or homerotic and therefore congruent with the homoeroticized language of clientage, cannot be known. See also, in particular, the last six lines of 41 and the opening quatrain, as well as the final couplet, of 42. It should be added, too, that the sonnets concerned with betrayal are followed by many celebrating the young man.

43. The emphasis of sonnet 67 on the perfect beauty of the youth, and its use of the 'rose' trope (which links it with sonnets 54 and 1, for example), imply the youth's androgyny. There is thus a likeness in the poem between the imaging of the young man and the imaging of Adonis in *Venus and Adonis*. That likeness has as another of its elements the notion that the youth is the epitome of natural beauty. Sonnet 68 of course continues that portrayal of the young man.

44. There is also an affinity with *Romeo and Juliet* in this poem. The speaker refers to 'a separable spite' which divides him from the young man (l. 6). Here, however, true friendship overcomes their being, as it were, 'star-crossed'. The discourses of friendship and of love are merged in sonnet 20, as has been argued earlier in this chapter.

45. Or he takes on a role equivalent to it. It appears, given the Petrarchan elements of 35–6, that he is more likely to be taking on that familiar role adopted so often by the speaker of the *Rime* and by his multifarious descendants.

46. See, for example, 'make my love engrafted' (l. 8) and especially the terms 'shadow', 'substance' and 'abundance' (ll. 10–11) within the second quatrain as a whole.

47. That is, he is either the speaker's patron or someone the speaker wants to have as his patron. And according to Shakespeare's speaker, of course, the young man is radically flawed – which Laura is not.

48. Although Ovid and Horace use the eternizing motif with reference to themselves, Propertius uses it, condescendingly, with reference to others; however, the dynamic of its use in the Sonnets most closely

resembles that in the *Rime*. The dynamic is, very simply put, that the object of desire inspires the lover to honour the ideal and to write; the lover, writing, praises and immortalizes the object of desire. Ennobled and empowered, he in turn celebrates and empowers (in immortalizing).

49. On the sinister aura given the rival poet by Shakespeare's speaker, see especially ll. 9–10: 'He, nor that affable familiar ghost/Which nightly gulls him with intelligence . . .'.

50. On the subject of the world's directly or indirectly impinging upon/ intruding into the relationship between the speaker and the young man, see also sonnet 107, ll. 1–4. Joan Grundy was one of the first modern Shakespeare critics to highlight the allusions to the world (that is, to the world of other people environing the speaker and the youth) in the Sonnets. See, again, her 'Shakespeare's Sonnets and the Elizabethan Sonneteers', *Shakespeare Survey*, 15 (1962), pp. 41–9. The speaker at times powerfully depicts himself as a man afflicted by the world.

51. That is, 'much in little' is transformed into 'not much, but everything, in little' – the same transformation Donne works upon the commonplace in poems such as 'The Sun Rising'.

52. The poem, although incomplete as a formal sonnet, is nonetheless complete as a 'little song' – the literal meaning of the word 'sonnet'. Disruption or sundering in the relationship between the speaker and the youth seems aptly signalled by an incomplete, formal sonnet, however.

53. See sonnet 82, ll. 5–8; cf. 84, ll. 13–14. On the Senecan theory of giving and receiving gifts, see Seneca, *De Beneficiis*, trans. J. W. Basore, *Loeb Classical Library* (1935; rpt. London and Cambridge, Mass: Heinemann and Harvard, 1964), and Edgar Wind, *Pagan Mysteries in the Renaissance* (1958; rpt. London: Penguin, 1967), pp. 26–35. The language of gift-giving may not be intended to evoke Seneca in this sonnet; its use here, particulary in the context of patronage/friendship, would seem nonetheless to do so.

54. His praise of the young man is ambiguous, on the other hand, especially prior to the poems focused on rivalry.

55. The words 'possessing' and 'estimate' overshadow, or contaminate, the meaning 'beloved' – especially in conjunction.

56. Ll. 11–12 could be read as implying that the youth has returned himself to himself – has taken back the gift of himself, as it were – with an increase in worth because he has become greater while in the keeping of the speaker as encomiastic, immortalizing poet.

57. Here the imaging of the youth as a 'lovely boy' resembles the depiction of him in sonnets 20 and 53 rather than that in sonnets 1–19. There are continuities between the portrayals of the young man in the two groups of poems, of course; however, in 1–19 he is Narcissus before he is Adonis although, again, he is both. He is feminized in the first nineteen poems; he is depicted as androgynous in the subsequent group. In sonnet 126 he is Adonis rather than Narcissus and, hence, implicitly

closer to the androgynous picture of him in 20 and in 53 than to the picture of him in, say, sonnet 1.

58. Elaborate praise and disparise coexist in sonnets 88–93; the disparise in those poems preludes the praise given the youth in sonnets such as 97–99.

59. It is compromised, as has been noted above, by having disparise as its prelude: the alternation of perspectives that one sees elsewhere in 20–126 occurs here, that is to say.

60. Agency is unclear at several points in the poem, which results chiefly from the fluidity of the sonnet's syntax. Line 11, of direct relevance here, does not indicate clearly how '[t]he summer's flower' (l. 9) 'with base infection meet[s]'. The latter word implies that a naturally transmitted contamination affects the 'flower' – but 'deeds' (l. 13), while not contradicting that, implies action *and* the possibility of choice, regardless of whether the 'infection' itself was chosen, allowed to happen, or just happened in the course of things. Certainly the emphasis on 'base' in l. 11 and the variation on that word, 'basest' in l. 12, suggest moral debasement which leads to social debasement, 'deeds' then seeming to evoke the possibility of choice: moral choice about how one will act.

61. I am well aware that the outline just given of what ll. 1–8 convey is only an outline and does not confront some issues of interpretation; on the other hand, the outline does suggest how I understand – in very general terms – the argument of ll. 1–8.

62. *Virtu* is contemporaneously identified in various ways, among them being as strength of will – the personal strength which allows people to confront the force of circumstance – and as individual talent. *Sdegno* is that pride which will not allow a gentleman to demean himself and which will give him an appropriate sense of superiority when dealing with his inferiors. Milton, in *Paradise Lost*, interestingly attributes the latter aspect of *sdegno* to Satan, who has of course abandoned the former.

63. Prudence is warmly urged upon the young man in sonnets 1–17; but the speaker portrays it as a generous as well as self-interested wisdom.

64. Sonnet 69, l. 12 is: 'To thy fair flow'r add the rank smell of weeds'.

65. Thus 93, ll. 1–4 and 13–14 are relevant here as well. Moreover, 94, ll. 9–10 may recall sonnets 1 and, in contradiction, 54. That is to say, the link between the generalizing first eight lines of the poem and its apparently particularizing last six lines may be an indirect allusion to self-sufficiency or self-regard, for which the young man has been so often condemned earlier in the Sonnets.

66. One should perhaps underline once more the affinities between 94, l. 14 and 69, l. 12. There would seem to be very little doubt that the affinity links (importantly if in part) the youth with the figures and situations of 94.

67. Cf. 93, especially ll. 13–14. At the end of 33 the youth is, of course, a stained sun/son of the world.

68. Reference to Herbert is from *The Works*, ed. F. E. Hutchinson (1941; rpt. Oxford: Clarendon Press, 1972).

69. On the young man's capacity for duplicity, see in particular 95, ll. 11–12 and 96, ll. 9–12.

70. But the two instances are not identical. In the former it is arguable that he did at least in part consider them, for he remedied failed fictionalizing with compensatory, self-conscious fictionalizing (self-conscious at that moment); in the latter, he proceeds at once to praise the youth as if no discrediting of the fiction of androgyny – as unfolded in sonnet 20 – had occurred. The speaker lays bare his fictionalizing at other moments in the Sonnets, and he does so in differing ways.

71. Kerrigan captures the spirit of the line well in the note on p. 277 of his edition (J. Kerrigan, *The Sonnets and A Lover's Complaint* (Harmondsworth: Penguin, 1986)).

72. Especially in l. 12, which implicitly contrasts his insight with the impercipience of his rival.

73. Given the stilnovistic representation of the young man, the speaker's allusion to the inexpressibility topos is a decorous and graceful conclusion to the sonnet. The physically perfect youth is flawed within, of course, which differentiates him from the trend of stilnovistic convention.

74. The words are Booth's, p. 387. His commentary on the poem remains, I think, the best we have.

75. See, for example, Booth pp. 384–92, Kerrigan pp. 53–4 and 332–5; W. G. Ingram and T. Redpath, *Shakespeare's Sonnets* (1964; rpt. London: Hodder & Stoughton, 1978), pp. 268–9; G. Blakemore Evans, *The Sonnets* (Cambridge: Cambridge University Press, 1996) pp. 227–9.

76. Shakespeare's speaker is primarily arguing, that is to say, by *ethos*; I would suggest that he argues by *pathos*, then *logos*, in order to do so.

77. One sees in that line the mingling of negation and emphasis recurrent throughout 116; the last line of the poem is, however, more direct in making its assertion.

78. See ll. 5–8.

79. Thus Shakespeare's speaker plays with the *nosce teipsum* topos as well as with the *exegi monumentum* topos, love being the monumental expression of his selflessness and the poem the monument to his love.

Chapter 5

Shakespeare's Sonnets 127–154: The Poet, the Dark Lady and the Young Man

(I) FICTIONS OF BEAUTY

In the last of the Sonnets one sees Petrarch's drama of the divided self, that drama performed so cunningly by Astrophil, played out by Shakespeare's speaker in relation to two objects of desire, not within devotion to a single, unpossessable beloved. It seems that the fair-haired young man remains a focus of the speaker's attachment; the so-called Dark Lady, perhaps the woman to whom allusion is made in sonnets 40–42, likewise enthrals him. The speaker does in fact claim that his involvement with the Dark Lady resembles imprisonment: that he, and the young man as well, are prisoners of their sexual obsessions with her.[1] There are clearly, then, important differences between the earlier sonnets, especially 20–126, and the later. There are nonetheless important similarities between sonnets 127–154 and their predecessors. For example, prior to the speaker's portrayal of the Dark Lady as a truly 'ugly beauty' – as profoundly antithetic both to Laura and to the young man – he depicts her through a process of wavering and oscillation, imposing fictions precariously upon her much as he did upon the youth.[2] (Thus his portrayal of her is initially ambiguous but not ultimately sceptical.) He continues, moreover, his unstable portrayal of the young man, evoking the contraries that pervade his earlier representations of the 'master mistress'. Again, too, he imposes fictions of empowerment and of disempowerment upon himself. He plays with and interplays the discourses of Petrarchism, friendship and misogyny: implicitly iterating his transference of the Petrarchan language and rhetoric of love to the young man, he also relates them to the Dark Lady, using them neither simply to parody her nor her simply to parody them; conventional notions of amity are at once followed and violated; the misogyny already intense within the discourse of friendship, and prominent in sonnets 20–126, is intensified. Where that play with and interplay of discourses begins is where the speaker begins everything in the final group of sonnets, with conflicting fictions of beauty.

In sonnets 127–130 Shakespeare's speaker sets those fictions before the reader and indicates the scope of their conflict. Offering a mock explanation, in sonnet 127, of how dark colouring in a woman has come to be thought beautiful, he indicates as well a genealogy of the rival and supplanted notion that only women with blonde hair and of light complexion possess true beauty. His problematic defence and celebration of 'black beauty', as it was called, may allude to and rework the seventh sonnet of *Astrophil and Stella*; more important, however, are comparisons and contrasts between what he says in sonnet 127 and what he has previously said in sonnet 20.[3] For instance, he invents histories in each of the poems: that of black beauty with its fictional triumph over its long-dominant rival, which ludically explains the Dark Lady's allure; that of the young man's surpassing the boundaries of gender, which ludically explains his physical perfection. The distant and tacit interaction of those histories, and hence of the sonnets containing them, implies how radically gender, sex and hue differentiate between the two beloveds. One difference appears with the speaker's opening words in sonnet 127: 'In the old age . . .'. 'In the olden days,' he begins by way of introducing a history that will focus on the Dark Lady, and legitimize her, as a creature of the present. But although in sonnet 20, through the playful history unfolded as the third quatrain, the speaker emphasizes that the young man has a numinous presence because manifesting beauty conferred uniquely by nature herself, he makes no suggestion that the youth is a creature of the moment. His not doing so accords with his assertions, made elsewhere, that the young man links the present with the Golden Age. Sonnet 67 ends with his describing nature's relationship to the youth as follows: 'O him she stores, to show what wealth she had,/ In days long since, before these last so bad.' Sonnet 68 opens with the speaker saying of the young man: 'Thus is his cheek the map of days outworn. . . .'[4] The Dark Lady is characterized on the basis of a contrast between past and present; the young man, not represented as of the moment if certainly portrayed in other of the sonnets as bound to time, embodies a continuity of the present with the past.[5] She emerges from the world's decline whereas he stands – or, at least, is said sometimes to stand – in antithesis to it.[6]

Other comparisons and contrasts between sonnets 127 and 20 become clear when the opposing fictions of beauty unfolded in sonnet 127 are considered more closely. The poem's mock history of black beauty unfolds one explicit fiction and coexists with an implicit fiction: the former is, of course, that of black beauty's triumph over 'fair' beauty; the latter is that of fair beauty itself. A problem with the fictions would seem to be, however, that although black beauty is claimed to have displaced its long-dominant rival, fair beauty remains the standard against which black beauty is judged: fair beauty remains, in short, to be regarded as true beauty by the speaker celebrating the triumph of its counterpart. He says:

> In the old age black was not counted fair,
> Or if it were it bore not beauty's name.
> But now is black beauty's successive heir,
> And beauty slandered with a bastard shame;
> For since each hand hath put on nature's pow'r,
> Fairing the foul with art's false borrowed face,
> Sweet beauty hath no name, no holy bow'r,
> But is profaned, if not lives in disgrace.
>
> (ll. 1–8)

According to the speaker, the use of cosmetics has made it imposs-ible to know whether someone is actually 'fair' or not.[7] Dark, and so notionally unfalsified, colouring has for that reason come to be con-sidered true beauty; in other words, the speaker's narrative explains black beauty's current pre-eminence as a triumph gained by default and in any case unreal. That fiction of black beauty's equivocal triumph then leads to an equivocal celebration of the Dark Lady as a type of black beauty. The speaker introduces her into the poem by declaring: 'Therefore my mistress' eyes are raven black . . .' (l. 9). He indicates that he chose her because of her genuine, fashionably beautiful appear-ance, that she has chosen to retain rather than to falsify her natural colouring, and also that she somehow chose her dark colouring in order to avoid the possible imputation of using cosmetics.[8] She is, then, a paragon of honesty; the speaker even suggests in line 10 that her dark eyes seem as if mourning the dishonesty of those who fake their appearance, 'who, not born fair, no beauty lack,/ Sland'ring creation with a false esteem' (ll. 11–12). But he ends with this: 'Yet so they mourn becoming of their woe,/ That every tongue says beauty should look so' (ll. 13–14). Complimentary though the couplet may be, it affirms what the mock history of black beauty has already suggested, namely, that fair beauty is truly beautiful and that black beauty is merely its now-successful double. Even while praising the attractive-ness of the Dark Lady's appearance the speaker's last lines intimate that, as a type of black beauty, she does not possess true beauty.

What the speaker will not or more probably does not see, of course, is that his history of black beauty, unfolding his fiction of black beauty triumphant, coexists with an implicit genealogy of fair beauty which indicates fair beauty itself to be a naturalized fiction. His emphasis on the blackness of his lady's eyes draws attention to the colour they are not; in doing so, it evokes that paradigm of beauty passed from the *fine amour* tradition to Petrarch and his successors, thereby foregrounding the paradigm's fictionality.[9] Whether or not Shakespeare's speaker does see that implication of his emphasis on the dark hue of his mistress's eye, the conflict he stages between black beauty and its counterpart has implications concerning the Dark Lady of which he can hardly be unaware. One, mentioned above, is that she does not possess true beauty. The speaker celebrates her attractiveness and tells of its celebration by others; however, obliquely identifying black beauty as merely the double of true beauty he thus implies her to be merely a double – that of a truly beautiful woman. Another implication is her vulnerability to fashion and opinion. They have made black beauty now pre-eminent; their having done so has contributed to the value set on her beauty by the speaker.[10] Those implications are important for several reasons. They reveal the speaker at first portraying the Dark Lady much as he portrays the young man in sonnet 20: through wavering, unstable idealization. In addition, they link the Dark Lady to the young man, to the speaker and even to Lucrece, for in sonnets 20–126 and in *Lucrece* each of the latter is significantly environed by others' judgements.[11] Finally, for the moment, they powerfully distinguish between the Dark Lady and the young man. The speaker suggests in sonnet 20 that the young man conforms better than do women to the ideal of beauty manifested by Laura. He suggests at the same time that the youth, in his androgyny, incarnates a femaleness which leaves to those who are solely female the flaws innate to women.[12] The speaker indicates that the beauty and femaleness of women form an imperfect double to the youth's beauty and femaleness. In sonnet 127, on the other hand, Shakespeare's speaker indicates that the Dark Lady's appearance establishes her as merely the shadow of, the double to a truly beautiful woman. Therefore he represents her as in effect a double to someone who would herself be just a double to the young man, without having yet said or implied, as he soon will, that she is the epitome of female duplicity – and hence more double than ordinarily duplicitous women. She is characterized from sonnet 127 onward as multiply a double to the youth; and in being so she forms a dark counterpart to Laura.[13] However she is also Laura's double in another respect, one which makes her seem a Laura demonized.[14] The Dark Lady's capacity to attract admiration is acknowledged at the end of sonnet 127, foretelling her ability to compel devotion, even obsession, as revealed in the following sonnets. The persona of the *Rime* associates his devotion to Laura with sexual desire but not exclusively with that; after sonnet 127, Shakespeare's speaker will associate his and the youth's devotion to the Dark Lady with concupiscence alone.[15] She is portrayed as having the power of Laura to generate desire, yet desire which is physical and nothing more. As the speaker complains again and again in the subsequent sonnets, nothing productive comes from his pursuing her – and nothing apparently does, except for his often bitterly playful poems of complaint, denigration and self-reproach.[16]

At the start of the later sonnets, then, the speaker's conflicting fictions of beauty present his dealings with the Dark Lady but simultaneously imply her relations to, if not yet her dealings with, the young man and likewise her relations to the more distant figure of Laura. As a type of black beauty the Dark Lady is set in obvious as well as in subtle opposition to the fair young man. Ultimately she is therefore set in opposition to Laura, her relations to that precursor seeming more straightforward than her relations to the androgynous youth. What the speaker has suggested initially through the two fictions he then develops in sonnets 128–130. In the first of those poems he elaborately expresses and also distinctly identifies his desire for his mistress; doing so, he both characterizes himself and moves toward subsequent caricature of her. The speaker's self-consciously indulgent expressing of desire, his elaborate pursuit of the conceit that he envies the virginal keys touched by his lady, is a display of artistic virtuosity to the mistress which implicitly compliments and complements the artistic virtuosity he attributes to her. At the start of sonnet 128 he celebrates the overwhelming artistry of the Dark Lady's performance at the virginal:

> How oft, when thou my music music play'st
> Upon that blessed wood whose motion sounds
> With thy sweet fingers when thou gently sway'st
> The wiry concord that mine ear confounds. . . .

> (ll. 1–4)

His praise of her skill seems an allusion to the contemporary aesthetic category *stupore*, which identifies a work of art, or an artistic performance, as being so extraordinary in its accomplishment that it stupefies the beholder because making extraordinary demands upon his or her senses.[17] The speaker goes on to say:

Do I envy those jacks that nimble leap
To kiss the tender inward of thy hand,
Whilst my poor lips, which should that harvest reap,
At the wood's boldness by thee blushing stand.
To be so tickled they would change their state
And situation with those dancing chips,
O'er whom thy fingers walk with gentle gait,
Making dead wood more blest than living lips.
> Since saucy jacks so happy are in this,
> Give them thy fingers, me thy lips to kiss.

(ll. 5–14)

For all the ostentatious inventiveness of the remaining lines of the sonnet, what seems important in them is not chiefly the speaker's display of his own artistic virtuosity, which implicitly complements his lady's. True, through that display he indicates his empowerment amid comic disempowerment. Although the virginal keys can be seen as sexually privileged at his expense, his portrayal of their intimacy with his mistress allows him to request from her that he be granted yet greater intimacy; although, as he suggests in the poem's opening lines, his artistry takes that of his lady as its starting point, it too brings the virginal to life – by means of half-personification and contrived analogy. More important, nonetheless, seems to be this: having associated his lady with musical harmony, the speaker proceeds to focus on what he sees as the eroticism with which she produces that harmony. He thus at once expresses and identifies his desire. In the sonnet's opening quatrain the speaker calls his lady 'my music' and mentions the 'wiry concord' of the music she makes at the keyboard.[18] According to neoplatonic thought, beauty is a manifestation of harmony. According to Ficino, moreover, when beauty is apprehended through the sight and (or) the hearing, rather than through the other senses, it is loved for its own sake: it is truly loved.[19] The speaker proceeds, of course, after the first quatrain to express his desire by insistent reference to the sense of touch. What begins like a poem voicing refined or tempered desire then gives voice instead to detailed preoccupation with the flesh. Thus the speaker reveals his love for the Dark Lady as akin rather to what Ficino calls 'bestial love' than to what Ficino, or Pico, would identify as 'divine' or 'human' love. Characterizing himself as concupiscent, perhaps he indicates at the same time that only concupiscence can be aroused by the Dark Lady, that she can evoke nothing higher. Certainly he will claim as much in subsequent poems.

In the immediately subsequent poem, however, he reflects upon concupiscence itself. Because he presumably does so with his mistress

as his point of reference, and because he totally excludes the notion
of spiritual desire from his reflections, sonnet 129 seems no less than
its predecessor to associate the Dark Lady with evocation of 'bestial
love' alone. The speaker's love for her is by implication 'lust in
action' (l. 1), lust wanting to be in action, or lust regretted. In sonnet
128 he sounds not unlike Venus when she talks to Adonis; here he
sounds like Tarquin when pondering sex with Lucrece. Nor is the
affinity between the speaker and Tarquin just a matter of verbal
echoes or resemblances. As has been argued in Chapter 2, Tarquin's
assault on Lucrece in effect makes her home a site where no civilized
law exists, where only desire is law: 'a wilderness where are no
laws'.[20] At the start of sonnet 129 Shakespeare's speaker says:

> Th' expense of spirit in a waste of shame
> Is lust in action, and till action lust
> Is perjured, murd'rous, bloody, full of blame,
> Savage, extreme, rude, cruel, not to trust. . . .
>
> (ll. 1–4)

The similarity is clear; furthermore, the opening lines of this poem,
like the lines quoted from or alluded to in *Lucrece*, can be usefully
related to Cicero's picture of pre-civil life in *De Inventione*. The
relevance of that picture to *Lucrece*, as has been argued in the second
chapter, is twofold. It illuminates the representation of Tarquin's
desire and it suggests the wisdom that Lucrece lacks, through no
fault of her own. It also has a twofold relevance to sonnet 129. On
the one hand, it illuminates the speaker's representation of his desire;
on the other, it indicates not that he lacks *prudentia*, as does Lucrece,
but that having a 'practical knowledge of things to be sought for and
of things to be avoided' he nonetheless does not avoid what he
knows he should.[21] Like Tarquin he is desire-driven, lust-impelled,
and like Tarquin he knows what he should not do in his particular
circumstances but cannot be guided by his knowledge. Like Tarquin,
if less dishonestly, the speaker laments the tyranny of physical desire.
Sententious and epigrammatic, but likewise staccato, embittered and
despairing, the poem is a wisdom poem on the powerlessness of
wisdom to deal with physical desire.[22]

   That lament at the power of physical desire, while concerned
with such desire in general, is of course also concerned with its
arousal by a specific woman. As has been remarked above, almost
from the start of the later sonnets the speaker associates the Dark
Lady with concupiscence alone, directly implying that he feels only
lust for her and indirectly implying that she is capable of arousing

lust and nothing more. As has likewise been remarked above, the latter will be claimed distinctly in subsequent poems – and it will be claimed as well that the Dark Lady herself experiences lust for others but nothing more. Yet from the very start of the later sonnets the speaker's mistress is indicated to be a dark counterpart to the young man and, ultimately, to Laura. In sonnet 130, having previously characterized himself and apparently the Dark Lady in terms of concupiscence, the speaker again relates her to Laura. This time he does so more overtly; nevertheless, he does so no less problematically. When first the speaker relates her to Laura, in sonnet 127, it is by way of the fictions of black and of fair beauty. The Dark Lady, as a type of black beauty, is suggested to be a double: to a truly beautiful woman, to the young man, and to Laura as the archetype of fair beauty. When the speaker once more relates her to Laura, the conflicting fictions of beauty are the background to his ambiguous contrast between her and her Petrarchan antecedent.

The speaker begins with unmistakable allusion to Petrarch's imaging of Laura and to the portrayals of her many successors:

> My mistress' eyes are nothing like the sun –
> Coral is far more red than her lips' red –
> If snow be white, why then her breasts are dun –
> If hairs be wires, black wires grow on her head. . . .
>
> (ll. 1–4)

His words implicitly mock the Petrarchan ideal of female beauty, as expressed in the *Rime* and recreated thereafter, and at the same time imply its displacement by a more realistic view of what an attractive woman may look like.[23] They are still sometimes taken as signalling merely that. For the most part, however, commentary on the sonnet now remarks on the conventionality of what the speaker says, for mocking displacement of the Petrarchan ideal was already long familiar, by Shakespeare's time, as a form of anti-Petrarchism generated within and contained by Petrarchan discourse. The speaker's words have another dimension, too. At the end of the sonnet he says: 'And yet by heav'n I think my love as rare/ As any she belied with false compare' (ll. 13–14). Unreliable comparison, and contrast, have been connected with the speaker's representation of his mistress from the first of the Dark Lady sonnets. So it is not only the objects of desire in other Petrarch-related love poems which have been disingenuously depicted. More important, the attractively undivine lady praised here is also the mistress associated in sonnets 128 and 129 with tyrannic concupiscence – and concupiscence alone. The Petrarchan language and rhetoric of 'My mistress' eyes . . .' are not used in simple parody of either Petrarchism or of the Dark Lady.

(II) THE DIVIDED SELF, MISOGYNY AND FRIENDSHIP

The speaker's apparently calm assurance in sonnet 130 contrasts with his violent emotion in the preceding poem; his image of the Dark Lady contrasts likewise with his obliquely damning reference to her in sonnet 129. The two poems, that is to say, interact in a way which recalls how some of the poems to or about the young man relate to each other. Thus in the later sonnets there is something akin to the oscillation as well as to the wavering that can be observed in their predecessors focused on the youth. But in the sonnets that follow, although contradiction as well as equivocation are strategies still used by the speaker and although the conflicting fictions of beauty continue to be manipulated by him, more interesting seems to be what develops from his uses of those strategies and fictions. First, there is his portrayal of himself as divided between desire for the Dark Lady and desire for the young man. Furthermore, because he increasingly devalues her – moving toward depiction of her as a truly ugly beauty – and depreciates her at the expense of the equivocally idealized young man, his divided desire brings powerfully together the discourses of misogyny and of friendship.[24] He begins his devaluation of her by alluding again to Petrarchan convention.

In sonnet 131 the speaker says:

> Thou art as tyrannous, so as thou art,
> As those whose beauties proudly make them cruel;
> For well thou know'st to my dear doting heart
> Thou art the fairest and most precious jewel.
> Yet in good faith some say that thee behold
> Thy face hath not the pow'r to make love groan;
> To say they err I dare not be so bold,
> Although I swear it to myself alone.
> And to be sure that is not false I swear
> A thousand groans but thinking on thy face
> One on another's neck do witness bear
> Thy black is fairest in my judgement's place.
>> In nothing art thou black save in thy deeds,
>> And thence this slander as I think proceeds.

Alluding to the Petrarchan convention of the proudly beautiful, tyrannic mistress, Shakespeare's speaker identifies the Dark Lady with that figure only to distinguish her from it. He evokes once more the conflicting fictions of beauty, and he evokes again as well the notion of opinion's power, in order to suggest yet more clearly what he indicated in sonnet 127: that the Dark Lady does not possess true beauty; that she is a double to a truly beautiful woman and, ultimately, to Laura. In doing so he reveals his own, cunning doubleness. He duplicitously affirms the beauty of his mistress by announcing that he thinks her pre-eminently attractive – 'fairest' is one of his key words – while also implying that his perception of her personal appearance is unreliable. Moreover, whereas at the end of sonnet 127 he drew on the authority of (allegedly) popular opinion in order to assert his mistress's exceptional beauty, here he cites the opinions of 'some' others in order to deny that she is in fact beautiful. With ostentatious humility he announces that, although he dare not publicly dispute with those others, in private he maintains his opinion against theirs, opposing the evidence of his groans to their expressions of disbelief. In the sonnet's final lines he is perhaps more cunningly and more brutally duplicitous. Having said to his mistress that her 'black is fairest in [his] judgement's place' (l. 12) – thus having suggested both that her black beauty transcends fair beauty and, in effect, that (her) black is white in his estimate – he then proceeds to relate blackness not to her appearance but to her behaviour. He claims in the last lines of the poem that she is 'black' only in her 'deeds', which may explain why some people don't think her beautiful. His remark about her behaviour might be just conventional, a reference to the supposed cruelty of a disdainful mistress, but it nonetheless gestures toward something beyond that. The speaker ends by indicating that the blackness of the Dark Lady comes from within and concerns who she is rather than what she looks like. Duplicitously he blackens her; soon he will castigate her for doubleness, intensifying the misogyny revealed in sonnet 20 and in many of the subsequent poems.

He castigates her for doubleness and, as has been mentioned above, for much else. She can arouse and experience only concupiscence, the speaker asserts; he accuses her, too, of being sexually insatiable.[25] Thus he attributes to her faults often assigned to women in misogynic writings, as duplicity is, for example, in sonnet 20, while also suggesting that she is worse than most other women. She becomes a caricature, not perhaps a type of the loathly lady set implicitly against that type of the lovely lady which is Laura but certainly an instance of truly ugly beauty set in opposition to the young man and distantly implied to be Laura's grotesque counterpart. Caricaturing her, moreover, the speaker all but caricatures himself, indicating with disgust that his

own concupiscence reduces him to virtually a distorted image of
what he would be if it did not dominate him, having been aroused
by her. In order to illustrate his castigating her for duplicity, one
could cite the first lines of sonnet 138: 'When my love swears that
she is made of truth,/ I do believe her though I knows she lies. . . .'
And there is this later remark by the speaker: 'Simply I credit her
false-speaking tongue' (l. 7). Further, in sonnet 142 he addresses the
Dark Lady and refers to

> those lips of thine,
> That have profaned their scarlet ornaments,
> And sealed false bonds of love as oft as mine,
> Robbed others' beds' revenues of their rents.
>
> (ll. 5–8)

To illustrate the speaker's view of the desire aroused and experienced
by the Dark Lady, one could hardly fail to cite sonnet 135. There
the insistent use of the word 'will', alluding probably to Shakespeare's
given name but certainly as well to the speaker's genitals and to his
mistress's, suggests both the concupiscence aroused by the Dark Lady
and her interest in no other form of desire.[26] The speaker says, for
example:

> Wilt thou, whose will is large and spacious,
> Not once vouchsafe to hide my will in thine?
> Shall will in others seem right gracious,
> And in my will no fair acceptance shine?
> The sea, all water, yet receives rain still,
> And in abundance addeth to his store;
> So thou being rich in will add to thy will
> One will of mine, to make thy large will more
>   Let no unkind, no fair beseechers kill;
>   Think all but one, and me in that one will.
>
> (ll. 5–14)

There are fourteen instances of 'will' in the poem (counting 'wilt' in
l. 5); one for every line, even though the word does not occur in
each line. '[W]ill in overplus' (l. 2) is, in that sense, surely right. The
speaker's phallic bravado, while linked to self-disgust in poems such as
129 and 141, here has another connection. His representations of desire
in the poem imply his for the Dark Lady to be concupiscence alone,
as has been remarked just above, and hers to be insatiable, universal
concupiscence – from which he hopes to benefit: by implication, she
can inspire nothing more, at least in him, and she experiences nothing

more. The Venus whom Adonis seeks to evade is, as it were, just the person whom the speaker wishes here both to know better and to deride. His desire for his mistress's body, his self-disgust at his desire, his misogyny, and his subsequent need to caricature his mistress are all indicated by his allusion in sonnet 137 to her 'bay where all men ride' (l. 6).

That image contrasts ironically with the end of Petrarch's '*Passe la nave . . .*', which Wyatt rendered as 'And I remain despairing of the port'.[27] More important, it suggests how marked an element of the speaker's misogyny is his fear of male rivalry. In the sonnets focused on the young man, the speaker portrays him as courted by other men, among them a rival poet, and as not unreceptive to the overtures of those who seek his favour. The speaker also reveals fear and jealousy of a woman who has forsaken him for the youth, that woman possibly being the Dark Lady. Be the latter who she may, in the sonnets undoubtedly concerning the Dark Lady the speaker's antagonism to the woman he desires seems to involve these things, among others: male fear of female sexuality because it is perceived as being beyond control or possession and, as might be expected, male fear of other males who do or will seek to win over the beloved. Hence of course the speaker's particular disturbance, in the later sonnets, when the sexually untameable woman is said by him to be the lover of the already much-pursued young man. The woman whom he admits that he desires obsessively yet claims he cannot monopolize is the lover of the young man to whom he claims to be devoted and whom he has long acknowledged to be beyond his 'possessing' (87, l. 1).

The speaker's self-division between those two flawed objects of flawed desire is elaborately presented in sonnet 133 and in the better-known 144. The former poem reveals not merely the speaker's being drawn at once to the Dark Lady and to the young man but, as well, his being divided between disgust at and delight in his own lust. An intricate, narcissistic fiction through which the speaker attempts to image a strange harmony of contrasts, the sonnet displays an uneasy cohabitation of discourses and presences: Petrarchism, friendship and misogyny are brought uneasily together in the speaker's representing of relations as they are and as they notionally could be among the three lovers. The speaker says:

Beshrew that heart that makes my heart to groan
For that deep wound it gives my friend and me.
Is't not enough to torture me alone,
But slave to slavery my sweet'st friend must be?

Me from myself thy cruel eye hath taken,
And my next self thou harder hast engrossed.
Of him, myself, and thee, I am forsaken –
A torment thrice threefold thus to be crossed.
Prison my heart in thy steel bosom's ward,
But then my friend's heart let my poor heart bail;
Whoe'er keeps me, let my heart be his guard,
Thou canst not then use rigor in my jail.
    And yet thou wilt, for I being pent in thee
    Perforce am thine, and all that is in me.

The tropes with which the speaker begins his fiction are conventional in Petrarchan love verse: the wounded heart, torture, slavery, loss of the self, all serving to imply the further trope of female tyranny. Yet almost from the start they are used unconventionally, for the speaker uses them in order to set heterosexual against homosocial desire, Petrarchan love against friendship.[28] The lady is figured as harder in her tyranny over the speaker and his friend than a conventional *domina petrosa* ('steel bosom's ward', l. 9), whereas the 'sweet'st friend' (l. 4) is pictured as her helpless, all but guiltless victim.[29] The speaker represents himself, on the other hand, as the disempowered devotee of his mistress, a devotee eager nonetheless to sacrifice himself for someone to whom he is even more devoted, the 'next self' (l. 6) who is the young man. Identifying the speaker's fiction of divided desire as narcissistic therefore seems justifiable because of his idealized self-portrayal. There is, however, another and better reason for doing so. In the third quatrain of the sonnet the speaker at once announces his wish to sacrifice himself for his friend and reveals his display of concern for his friend throughout the poem to be ultimately self-serving, no less a joke than his quibbling acknowlegement of power-lessness in the poem's last couple of lines. After all, to sacrifice himself for his friend in the manner proposed would obviously allow him uncontested possession of both mistress and friend.[30] His fiction of divided desire is an elegant fantasy of desire fulfilled, one aspect of its elegance being the speaker's fantastically denying his fantasy at the last and turning his joke upon himself.

Sonnet 144, more widely admired than the poem just now con-sidered, likewise sets heterosexual against homosocial desire but inter-plays the two with emphases interestingly different from those given them in the earlier poem. Producing those differences of emphasis by using a religious discourse to describe the relationship between the young man and the Dark Lady, between them and himself, the speaker reminds one of something indicated in the very early sonnets, those which call Narcissus to account: how of this world the Sonnets are. More directly, however, the speaker's carnally religious discourse can be seen to subsume the fictions of black and of fair beauty and, at the same time, to heighten the Petrarch-related imagings of the young man and of the Dark Lady presented or implied elsewhere in sonnets 127–152. Thus the young man is pictured not merely as 'a man right fair' (l. 3) but as the speaker's 'better angel' (*ibid.*) and his 'saint' (l. 7); the Dark Lady is 'a woman coloured ill' (l. 4) and the 'worser spirit', 'a devil' and 'fiend' (ll. 4, 7 and 9 respectively).[31] Furthermore, if misogyny seems latent in the intensified *domina petrosa* motif of sonnet 133 it becomes explicit and virulent in sonnet 144, as the speaker's demonizing tropes for his mistress unmistakably suggest and likewise his phrase 'my female evil' (l. 5). The interplay between heterosexual and homosocial desire is therefore markedly different in its emphases from that fashioned in sonnet 133. It is most different, one could suggest by way of summary, because the speaker crudely caricatures the Dark Lady and disingenuously caricatures the young man. She becomes a type of truly ugly beauty, he an angelic, saintly companion who is revealed as not able to sustain such idealization. The speaker in effect flaunts the wilfulness of his religious analogies as a means of expressing his divided desire.

No account of self-division, misogyny and friendship as they are portrayed in the later sonnets could end without some consideration having been given to sonnet 137. A complaint against the power of physical desire to set the speaker's eyes and heart at odds with their several capacities to see and to feel truly, that is, at odds with themselves, the poem mingles misogyny, Petrarchism, fear, a various desire, and self-disgust. The speaker says:

> Thou blind fool love, what dost thou to mine eyes,
> That they behold and see not what they see?
> They know what beauty is, see where it lies,
> Yet what the best is take the worst to be.
> If eyes corrupt by over-partial looks
> Be anchored in the bay where all men ride,
> Why of eyes' falsehood hast thou forged hooks,
> Whereto the judgement of my heart is tied?
> Why should my heart think that a several plot,
> Which my heart knows the wide world's common place?
> Or mine eyes, seeing this, say this is not
> To put fair truth upon so foul a face?
> > In things right true my heart and eyes have erred,
> > And to this false plague are they now transferred.

Acknowledging the strange, irresistible power of the god of love and alluding to the 'hooks' with which he ensares his victims, the speaker uses those familiarly Petrarchan tropes to evoke a state recurrently voiced by the speaker of the *Rime*: powerless insight into being self-divided, self-alienated.[32] Yet although it is not unusual for the persona of the *Rime* to expresses self-disgust at his domination by desire, and so too does Shakespeare's speaker in this sonnet, the latter's disgust with himself is unlike that uttered by his Petrarchan antecedent because linked with misogyny and with fear: misogynically articulated fear of uncontrollable, unownable female sexuality. The speaker refers to his mistress's genitals as 'the bay where all men ride', and says that in between her legs doesn't lie his 'several plot' but 'the wide world's common place' (ll. 6, 9 and 10 respectively). Perhaps the speaker's fear, misogyny and disgust with himself gesture, after a fashion, back to Petrarchism. The second and twelfth lines of the sonnet, particularly the twelfth line with its opposing 'fair truth' to 'foul a face', repudiate black beauty. One implication of the speaker's repudiating it, especially when his doing so is taken in conjunction with his misogyny, fear and self-disgust, would seem to be elevation of the youth, a tacit exaltation of that male friend who figures throughout the Sonnets as a unique manifestation of Petrarchan beauty. In focusing on his self-division the speaker may be simultaneously denigrating a *Venus Victrix* and expressing nostalgia for an Adonis.[33]

(III) ENDING WITH CUPID

Whether or not Venus and Adonis can be glimpsed in sonnet 137, Cupid is certainly there from the beginning. Blind desire turns the speaker against himself, as he complains directly in that poem and has implied earlier. Amid his subsequent laments at being irremediably self-divided, the speaker even hints that he has become a parodic counterpart to Blind Cupid.[34] The power of the little, but terrible, god of love is therefore appropriately the focus of those poems that bring the Sonnets to an end – an end without resolution, for the speaker indicates that his desire continues unabated.[35] It is true that, before the power of the alexandrian Cupid is playfully if not lightly considered in sonnets 153–154, in sonnet 146 the speaker considers his self-division from a Christian perspective. He seems however to abandon and almost to mock that perspective in the sonnets which immediately follow. The only religious poem in the collection thus serves to emphasize the secularity of the Sonnets as a whole: further to confirm, as it were, the power of Cupid and the Dark Lady over the speaker. Like some other palinodes it is a moment of devout meditation expressing wisdom which its speaker will not deny but upon which he will not act. That the speaker of the Sonnets does not act upon it appears the less surprising given his previous, indirectly acknowledged failure to be guided by wisdom in the more mundane guise of *prudentia*.

The isolation of sonnet 146 is arguably more important than any other aspect of the poem. It cannot be said to exist in perfect isolation, of course. The speaker's words are not unlike those used by the narrator of *Lucrece* to describe Tarquin's self-violation; then, too, the speaker's exhorting himself to redeem the time seems as if a sacred parody of his urging the youth, in sonnets 1–17, to seize the day. Particularly telling in that regard is his use of economic imagery to evoke not merely the notion of the economy of nature but also that of the four last things.[36] His allusion, in the last line of the sonnet, to the Pauline topos of death's ultimate mortality anticipates Donne's allusion to it at the close of 'Death be not proud . . .'. Moreover it is interesting to compare the Donne speaker's insistent suggestion of his own fearlessness throughout that Holy Sonnet with the grotesque depiction of self-empowerment by Shakespeare's speaker at the end of sonnet 146.[37] The poem is, nevertheless, isolated. In sonnet 147 the speaker does not again use conventional religious discourse – the mode of discourse profaned in sonnet 144 – but that of Petrarchan love-psychology. For example, he says:

> My reason, the physician to my love,
> Angry that his prescriptions are not kept,
> Hath left me, and I desp'rate now approve
> Desire is death, which physic did except.

> (ll. 5–8)

He continues:

> Past cure I am, now reason is past care,
> And frantic mad with evermore unrest,
> My thoughts and my discourse as madmen's are,
> At random from the truth vainly expressed;
> > For I have sworn thee fair, and thought thee bright,
> > Who art as black as hell, as dark as night.

> (ll. 9–14)[38]

His demonizing the Dark Lady, while broadly consonant with the religious language and rhetoric of sonnet 146, accords more distinctly with his portrayal of her in 144 and his oblique allusion to her in the final couplet of 129.[39] His picturing himself as a man maddened by desire accords, too, with what he says about lust in these lines from 129:

> Past reason hunted, and no sooner had,
> Past reason hated as a swallowed bait,
> On purpose laid to make the taker mad;
> Mad in pursuit, and in possession so. . . .

(ll. 6–9)

The speaker's picture of himself as a madman also forms an embittered counterpart to these later, joking announcements by Drayton's persona in *Idea*: 'I am lunaticke . . .'; 'Reason and I (you must conceive) are twaine . . .' (9, ll. 5 and 10). In any event, immediately thereafter Shakespeare's speaker returns to consideration of Cupid's power to distort his perceptions, to warp his judgement and to divide him against himself.

The beginning of sonnet 148 clearly illustrates the speaker's return to those preoccupations:

> O me! what eyes hath love put in my head,
> Which have no correspondence with true sight!
> Or if they have, where is my judgment fled,
> That censures falsely what they see aright?

(ll. 1–4)[40]

Yet it is a return that involves more than mere repetition. For a start, in this poem the judgement of 'the world' (l. 6) is said to have an authority by no means always conceded it in the poems focused on the young man: 'Love's eye is not so true as all men's: no' (l. 8). Further, when the speaker then asks himself, 'How can it? O how can love's eye be true,/ That is so vexed with watching and with tears?' (ll. 9–11), his answer takes one back suddenly to sonnets 18, 33 and 34. He says: 'No marvell then though I mistake my view;/ The sun itself sees not till heaven clears' (ll. 11–12). In the earlier sonnets Shakespeare's speaker uses the imperfections of the sun or, at least, its limitations as ways to suggest the perfections or the (excusable) imperfections of the youth. Here he uses the sun's limitations to excuse his own error: he compares his vision, as a lover, with that of the clouded eye of heaven. Finally, in connection with sonnet 148, it should also be mentioned that the speaker implies love/the little love god to have transformed him so that he might not perceive the faults in both the Dark Lady and love/Cupid themselves. He laments: 'O cunning love, with tears thou keep'st me blind,/ Lest eyes, well seeing, thy foul faults should find' (ll. 13–14). He has become a parodic counterpart to Blind Cupid.[41]

So he indicates too at the close of the following sonnet; but he implies, before its final lines, that he has been subjected as well to another, ironic transformation by his desire. He reproaches his mistress, saying: 'Do I not think on thee when I forgot/ Am of myself all tyrant for thy sake?' (149, ll. 3–4). The speaker suggests her tyranny over him to be complete, for he suggests that he replicates it by tyrannizing over himself in total submission to her will. Desire compels him to be, in that respect, her double. Of course he has already revealed himself to be like her in a couple of other respects: his concupiscence and duplicity. An unwittingly pertinent commentary on the speaker's situation is offered by the persona of Chapman's *A Coronet for His Mistresse Philosophie*.[42] In the second poem of that sonnet-sequence Chapman's persona tells lovers whose concern is with the flesh alone:

> But dwell in darknes, for your God is blinde,
>> Humor poures downe such torrents on his eyes,
>> Which (as from Mountaines) fall on his base kind,
>> And eate your entrails out with exstasies.
> Colour, (whose hands for faintnes are not felt)
>> Can binde your waxen thoughts in Adamant,
>> And with her painted fires your harts doth melt
>> Which beate your soules in peeces with a pant. . . .
>
> (ll. 1–8)

His words interestingly complement what Shakespeare's speaker discloses about himself in sonnets 129, 144 and 146.

While the isolation of sonnet 146 within the collection as a whole is marked by the speaker's immediate return in the subsequent poems to preoccupation with his marred perceptions and judgements, with his self-division, it is also emphasized in those poems by his play with or violation of the sacred. At the end of sonnet 150 the speaker says to his mistress: 'If thy unworthiness raised love in me,/ More worthy I to be belov'd of thee.' There he seems to be parodying the notion of the divine *agape*.[43] His lady's 'unworthiness', he asserts, moved him to love her – not her merit; therefore, his generosity in loving her should evoke love from her in response. He comically dignifies a plea for love with an outrageous, and by no means uninsulting, condescension.[44] In sonnet 151, on the other hand, the speaker plays with the notion of conscience. Alluding to the relations between his body and his soul much as he did in sonnet 146, and to the irresistible power of physical desire much as he did in sonnet 129, he proceeds to offer mock-evidence of love's having a conscience. He says:

> My soul doth tell my body that he may
> Triumph in love; flesh stays no farther reason,
> But rising at thy name doth point out thee,
> As his triumphant prize – proud of this pride,
> He is contented thy poor drudge to be,
> To stand in thy affairs, fall by thy side.
>   No want of conscience hold it that I call
>   Her love for whose dear love I rise and fall.
>
> (ll. 7–14)

The speaker proposes lust and pride, specifically, tumescence and detumescence, as proofs of love's having a conscience. His phallic bravado recalls that expressed by him in sonnets 135–6, although here the context of his self-display is theological and ethical. His 'flesh', he tells his lady, is her good and faithful servant. He acknowledges and seems finally to accept, even to delight in, the impotence of his soul.

It is therefore by no means inappropriate that the Sonnets end with consideration of Cupid's power. In 152 the speaker says to his mistress:

> For I have sworn deep oaths of thy deep kindness,
> Oaths of thy love, thy truth, thy constancy,
> And to enlighten thee gave eyes to blindness,
> Or made them swear against the thing they see,
>   For I have sworn thee fair: more perjured eye,
>   To swear against the truth so foul a lie.
>
> (ll. 9–14)

He associates himself yet once more with Blind Cupid, stressing his 'blindness' and his 'perjured eye'. He cannot say, as can the persona of sonnet 84 in Greville's *Caelica* when addressing Cupid:

> The spectacles to my life was thy blindnesse:
>   But Cupid now farewell, I will goe play me,
>   With thoughts that please me lesse, and lesse betray me.[45]

On the contrary, he proceeds to the anacreontic narratives which tell of Cupid's – and of his mistress's – dominion over him, of unceasing desire.

The links between sonnets 153–154 and the emblem tradition have been carefully studied; so, too, have the poems' joking allusions to disease.[46] But their play with emblematic conceit and with reference to venereal disease serve primarily to emphasize desire's insistence and persistence. Sonnet 153 begins:

> Cupid laid by his brand and fell asleep.
> A maid of Dian's this advantage found,
> And his love-kindling fire did quickly steep
> In a cold valley-fountain of that ground,
> Which borrowed from this holy fire of love
> A dateless lively heat, still to endure,
> And grew a seething bath which yet men prove
> Against strange maladies a sovereign cure.
>
> (ll. 1–8)

A variation on the motif of the conflict between Venus and Diana, this narrative portrays Cupid as a conqueror over opposition to desire. For a start, his power can be displaced, not negated; and the last lines of the sonnet elaborate on the notion of displaced power. The speaker says:

> But at my mistress' eye love's brand new-fired,
> The boy for trial needs would touch my breast.
> I sick withal the help of bath desired,
> And thither hied, a sad distempered guest,
>   But found no cure; the bath for my help lies
>   Where Cupid got new fire – my mistress' eye.
>
> (ll. 9–14)

Beauty generates desire and beauty alone can ease it – by implication, through promise of fulfilment and, ultimately, fulfilment itself. According to the speaker, not repudiation but satisfaction allows humankind, as distinct from 'maid[s] of Dian', to cope with desire. The lady's eye is focused on here, not the speaker's own 'perjured eye'. In 154 the narrative of the preceeding sonnet is varied but the power of desire is again affirmed. The speaker relates that a nymph 'that vowed chaste life to keep' (l. 3) extinguished Cupid's torch

> in a cool well by,
> Which from love's fire took heat perpetual,
> Growing a bath and healthful remedy
> For men diseased; but I, my mistress' thrall,
>   Came there for cure, and this by that I prove:
>   Love's fire heats water, water cools not love.
>
> (ll. 9–14)

Bitterly playful acknowledgement of desire's power ends the Sonnets, an affirmation that both exalts and implicitly denigrates the speaker's mistress. Perhaps the speaker also implies that he is resigned to domination by desire. Be that as it may, his final words appeal both to nature and to Scripture in conceding his desire to be without end and his predicament without resolution.[47]

NOTES

1. See, for example, sonnet 133.
2. For the most recent and informed discussion of the 'ugly beauty' tradition see Heather Dubrow's *Echoes of Desire: English Petrarchism and Its Counterdiscourses* (Ithaca and London: Cornell University Press, 1995), pp. 163–201, 233–44.
3. The phrase 'black beauty' was in Shakespeare's time an oxymoron, since the categories 'black' and 'ugly' were thought cognate when applied to people, by contrast with 'fair' and 'beautiful'. In terms of colouration, to be 'black' – leaving aside negritude or having black hair – meant such things as having brown hair or a brown complexion and not having blue or grey eyes.
4. See also sonnet 59. Sonnet 68, like 127, attacks the use of cosmetics: the pretence to beauty.
5. In other of the sonnets the young man is of course shown as needing to seize the moment.
6. It could be said that the Dark Lady is timely, the young man untimely (as it were). He is not merely of the time – as is the Dark Lady – nor is he present at the wrong time; but he is said occasionally, as in 67–8, to be someone whose perfection makes him at odds with the times. Of course he cannot be said to be timeless, for he is shown again and again in the Sonnets to be trapped in the cycles of time. One could add here that whereas the young man seems to be the heir to some aristocratic family, the Dark Lady seems to have a husband but nothing more: Shakespeare's speaker alludes to the genealogy of the youth but not to hers.
7. The idea is that only someone blonde can be beautiful/ someone beautiful can be only blonde. In the context of sonnet 127 as a whole, the 'someone' is to be thought of as female; but given that sonnet 126 addresses the youth, and that the Dark Lady is introduced into sonnet 127 from l. 9, one can reasonably take ll. 1–8 of the sonnet as referring to people in general.
8. On the latter, see Kerrigan's note to l. 9 on p. 354 of his edition (J. Kerrigan, *The Sonnets and A Lover's Complaint* (Harmondsworth, Penguin: 1986)); as regards what I list as the first and last implications of the line see Evans's note on p. 244 of his edition (G. Blakemore Evans, *The Sonnets* (Cambridge: Cambridge University Press, 1996).

9. One might see the literariness of the allusion and nonetheless think that, privileging fair beauty, *fine amour* and Petrarchan tradition were to follow the dictates of nature; however, the allusion does foreground the literariness of the fair beauty paradigm and therefore allow one to perceive its conventionality. It should be mentioned here that the colour of Laura's eyes, though not the rest of her colouring save for that of her eyebrows, is in fact black – despite the recurrence in Petrarch-derived love verse of blue or grey as the colour of a mistress's eyes. The rest of Laura's colouring is golden, white and red.

10. As ll. 9 and 13–14 make very plain.

11. Fear of rumour is alluded to by Venus in her attempted seduction of Adonis.

12. As has been pointed out, in those words, in the third chapter's discussion of sonnet 20. It is also indicated in sonnet 20 that, because of his androgyny, the youth transcends Laura.

13. The speaker implies that the Dark Lady is beneath Laura, whereas the youth overgoes her.

14. The speaker attests in the last lines of sonnet 127 to the Dark Lady's capacity to attract admiration.

15. Astrophil connects his love for Stella with concupiscence but, more broadly, with *concupiscentia*. Petrarch's speaker finally, of course, links his love for Laura with *cupiditas*; but his love is ultimately and not simply associated with *cupiditas*.

16. 'Denigration' because instead of proceeding to celebrate the black beauty of his lady in subsequent poems he uses it – or, at least, her colouring – to blacken her: to create a blackened representation of her.

17. The beholder and (or) auditor. Here I follow David Summers, *Michelangelo and the Language of Art* (Princeton, N.J.: Princeton University Press, 1981), pp. 171–6, especially at pp. 172–3.

18. The 'wiry concord' of her music 'confounds' his 'ear', that is to say, it effects in him a *concordia discors*.

19. See Ficino's *Commentary*, at 5, 2, p. 86 (*Commentary on Plato's Symposium*, ed. Sears Jayne (1985; rpt. Woodstock: Spring, 1994)).

20. *Lucrece*, l. 544; see also ll. 545–6.

21. The phrase quoted is Cicero's, as used and identified in Chapter 2.

22. The implied powerlessness of wisdom is matched by the implied failure of spirituality, suggested by the sexual figuring of heaven and of hell in the poem's final lines.

23. Contrast 130 with *Amoretti* 15, 17, 37 and 81. Reference is to W. A. Oram *et al.* (eds), *The Yale Edition of the Shorter Poems of Edmund Spenser* (New Haven and London: Yale University Press, 1989).

24. As has been shown in Chapter 3, those discourses had of course already been long connected.

25. See *Amoretti* 8, ll. 9–12 and 84, *passim*. By way of immediate comparison and contrast with 131, see *Amoretti* 5, 6, 10, 20, 27.

26. The word 'will' is used in other senses as well but they do not downplay or deny the sexual meanings so often evoked by the word as used in the poem and in its successor. Sonnet 136 uses 'will' seven times and ends by using it apparently in reference to Shakespeare.

27. Reference is to *Collected Poems*, ed. J. Daalder (London: Oxford University Press, 1975). See also *Amoretti* 34 and 63.

28. More obviously unconventional is the fact that the Dark Lady is mistress to both men at the same time.

29. For another example of the *domina petrosa* motif, see *Amoretti* 54, l. 14.

30. Uncontested in terms of relations among the three.

31. It is not uncommon for the female beloved to be called a 'saint' in Petrarch-derived love verse. In addition, while the Dark Lady is not called a 'fiend' she is clearly signalled to be one. Cf. Drayton's 'An evill spirit your beautie haunts me still . . .', in *Idea* (20). Reference is to *The Works of Michael Drayton*, ed. J. W. Hebel, 5 vols, corr. edn (Oxford: Blackwell, 1961), 2, 320. With portrayal of the Dark Lady in 144, contrast also *Amoretti* 8, ll. 1–8.

32. I am not suggesting that those tropes are exclusively Petrarchan, merely that they are tropes used by Petrarch and often to be seen in sixteenth-century English verse imitating or otherwise linked to Petrarch's.

33. The sonnet could be seen as depicting a triumph of Cupid, a parodic Venus the Conqueror, and desire for an absent or, at least, not possessed Adonis.

34. See sonnets 148–149, ll. 13–14 in each case.

35. In his edition of the Sonnets, Kerrigan interestingly argues that the anacreontic, final poems lead to *A Lover's Complaint*, which forms an ending to the Sonnets as a whole. See especially pp. 12–18, 389–90.

36. The 'four last things' are death, judgement, hell and heaven.

37. The final lines of 146 seem as if a sacred parody of the *tempus edax rerum* topos, thus implicitly complementing the first lines of sonnet 19.

38. Cf. *Amoretti* 50.

39. I do not mean that he alludes to her only in the final couplet of 129 – for the whole poem is written in allusion to her – but that the final couplet of 129 accords with that of 147.

40. By way of contrast, see Davies's *Ten Sonnets, to Philomel* 1, ll. 1–8. Reference is to *The Poems of Sir John Davies*, ed. R. Kreuger (Oxford: Clarendon Press, 1975).

41. See Booth's note to 148, ll. 13–14 on p. 521 of his edition (*Shakespeare's Sonnets* (New Haven and London: Yale University Press, 1977)). As he points out, given the phrase 'thy foul faults' then 'love' must also include reference to the mistress.

42. Reference is to *The Poems of George Chapman*, ed. P. B. Bartlett (1941; rpt. New York: Russell & Russell, 1962).

43. In Protestant theology, the divine *agape* is the freely given, unmerited love of God compassionately bestowed from above upon fallen humankind.

44. Perhaps the final couplet of the sonnet could likewise be seen as expressing *sdegno*, a courtly disdain. For other aspects of the final couplet, see the comments by Booth, Kerrigan and Evans.

45. Reference is to Greville's *Certaine Learned and Elegant Workes (1633)*, introd. A. D. Cousins (New York: Scholars' Facsimiles and Reprints, 1990).

46. See J. Hutton, 'Analogues of Shakespeare's Sonnets 153–4: Contributions to the History of a Theme', *MP*, 38 (1940–1), 385–403; see also, M. Praz, *Studies in Seventeenth-Century Imagery*, 2 vols (London: Warburg Institute, 1939), 1, pp. 82 and 91–2. On the allusions to venereal disease and its treatment, see Booth's edition, pp. 533–8.

47. In the last line of the poem the speaker alludes to the Song of Solomon, 8:7. That allusion was first noted, as far as I am aware, by R. Jaeger; Booth cites Jaeger on p. 538 of his edition.

Conclusion

Conclusions of many and often different kinds have been drawn about Shakespeare's non-dramatic verse. That is partly because it is by him, partly because the Sonnets in particular can seem, and maybe are, intensely and enigmatically personal, and also because so many readers, so many readerships, have tried to possess it. To say as much is not to make any claims for one's own readings of the Sonnets and of the narrative poems other than this: centuries of conclusions having been delivered on the non-dramatic verse, one is necessarily wary in adding one's own. Nevertheless these conclusions might be hazarded on the basis of what has been argued in the preceding chapters.

First, the elusiveness of the non-dramatic verse can be identified only to some extent in terms of what we do not yet and may never know about it: for example the relations, if directly any, between Shakespeare and Southampton; what Shakespeare's narrative poems were meant exactly to get from the Earl; the identity of Mr W. H. and whether knowing that would tell us more about the Sonnets than about how we have chosen to read them. The elusiveness of the narrative poems can be identified as well in terms of a sceptical play with myth, meta-Ovidian in *Venus and Adonis*, meta-Ovidian likewise in *Lucrece* but also congruent in some ways with the method of Pyrrhonian scepticism. The scepticism of *Lucrece* has as its counterpart in the Sonnets, a scepticism which, while not strictly Pyrrhonian, seems closer to that than to scepticisms of other forms in later Elizabethan literary culture. As has been suggested earlier, however, and perhaps should be repeated, just as scepticism in the non-dramatic verse is not of one form neither is it all-pervasive nor equally exercised.[1] It could be said, by way of brief illustration, that although exemplarity receives close examination from a sceptical perspective, the notion of natural law is examined sceptically but not consistently, much less systematically. Moreover, it does not seem that Christian belief is sceptically interrogated in the non-dramatic verse. Obvious social and political constraints would have inhibited its being so, assuming for the moment that Shakespeare might have wanted to have focused on it sceptically; on the other hand, the narrative poems and Sonnets appear to be very much of this world and not otherworldly in their preoccupations.[2]

One of their worldly preoccupations is of course wisdom. They seem not greatly interested in contemplative wisdom (*sapientia*). Adonis and Lucrece engage in metaphysical speculation: Adonis when confronted by what he sees as sexual threat; Lucrece after sexual assault. The speculations of both are flawed, bespeaking desperation. The speaker of the Sonnets parodies or engages in theological reflection when sexually intimidated by the Dark Lady. But his moment of apparently serious, certainly conventional religious reflection is isolated within his insistent and various reflections on more worldly desires. It is rather prudence (*prudentia*) with which the narrative poems and the Sonnets are concerned. Adonis unknowingly lacks it and thus cannot see how to gain it. He has no concept of self-knowledge in relation to prudence. And in any event the relationship between the two is indicated to be problematic. Venus also lacks it but, being a goddess, can blunder on into eternity. Collatine spectacularly and tragically lacks prudence – the tragedy being his wife's; Lucrece has been deprived of prudence. Hence she is doubly vulnerable. The young man of the Sonnets is confronted with prudence by Shakespeare's speaker but seems to reject it. The speaker seeks to make good that lack only to reveal, subsequently, his own inability to act upon his knowledge of what prudence is in his circumstances. The non-dramatic verse suggests that prudence is a necessary, difficult and elusive ideal.

Prudence is often associated in treatises and in iconography with gaining or seeking to gain control over time: by taking advantage of an opportunity rather than wasting it; by learning from the past in order to manage the present and prepare for the future. That association is implied in the non-dramatic verse but of course the narrative poems and Sonnets have much else to suggest and to consider about time. For example, they all express a sensitivity to the movement of time, an awareness of how dominated by time human life is. Venus appeals to the *carpe diem* motif when rushing to seduce Adonis; Adonis implicitly counters the notion of seizing the day by appealing to another, namely, that there is a time needed for maturation which should not be disrupted. Lucrece's experience and understanding of time change after her sexual assault and she denounces time itself as being partly responsible for her suffering. Shakespeare's speaker in the Sonnets confronts the young man with portrayals of Father Time the Saturnian devourer and claims to war with Time on the young man's behalf.[3] Nevertheless among the many things that the non-dramatic verse suggests and considers about time is indeed a connection between time and prudence.

As was mentioned above, time is connected with prudence in the narrative poems and Sonnets by the suggestion of a link between prudence and an opportunity grasped and therefore between imprudence and one let slip. The association between prudence or imprudence and opportunity is not always so straightforwardly represented, however; nor is the association, in any event, simple. Whereas Tarquin unwisely grasps the opportunity offered by Collatine's imprudence, Brutus prudently, meanly, effectively uses the opportunity made available by Lucrece's death. The young man, apparently, lets slip the opportunity to be prudent and espouses imprudence; Shakespeare's speaker in the Sonnets prudently takes the opportunity of the young man's imprudence to become his champion against Time. Yet from his cliently prudence follow many imprudences. Acting wisely, or otherwise, is nonetheless not associated in the narrative poems and Sonnets with opportunity alone. As was also mentioned above, prudence is connected with learning from the past. But the non-dramatic verse indicates how difficult it can be to know the past. Venus invites Adonis to learn from nature. And by reminding Adonis that she who now courts him is the conqueror of Mars, she also invites him to learn from the past about his beauty's singularity and hence of his importance. She invites him to learn from the past and to seize the day; but her version of the past is incomplete, for she does not tell him what happened after she had conquered Mars. She suppresses knowledge of the past and Adonis may or may not be aware of that. Adonis, on the other hand, invents the past so that he can explain, if not come to terms with, the present. He imagines that spiritual love has fled the earth, having been supplanted by a carnal successor. Lucrece, when pleading with Tarquin, reveals that she has never really understood the recent past. She has never understood the nature of rule by Tarquin's family. She does recognize, however, that knowledge of the past is fragile and must be safeguarded from falsification. After her death, Brutus more than justifies her anxiety. In the Sonnets, Shakespeare's speaker wilfully reinvents the young man's own past in order to exculpate him. Like Brutus, if perhaps less cynically, the speaker can remake the past to suit himself. His doing so confirms his admitted distrust of historical record and adds an ironic note to his claim that his portrayals of the youth will hand down truth to posterity.

If the narrative poems and Sonnets suggest, amid displaying invention and reinvention of the past, how difficult it can be to know the past, they also suggest the problematic relations among self-knowledge, sexuality and death. The paradigm for Shakespeare's exploring those relations appears to be the myth of Narcissus, yet he evokes that paradigm only to depart significantly from it. Venus wrongly implies that Adonis resembles Narcissus: as has been argued above, he is virtually an anti-Narcissus. Lucrece, although recurrently characterized in terms of Petrarchan discourse, proves not to be the narcissist that certainly Laura, and often her successors, are accused of being. Further, in her case, self-knowledge does not come from her own sexuality but from Tarquin's imposition of his sexuality upon her. That is to say, Adonis repudiates gaining self-knowledge through sexual experience; Lucrece gains self-knowledge by the tyrannic imposition on her of sexual violence. In the Sonnets, the young man so clearly identified with Narcissus has his narcissism and its terminal consequences explained to him: apparently rejecting the self-knowledge set before him, the young man rejects sexual reproduction and therefore chooses self-extinction. Moreover, the speaker who counsels him, and who claims to offer him textual reproduction, comes to reveal himself as variously and inescapably narcissistic.

What also seems important in Shakespeare's reworking of the Narcissus myth is, however, his elaborate play with the myth's ambiguous gendering of its main figure. Thus his narrator in *Venus and Adonis* puts forward that feminized anti-Narcissus, so to speak, who is Adonis as the notional object of male desire, at the expense of the goddess of love and beauty. So, in the Sonnets, Shakespeare's speaker celebrates the Narcissus-like young man – whom he implicitly associates, too, with Adonis – as more purely female in beauty than women themselves. His view of the young man may alter but his responsiveness to the young man's androgyny seems never in doubt. But what the nature of that responsiveness may be, and how one is to interpret the foregrounding of Adonis' androgyny, remain less than wholly clear. What does Shakespeare's choice of a homoerotic narrative through which to seek the patronage of Southampton indicate, for example? Does the speaker's responsiveness to the androgyny of the young man in the Sonnets indicate anything in particular about Shakespeare's notions of gender – and his sexual preferences? Answers to those questions are sometimes determined by faith in or hostility to Foucault's version of the history of early modern sexuality. Answers are sometimes determined, likewise, by whether one wants to have a partisan view of Shakespeare's sexual preferences. It is clear that the non-dramatic verse is often homoerotic or homosocial and misogynic. It is clear that those elements can be seen often in the plays.[4] But some of the implications of their being so can be only the subjects of speculation.

How the narrative poems and Sonnets relate to verse by Shakespeare's predecessors or contemporaries can perhaps be less speculatively described. Among those later Elizabethan minor epics focused on the erotic to the exclusion of the heroic, *Venus and Adonis* is surely rivalled by *Hero and Leander* alone in sophistication and scope. They are virtuoso performances in a new kind of writing that involved an unmoralized way of recreating Ovidian narrative and, at the same time, they are powerful imagings of unresolved contrariety in human experience. It could be suggested, however, that Shakespeare's poem has dimensions lacked by Marlowe's. For example in *Venus and Adonis* the characterizations of the poem's main figures are intricate; through (primarily) the characterization of Venus, moreover, the notion of 'love' is refracted. And in Shakespeare's poem not only the notion of love but that of nature is unstable, different versions of what nature or the natural is competing for dominance. The implicit scepticism of *Venus and Adonis* goes beyond the paradoxicality with which *Hero and Leander* represents human experience.[5]

Lucrece seems to subsume the complaint as fashioned anew by Daniel and in fact to transcend the complaint as a genre. For a start, the poem is not so much a complaint as a minor epic which incorporates elements from *de casibus* tragedy, the complaint, and the tyrant play; further, it is a minor epic that highlights the epic in addition to the erotic. No less to the point, sophistication as well as scope separates Shakespeare's second narrative poem from later Elizabethan complaints, just as both those qualities separate *Venus and Adonis* from other Elizabethan erotic epyllia. Its sophistication can be attributed in part to the complexity of its characterization, in part to the complex interplay of discourse effected by that characterization. Thus one must add, returning to the notion of scope, that the poem brings together not merely the epic and the erotic but the epic and (among other things) scepticism. *Lucrece* is in no sense a small work. To suggest that it overshadows *Rosamond* is merely to indicate that it also overshadows other complaints of the 1590s and those written previously.

Tropes of incorporation and of transcendence cannot be so readily used, of course, when the Sonnets are set against the sonnet sequences by Shakespeare's contemporaries. But one can discuss innovation. It is true that in the Sonnets can be seen motifs familiar from Petrarchan and anti-Petrarchan verse; nevertheless, they indicate innovation rather than simple conventionality. Certainly no Astrophil performs before the reader, alluding to the burden of the Petrarchan inheritance, insisting on his courtliness, alternately indicating and denying his total fictionality. But there is a speaker who, alluding to the persona of the *Rime* and to Astrophil, implies the courtliness of his art despite his own distance from the courtly world. There is a client who courts a young man, mingling counsel with praise, heroic self-assertion with studied self-effacement, and who deploys the discourses of friendship and of Petrarchism in fashioning precariously, sceptically idealizing images of the young man and of himself. The Sonnets do not so much deny or invert Petrarchism as appropriate it, radically altering the emphases on some of its elements, as the speaker's play with the myth of Narcissus suggests from the start. And from almost the start one sees that, if no Astrophil speaks from the page, neither will nor will be seen a woman such as Stella or such as Spenser presents in his *Amoretti*. There will be a woman who, like Laura, the feminized Adonis, and the lady of Spenser's sonnets, can be represented as a *domina petrosa*, but not one who can be likened to a star or, save in parody, to a saint. Instead of a Laura reborn there is a Laura demonized by Shakespeare's duplicitous speaker. The Sonnets end with acknowledgement of both her power and Blind Cupid's; the speaker seems nonetheless, toward the last of the Sonnets, to be focused rather on the flawed male friend from whom his desire for the Dark Lady, and also the friend's for her, separates him. For Shakespeare's speaker, unlike Petrarch's persona, there is no renunciation of a lesser object of desire. He does not experience desire that can be fulfilled in marriage, as does the speaker in *Amoretti*. There is unending desire, as there is likewise for Astrophil, but desire divided between two less than ideal objects and strongly, if partly, against itself. A final conclusion, at this point, might then be as follows. So to have described the innovativeness of the Sonnets, in conjunction with what has been claimed for the narrative poems, is to have suggested that if Shakespeare had written the non-dramatic verse and nothing more he would still be among the greatest of the Elizabethan poets.

NOTES

1. It cannot be said, then, that Shakespeare chooses all the targets of his scepticism: he might choose some but not others; he might indeed choose them all (but that cannot be demonstrated). If he does choose them all, we still do not know the relations between what was chosen and what was not.

2. Christian belief is not irrelevant to the non-dramatic verse — and not merely because of sonnets 144 and 146 in particular. Issues bearing on Christian belief are evoked in *Venus and Adonis*, more obviously so in *Lucrece*. Maybe Shakespeare devoutly rejected or avoided sceptical inquiry into Christian orthodoxy; maybe he fearfully or prudently did so; maybe both sets of reasons applied; maybe he just did not want to pursue matters religious. The last seems to me to be the most likely.

3. Other instances could be given; those are merely a representative few.

4. Some of the most important moments in the plays are connected, for example, with male intimacy. One could cite Harry's reproach of Scrope or Antonio's farewell to Bassanio as merely a couple of instances.

5. By far the most comprehensive and interesting discussion of Marlowe's poem is by P. Cheney in his *Marlowe's Counterfeit Profession: Ovid, Spenser, Counter-Nationhood* (Toronto: University of Toronto Press, 1997). He reads the poem as a critique of the cult of Elizabeth. Unfortunately his study was not yet in print when I was working on *Venus and Adonis*.

Index

LONGMAN MEDIEVAL AND RENAISSANCE LIBRARY

General Editors:
CHARLOTTE BREWER, Hertford College, Oxford
N. H. KEEBLE, University of Stirling

Published Titles:

Piers Plowman: An Introduction to the B-Text
James Simpson

Shakespeare's Mouldy Tales: Recurrent Plot Motifs in Shakespearian Drama
Leah Scragg

The Fabliau in English
John Hines

English Medieval Mystics: Games of Faith
Marion Glasscoe

Speaking Pictures: English Emblem Books and Renaissance Culture
Michael Bath

The Classical Legacy in Renaissance Poetry
Robin Sowerby

Regaining Paradise Lost
Thomas N. Corns

English and Italian Literature from Dante to Shakespeare: A Study of Source, Analogue and Divergence
Robin Kirkpatrick

Shakespeare's Alternative Tales
Leah Scragg

The Gawain-*Poet*
Ad Putter

Donne's Religious Writing: A Discourse of Feigned Devotion
P. M. Oliver

Images of Faith in English Literature 700–1500: An Introduction
Dee Dyas

Courtliness and Literature in Medieval England
David Burnley

Wyatt, Surrey and Early Tudor Poetry
Elizabeth Heale

A New Introduction to Chaucer
Derek Brewer

SHAKESPEARE'S SONNETS AND NARRATIVE POEMS